In memory of my darling Dad, the very
special Maurice Fine, who was so proud to be
Myrna Rosen's father!

STRUIK

Struik Publishers (Pty) Ltd
(a member of The Struik Publishing Group (Pty) Ltd)
Cornelis Struik House
80 McKenzie Street
Cape Town
8001

Reg. No.: 63/00203/07

© Text and photographs Myrna Rosen 1978, except cover photograph © Meat Board

First published by Howard Timmins (Pty) Ltd S.A. in 1978
Second impression 1979
Third impression 1979
Fourth impression 1979
Fifth impression 1980
Sixth impression 1981
Seventh impression 1982
Eighth impression 1986
This edition published by Struik Publishers (Pty) Ltd in 1992

All rights reserved. No part of this publication may be reproduced, stored in a retrieval system or transmitted in any form or by any means, electronic, mechanical, photocopying, recording or otherwise, without the permission in writing of the copyright owners.

ISBN 1 86825 298 1

CONTENTS

CONVERSION TABLE	ix
INTRODUCTION	xi
1. APPETISERS & HORS-D'OEUVRES	1
2. SOUPS	15
3. FISH	23
4. POULTRY	41
5. MEAT SECTION	55
1. Beef	57
2. Lamb	68
3. Veal	72
6. VEGETABLES	75
7. SALADS & DRESSINGS	81
8. DESSERTS	87
1. Hot	89
2. Cold	98
9. CAKES	111
10. TARTS	141
11. SMALL CAKES & BISCUITS	153

12.	BREAD, WAFFLES & SCONES	169
13.	TRADITIONAL JEWISH DISHES	175
	INDEX	183

ILLUSTRATIONS

1. DUTCH CURRIED PEA SOUP
   WITH HERBED BREAD 28
2. TROPICAL DUCK 44
3. ROAST SCOTCH FILLET 60
4. STRAWBERRY SPICE CAKE
   WITH WALNUT LAYER CAKE 92
5. ORANGE CHIFFON CAKE 108
6. GRAPE TART 122
7. YEAST CAKES 136

CONVERSION TABLE

grams	ozs	°C	°F	ml	cups
30	1	100	200	60	¼
60	2	120	250	80	
90	3	140	275	125	½
125	4	160	325	200	¾
150	5	180	350	250	1
180	6	200	400	375	1½
210	7	220	425	500	2
250	8	240	475	625	2½
280	9	260	500	750	3
310	10	280	550	875	3½
340	11			1000	4
370	12			1125	4½
400	13			1250	5
430	14			1375	5½
460	15			1500	6
500	16				

Boiling point 100 degrees Centigrade
Boiling point 212 degrees Fahrenheit

Mass & Liquid

¼ pint = 125 ml   1 quart = 1 litre
½ pint = 250 ml   1 teaspoon = 5 ml
¾ pint = 375 ml   2 teaspoons = 10 ml
1 pint = 500 ml   1 tablespoon = 12,5 ml

2 level tablespoons sugar = 30 g
1 level tablespoon fat   = 30 g
3 level tablespoons flour = 30 g
2 level tablespoons oil   = 30 g
2 level tablespoons salt   = 30 g
1 cup butter   = 198 g
1 cup flour   = 110 g
1 cup breadcrumbs   = 113 g

Baking Utensils

Loaf tins
17 x 7 cm = 7 x 3 inches
23 x 13 cm = 9 x 5 inches

Baking Tins/Dishes
20 x 30 cm = 8 x 12 inches
21 x 33 cm = 8 x 13 inches
30 x 10 cm = 12 x 4 inches
28 x 18 cm = 11 x 7 inches

Ring & Round Tins
20 cm diameter = 8 inches diameter

Square Tins/Dishes
15 cm = 6 inches
23 cm = 9 inches

INTRODUCTION

I could sit down and write an encyclopaedia full of recipes – but because I am very particular, I will only endeavour to present recipes, which to me, are simply delicious or exceptional and, most important of all, successful. I have, therefore, restricted myself, and in so doing, given you quality more than quantity. I hope that, in this way, I will stimulate an interest in everyone, whatever their particular fancies.

Although I have used the word 'restricted', this does not apply to the variety, as I feel that, in this book, there will be recipes of interest and within the capabilities of newly-weds, for those who prefer simple family meals and indeed, many to satisfy the most discriminating appetite.

I, personally, have always loved entertaining and consequently many recipes included will be of special interest to those who enjoy giving dinner parties and surprising guests with new and exciting dishes.

At this point, I would like to pay tribute to my late grandmother, Leah Chait, who really was a grand old lady and the most wonderful cook. When she immigrated to this country from Lithuania, she had a restaurant at the gold diggings, and my mother, who was the second youngest of the five sisters, used to help her at the restaurant and at home, to cook and bake. So, as you can well imagine, my mother, Mercia Fine, also became a fantastic cook, even better than my late grandmother – and that is really saying something! Cooking has been a trait in our family for many generations, and my knowledge and love of cooking is entirely due to the interest created in me by my mother; and her experience and knowledge have been an endless source of inspiration to me.

I sincerely hope that you will not only enjoy preparing, but also presenting, these dishes to your family and friends and achieve the satisfaction, or even part thereof, that I have derived from it all.

Success is the key and the stimulant in any field, and that is why I am so confident that you will enjoy using this book, from the simplest to the most exotic dishes, for it is with these very thoughts, first and foremost in my mind and my genuine love for cooking and baking, that has inspired me to present these recipes to you.

In conclusion, I would like to express my eternal gratitude to my mother, who has helped me all along, for, there is no doubt, that without her, this book would never have been possible.

I would also like to extend my very sincere thanks to all the women who have attended my demonstrations etc., for it is through their dedication, appreciation and loyalty that I have built up my reputation and am in the position I enjoy today.

Without you all, this dream of mine could never have materialised, and for this I will always remember and be grateful.

So here's to happy cooking and "Bon Appetit"!

MYRNA ROSEN

1. APPETISERS & HORS-D'OEUVRES

ASPARAGUS À LA ROQUEFORT

8 slices smoked salmon
8 large asparagus (mammoth)
50 g roquefort cheese (2 oz)
2 cups milk
125 g butter (4 oz)
½ cup flour
½ cup cream (125 mℓ)
½ cup white wine
  salt, pepper, nutmeg

Method: Melt butter, stir in flour and then add milk, wine and cream, stirring over low heat till smooth and thickened. Crumble cheese into sauce and season with salt, pepper and nutmeg to taste.

Wrap each asparagus in a slice of salmon and place side by side in a buttered pyrex dish. Spoon sauce over, sprinkle with additional nutmeg and bake in 200°C (400°F) oven 15 to 20 minutes, or till hot and bubbling.

Special hint: The salmon wrapped asparagus can also be rolled in a crêpe before spooning over the sauce.

AVOCADO DIP

175 g cream cheese (6 oz)
3 tablespoons lemon juice
2 tablespoons vinegar
½ teaspoon salt
⅛ teaspoon mustard
2 sieved ripe avocado pears
125 mℓ sour cream (½ cup)
125 mℓ mayonnaise (½ cup)
1 tablespoon anchovy sauce or paste
  dash tobasco

Method: Blend all together till smooth. Adjust seasonings. Serve with crisps or carrot sticks, sliced fresh mushrooms, radishes and celery sticks.

AVOCADO MOULD

1 level dessertspoon gelatine
¼ cup cold water
½ cup boiling water
1 cup mayonnaise
2 cups sieved avocado pear or 3 large mashed
  avocados
3 tablespoons lemon juice or vinegar
1 cup thick sour cream/orley whip
½–1 cup chopped celery and 1 dessertspoon
  finely grated onion
1 teaspoon sugar
  onion salt
  salt, pepper
(optional 125 g (4 oz) cream cheese)

Method: Soften the gelatine in cold water for 5 minutes. Add boiling water and sugar and stir until dissolved. Mix remaining ingredients together. Add gelatine and set in oiled mould. Fill centre with beetroot or any other salad of your choice.

Special hint: Fill with lobster or prawn cocktail. To do this boil lobster or prawns in salted water. Shell and dice. Mix together 1 cup mayonnaise, ½ cup tomato sauce, 1 teaspoon vinegar, 1 teaspoon Worcestershire sauce, few drops tobasco, dash salt and 1 teaspoon sugar. Pour over lobster or prawns.

CHEESE BOUREKAS

2 cups flour
125 g butter (4 oz)
1 teaspoon salt
8 tablespoons iced water

For filling
125 g butter (4 oz)
1 cup milk
4 tablespoons flour
250 g cheddar cheese (8 oz)

Method: Make the pastry by sifting the flour and salt. Grate in butter then blend into a dough with the cold water. Refrigerate whilst preparing the filling.

To prepare filling, melt the butter in a pan, stir in the flour, slowly add the milk, stirring constantly till smooth and thickened. Fold in grated cheese and remove from heat immediately. Allow to cool thoroughly.

Roll out the dough on a floured board about 1 centimetre thick, cut into rounds with a tumbler, place a teaspoon of filling and fold over and press edges together with a fork. Fry in oil, about 1 cup, till golden brown. Drain well on absorbent paper. These bourekas may be fried early in the the day and reheated in the oven on a biscuit tray when ready to serve. Heat in 180°C (350°F) oven for 10 to 15 minutes.

Special hint: Other fillings can also be used instead of the cheese such as tuna, or diced mushrooms.

CHEESE SOUFFLÉ

75 g butter (3 oz)
$\frac{1}{2}$ cup flour
3 eggs
1 cup hot milk
1 cup finely grated cheddar cheese
   salt, pepper, paprika

Method: Make a white sauce with the butter, flour and hot milk. Add cheddar cheese and well beaten egg yolks. Season with salt, pepper and paprika. Beat the egg whites stiffly and fold the cheese mixture into the egg whites. Butter a soufflé dish, pour the mixture in and bake in 200°C (400°F) oven for 25 minutes. Must be served immediately.

CHEESE & SOUR CREAM DIP

250 g cream cheese (8 oz)
500 mℓ (2 cups) sour cream
1 tablespoon prepared horseradish
1 tablespoon paprika
1 tablespoon chopped spring onions
1 teaspoon salt
1 teaspoon dill (fresh or dried)
$\frac{1}{4}$ teaspoon garlic salt
$\frac{1}{4}$ teaspoon black pepper
1 clove crushed garlic

Method: Mix all together well. Leave in fridge a few hours for flavours to blend.

Special hint: Serve with crudites, i.e. raw sliced vegetables (carrots, mushrooms, celery sticks, whole radishes, cucumber sticks, cauliflouwerettes).

CREAMY CAVIAR MOULD

1 level dessertspoon gelatine
125 g caviar (4 oz)
   pinch paprika
   pepper to taste
250 mℓ whipped cream ($\frac{1}{2}$ pint)
$\frac{1}{2}$ cup mayonnaise
1 dessertspoon finely grated onion
$\frac{1}{2}$ cup tomato sauce
125 mℓ sour cream ($\frac{1}{2}$ cup)
   dash of tobasco
$\frac{1}{4}$ cup cold water
$\frac{1}{2}$ cup boiling water

Method: Dissolve gelatine in cold water, then add boiling water and stir over low heat until completely dissolved. Cool. Mix together whipped cream, sour cream, mayonnaise, tomato sauce, gelatine and seasonings. Lastly fold in caviar very lightly. Pour into the mould which has been rinsed with oil and water, and allow to set overnight. Turn onto a platter of lettuce, drizzle a little sour cream over mould and garnish with chopped spring onion and hard boiled egg. Surround with little savoury pancakes which have been topped with cream and caviar.

SAVOURY PANCAKES

2 eggs, separated
½ cup cream (125 mℓ)
½ cup flour
½ teaspoon baking powder
  pinch salt

Method: Sift flour with baking powder and salt. Beat egg yolks till light and creamy, stir in cream and then add sifted dry ingredients. Beat till smooth. Lastly fold in stiffly beaten egg whites. Drop teaspoonsful into oiled frying pan and fry on both sides till golden brown.

These may be prepared in advance and frozen.

CREAM CHEESE CAVIAR BLINIS

Blinis: Beat 3 eggs with 2½ cups cold water. Add 1½ cups flour sifted with a pinch salt and ½ teaspoon baking powder. Grease pan with oil and fry on one side only.

Filling: 250 g (½ lb) cream cheese mixed with one or two tablespoons thick cream, 1 egg and 1 dessertspoon flour, 125 g caviar. (4 oz)

To assemble: Place a spoonful of cream cheese on the uncooked side of each crêpe and top with a teaspoon of caviar. Roll up and place in pyrex dish. Dot with butter and bake in medium oven till golden brown. Remove from oven and pour over dollops of thick sour cream and serve piping hot.

ESCARGOT

Method: Drain a tin of snails and rinse them under cold water. Cream 125 g butter (4 oz) with 1 dessertspoon chopped parsley, 2 teaspoons chopped garlic, salt, pepper, a few drops of Worcestershire sauce and a few drops of lemon juice.

Place a little of the mixture in the shells, insert a snail, then more of the mixture. Chill till required. To cook, place shells in a baking dish or in snail dishes and bake in a hot oven for about 10–15 minutes or until the butter begins to sizzle. Serve with very thin slices of brown bread.

LIVER PÂTÉ ROLL

500 g chicken livers (1 lb)
2–3 onions, sliced and fried in 4 tablespoons
  oil and 2 tablespoons chicken fat
1 dessertspoon sherry
  salt and pepper to taste
4 hard boiled eggs

Method: Wash liver under cold water thoroughly. Place in a small saucepan of boiling water and season well with salt and pepper. Continue to boil for about 3 minutes. Drain well, then rinse off with cold water. Mince the fried onions with the liver and 2 hard boiled eggs. Stir in the sherry and season very well with salt and pepper. Spread onto a sheet of oiled foil into a rectangular shape. Roll up as you would for a swiss roll. Sprinkle the remaining two grated hard boiled eggs on the foil and then roll the liver back and forth so that it is coated with the egg.

Leave in fridge to set for a few hours. Place on a bed of lettuce and garnish with overlapping slices of cucumber and tomato and sprigs of parsley. Use some black olives as well for colour. Serve with thin slices of rye bread or french loaf, spread with a thin film of hot mustard.

Special hints: For an extra creamy texture, add 1 sachet unwhipped orley whip.

After spreading out in a rectangular shape, you could place a row of stuffed green olives in the centre, then roll up. This way you would have a contrasting centre when sliced.

MUSHROOM & CHEESE QUICHE

Basic Quiche Pastry
1 cup flour
½ teaspoon salt
½ teaspoon lemon juice
175 g butter (6 oz)
Approximately 3 tablespoons iced water

Method: Sift together flour and salt. Grate in butter. Stir in iced water and lemon juice. Knead lightly. Wrap and chill 1 hour. Roll out pastry to fit 22 cm (9-inch) tart base, prick very lightly and bake blind in hot oven 10–15 minutes. Allow to cool.

Filling:
1½ cups grated cheddar or mozzarella cheese
1 tablespoon flour
2 eggs and 2 yolks
1 cup milk
½ teaspoon salt
 dash tobasco
1 packet sliced fresh mushrooms sautéed in butter
1 cup cream
½ teaspoon curry powder
 chopped parsley

Method: Mix together cheese and flour and sprinkle over base of quiche. Set aside 1 tablespoon of the mushrooms, and place the balance on top of the cheese. Beat eggs and yolks with seasonings and stir in the milk and cream. Carefully pour over cheese and mushrooms and bake in 200°C (400°F) oven for 15 minutes. Reduce heat to 180°C (350°F) and bake 15 minutes longer. When quiche is done, arrange mushrooms slices in centre and sprinkle a border of chopped parsley around them.

Special hint: This quiche may be varied by substituting smoked salmon titbits, chipped beef or lobster and/or fried onions for the mushrooms.

MUSHROOMS COQUILLES MORNAY

500 g (2 packets) large mushrooms (black or white)
4 tablespoons breadcrumbs
1 egg yolk ⎫
2–3 tablespoons cream ⎬ mix together
2 cloves crushed garlic
 salt, black pepper, garlic salt
1 tablespoon dried parsley
1 dessertspoon finely chopped spring onions

Method: Soak mushrooms in salt water for a few hours then wash off well. Remove the stalks and set aside.

Chop the stalks and fry together with garlic in a little butter till lightly browned. Add the breadcrumbs, egg yolk and cream. Add spring onions and season to taste with salt, pepper and garlic salt. Place the mushroom caps in a thickly buttered pyrex dish and fill with the breadcrumb mixture.

For Mornay Sauce
2 tablespoons butter
2 tablespoons flour
1½–2 cups milk
125 g grated cheddar cheese (4 oz)
250 g pink, peeled prawns (8 oz)

Method: Melt the 2 tablespoons butter, stir in the flour and add milk slowly, stirring constantly till smooth. Add grated cheese and prawns and stir till cheese has melted. Spoon over mushrooms, sprinkle with dried parsley, additional breadcrumbs and dot with butter. Bake 180°C (350°F) oven 25–30 minutes.

MUSSELS WITH WINE AND CREAM

5 kilos mussels (10 lb)
3–4 sticks celery, finely diced
1 bunch chopped parsley
3 onions, finely diced
250 g butter ($\frac{1}{2}$ lb)
3–4 cups semi-sweet white wine
250 ml ($\frac{1}{2}$ pint) thick or sour cream
   salt and black pepper

Method: Melt butter in a large saucepan. Add celery, parsley and onions and sauté for 3–5 minutes. Add mussels and wine. The wine *must not* cover the mussels. Simmer gently till mussels open, shaking the pot constantly to turn the mussels.

When the mussels have opened remove from saucepan and add cream and seasonings to the remaining juices, then pour over mussels. Serve immediately with garlic bread.

PIZZA ITALIANO

4 cups flour
1 cake yeast (20 g)
2 teaspoons oil
2 cups warm water
2 teaspoons salt
1 teaspoon sugar

Method: Place the yeast in a shallow bowl. Mix to a liquid with sugar. Pour over the warm water and allow to stand for 10–15 minutes. Place unsifted flour in a large bowl and make a well in the middle. Stir the oil and salt into the yeast mixture then pour into the well and mix till all the flour has been incorporated. Knead until smooth (approximately 5 minutes) cover with a cloth and allow to stand in a warm place overnight or till doubled in bulk, punch down, roll out to fit a very large swiss roll tin or 2 round pizza tins, which have been sprinkled with 2–3 tablespoons oil.

N.B. In the summer, you need only place the yeast dough in an air tight container in the refrigerator overnight.

Topping:
5 or 6 ripe tomatoes, skinned and sliced
2 onions diced
2 cloves garlic, optional
2–3 tablespoons butter or oil
2–3 tablespoons tomato puree or sauce
500 g mozzarella or cheddar cheese (1 lb)
1 egg
2–3 tablespoons cream or milk
1 tin anchovies
   sliced stuffed olives
1 teaspoon mixed herbs, basil or origanum

Method: Sauté onion lightly in butter. Stir in crushed garlic. Allow to cool. Spread tomato purée over dough, then dot with onions. Mix together the grated cheese, egg and cream or milk. Dot evenly on top of pizza. Cover with slices of tomato. Place anchovies in lattice pattern on top, placing a sliced olive in each window. Sprinkle with herbs and the anchovy oil. Leave to rise for ± 1 hour and then bake in a hot oven 210–225°C (425–450°F) for about 20–30 minutes.

Special Hint: To avoid the top from burning, cover with foil after 15 minutes.

Variations

MUSHROOM & TUNA PIZZA
Substitute tuna for anchovies and sauté mushrooms and onions. Omit garlic.

PRAWNS

May be used but must first be sautéed in butter together with the onions and garlic.

PIZZA WITH SAUSAGE, POLONY AND EGGS

Omit cheese mixture. Fry onions in oil with garlic. Cover dough with tomato purée or sauce, slices of sausage or polony, then tomato slices, sprinkle with herbs and 1 or 2 tablespoons of oil. Bake as directed. 10 minutes before pizza is ready, remove from oven, break 2 or 3 eggs onto pizza. Drizzle oil over eggs. Return to oven for a further 10 minutes, or till eggs are cooked.

QUICK AND EASY PIZZA DOUGH

2 cups flour
4 teaspoons baking powder
½ cup milk
  pinch salt
⅓ cup oil

Method: Sift together flour, salt and baking powder. Make a well in the centre. Add the milk and oil and stir then knead into a dough adding more milk if necessary. Knead well for 2–3 minutes then roll out to fit round 30 cm (12-inch) pizza tin.

Toppings: as for previous pizza recipe.

SAVOURY TARTLETS

QUICK PUFF PASTRY

250 g (½ lb) butter or vegetable fat
½ cup boiling water
2 cups flour
  pinch salt

Method: Grate fat into bowl. Add boiling water. Stir quickly with fork till mushy, then add salt and flour. Place in waxproof paper and chill overnight.

Roll out the dough, cut into rounds, place in patty tins and fill with any of the following fillings. Bake in hot oven (225°C–450°F) for 10 minutes. Then turn down to 200°C (400°F) and continue to bake till nicely browned.

TUNA

3 tablespoons butter (75 g)
1 cup milk
½ teaspoon salt
2 chopped hard boiled eggs
3 tablespoons flour
1 tin flaked tuna, drained
1 tablespoon tomato sauce
1 teaspoon Worcestershire sauce

Method: Melt butter, stir in flour, add milk and cook till thickened, stirring constantly. Add remaining ingredients and mix well.

SWISS CHEESE TARTLETS

175 g (6 oz) grated cheddar cheese
1 level tablespoon flour
½ cup yoghurt
¼ cup cream
½ teaspoon salt
1 tablespoon grated onion sautéed till soft in 1 tablespoon butter
½ cup milk
½ teaspoon mustard powder
2 eggs

Method: Beat the eggs and add all the other ingredients. Three quarter fill each tartlet and bake 15–20 minutes.

ASPARAGUS FILLING

1 tin asparagus cuts (410 g)
50 g (2 oz) butter
125 g (4 oz) grated cheddar cheese
1 beaten egg
3 tablespoons flour
125 ml cream ($\frac{1}{2}$ cup)
 pinch salt

Method: Drain asparagus, reserving juice. Melt butter, add flour mixing well. Add asparagus juice and stir. Add cream, grated cheese and stir over medium heat until sauce thickens. Add beaten egg, fold in asparagus. Three quarter fill tartlets, sprinkle with caraway seed, place half a round anchovy on top. Bake 15–20 minutes.

SNOEK PÂTÉ

500 g smoked snoek (deboned) (1 lb)
1 onion, diced
$\frac{1}{2}$ teaspoon black pepper
125 g butter (4 oz)
 juice of $\frac{1}{2}$ lemon
1–2 tablespoons mayonnaise

Method: Sauté onion in butter. Mince or place in food processor with deboned snoek. Add seasonings. Adjust if necessary. Serve with wholewheat bread.

SALMON BRIOCHE

$\frac{3}{4}$ cake yeast (15 g)
2 tablespoons lukewarm water
$\frac{2}{3}$ cup milk
175 g (6 oz) butter
$3\frac{1}{2}$ cups flour
 pinch salt
2 eggs, lightly beaten

Method: In a small bowl, liquify the yeast with 1 teaspoon sugar, then add the warm water. Set the bowl aside in a warm, draught free place for 20 minutes, or till the mixture is frothy. Place the milk in a saucepan with 125 g (4 oz) butter and stir till melted. Cool to lukewarm.

Sift the flour and salt, make a well in the centre and add the yeast, milk and butter mixture and the eggs. Stir the ingredients until all the flour has been incorporated and then knead in mixmaster or by hand, adding a little more warm water if necessary. Place the dough in an oiled bowl, sprinkle lightly with flour, and leave covered in a warm, draught free place to rise till doubled in bulk, or overnight. Punch the dough down and knead again for a few minutes, then roll out to a rectangle about 1 cm (quarter inch) thick. Trim the sides and cut into 16 squares. Place a dessertspoon of filling on each square, gather up the sides of each square over the filling and press together to form a bundle.

Melt the remaining 50 g (2 oz) butter in a saucepan, and dip each bundle in the melted butter then place seam side down in a 22 cm (9-inch) springform pan, arranging bundles in a circular pattern. Dribble any remaining butter over the bundles. Cover the tin with a cloth and stand in a warm place for half an hour. Bake in a 180°C (350°F) oven for 30 minutes, or till golden brown. Serve with caviar butter, made by melting butter and stirring in a few tablespoons of caviar.

Filling:
1 tin salmon or 250 g smoked salmon
 titbits.
$\frac{3}{4}$ cup cold cooked rice
$\frac{1}{2}$ cup melted butter
2 hard boiled eggs, coarsely chopped
$\frac{1}{2}$ cup sour cream
1 finely chopped pickled cucumber
 dash black pepper

Method: Combine all above ingredients.

SALMON PIE

2 tins pink salmon, drained
1 dessertspoon grated onion
125 mℓ cream (half cup)
½ cup breadcrumbs
50 g (2 oz) melted butter
3 eggs, separated
    dash pepper

Method: Mash salmon. Add all remaining ingredients except egg whites. Lastly fold in stiffly beaten egg whites. Bake in greased pyrex dish (20 cm (8 inch) diameter) in a 180°C (350°F) oven for 30 minutes. Must be served immediately.

SALMON SOUFFLÉ ROLL

125 g butter (4 oz)
1 cup flour
1¼ cups milk
7 eggs, separated
½ teaspoon salt
¼ teaspoon cream of tartar
    dash black pepper
½ cup cheddar cheese
2 tablespoons finely grated parmesan cheese

Method: Place milk and butter in a saucepan and bring to the boil. Add flour all at once and stir quickly till it comes away from the side of the pan. This mixture is called a "panade". Stir in the cheddar and parmesan cheese.

Beat the egg yolks very well in mixmaster, then add the panade, salt and pepper and continue to beat till well blended.

Beat the egg whites till frothy. Add the salt and cream of tartar and continue to beat until very stiff.

Fold ¼ of the egg whites into the yolk mixture, then fold in the balance of the egg whites.

Pour into wax lined and greased swiss roll tin 35 x 25 cm (14 x 10 inch) and bake on centre shelf in 180°C (350°F) oven for 12 minutes.

Turn out onto clean cloth. Spread with the filling given below and roll up from long side. Place on greased baking sheet. Arrange slices of cheese (mozzarella is best) on top and place under the griller till the cheese melts.

Use spatula to remove to serving dish.

Filling:
1 tin drained salmon
1 chopped onion
½ green pepper diced (optional)
125 mℓ (½ cup) cream
1 tin cream of mushroom soup (225 g)
1 cup grated cheddar cheese
    salt and black pepper
1 tablespoon maizena, mixed to a paste with a little cold water

Method: Sauté onion and green pepper in butter. Add flaked salmon, soup, cheese and seasonings. Thicken with maizena.

Special hint: You may also use an ordinary creamed spinach for the filling if desired.

SOUFFLÉD CREAM & CAVIAR BLINIS

¾ cup flour
¼ teaspoon baking powder
¼ teaspoon salt
3 eggs separated
¾ cup thin cream

Method: Sift flour with baking powder and salt. Beat the egg whites till they form thick, satiny peaks. Using your mixmaster, beat the egg yolks slightly, mix in cream, and gradually add the flour mixture, beating until smooth.

Fold whites into the egg yolk mixture till thoroughly blended. Fry in a small frying pan which has been generously buttered. Use about $\frac{1}{2}$ cup batter for each, and fry on both sides till golden brown. Stack until ready to use.

Place a crêpe on each plate, pour over thick cream, sprinkle with caviar and serve with chopped hard boiled egg and chopped onion, which has previously been marinated in vinegar, to remove the bitterness.

SPINACH AND FETA CHEESE FLAN

250 g ($\frac{1}{2}$ lb) butter
$\frac{3}{4}$ cup iced water
2 cups flour
1 dessertspoon lemon juice
$\frac{1}{2}$ teaspoon salt

Method: Sift flour and salt. Cut one third of the butter into the flour, then make into a dough with the water and lemon juice. On a floured board roll out in a large rectangle ± 1 cm ($\frac{1}{4}$ inch) thick. Spread $\frac{2}{3}$ of the dough with $\frac{1}{4}$ of remaining butter. Fold the unbuttered third over the centre third and the remaining third fold over to cover the first third, buttered side down, making 3 layers of dough with butter in between each. Turn the dough quarter of the way round and roll out again to 1 cm ($\frac{1}{4}$ inch) thickness. Spread with another $\frac{1}{4}$ of the butter, fold as before and chill for 20 minutes. Roll out, spread with butter, fold and chill twice more. This pastry may be used at once, or wrapped in grease proof paper and refrigerated 12–24 hours or deep-frozen indefinitely.

Filling:
500 g (2 pkts) frozen chopped spinach
4 tablespoons crumbled feta cheese
1 carton (250 g) cottage cheese
50 g (2 oz) grated cheddar cheese
250 mℓ fresh cream (1 cup)
2 eggs, slightly beaten
1 cup milk
$\frac{1}{2}$ onion, grated
2 tablespoons flour
2 tablespoons butter
   nutmeg and salt
   black pepper

Method: Boil spinach in water for 10 minutes and drain well. Sauté onion in butter, stir in flour and make into white sauce with milk and cream. Remove from stove, add beaten eggs *very* slowly and then return to heat and cook until thickened. Add all the cheeses, and the spinach and season to taste with salt, pepper and nutmeg. Spoon into pastry shell, decorate pastry in lattice pattern on top. Bake at 225°C (450°F) until pastry is golden. Serve hot.

Special Hint: Feta cheese should always be soaked in cold water for a few hours to remove saltiness.

SPINACH GNOCCHI

500 g chopped frozen spinach (1 lb)
$\frac{1}{4}$ cup cheddar cheese grated
375 g ricotta cheese ($\frac{3}{4}$ lb)
2 eggs beaten
1 tablespoon parmesan cheese
2 tablespoons flour
1$\frac{1}{2}$ teaspoon salt
$\frac{1}{4}$ teaspoon pepper
1 level teaspoon nutmeg

Method: Cook spinach and drain well. Combine with remaining ingredients and mix well. Shape in balls, (size of a walnut) using wet hands. Poach in salted water, a few at a time, till they rise to the surface. Remove with slotted spoon.

Place in greased pyrex dish. Pour over white sauce made with 2 tablespoons butter, 2 tablespoons flour, 2 cups milk. Season with salt, pepper and nutmeg. Sprinkle with additional parmesan and cheddar cheese. Dot with butter and bake 180°C (350°F) till hot and bubbling. Place under griller to brown.

Special hint: Can substitute cottage cheese if ricotta is unobtainable.

STACKED CRÊPES FLORENTINE

$1\frac{1}{2}$ cups cold water
$1\frac{1}{2}$ cups cold milk
4 eggs
$\frac{1}{2}$ teaspoon salt
2 cups flour
4 tablespoons melted butter or oil

Method: Beat eggs very well. Add water and milk and beat again. Add sifted flour and salt and blend till smooth. Lastly stir in melted butter. Pour through a sieve and refrigerate for 2 hours. When frying you will find it necessary to grease the pan slightly with oil occasionally. Stack one on top of another when cool. For the crêpes florentine you will only require some of the crêpes, the balance of the crêpes may be used for salmon blinis etc.

Filling:
4 tablespoons butter (125 g)
5 tablespoons flour
$2\frac{3}{4}$ cups hot milk
$\frac{1}{2}$ teaspoon salt
1 packet frozen chopped cooked spinach (250 g)
1 carton cream cheese (250 g)
pepper, nutmeg
$\frac{1}{4}$ cup thick cream
1 cup grated swiss cheese or mozzarella cheese
1 egg
1 tin cream of mushroom soup (410 g)
1 packet fresh mushrooms (400 g) chopped and fried in butter

Method: Melt the butter, stir in the flour and then add milk, salt, pepper and nutmeg, as for a white sauce. Stir in the cream and all except two tablespoons of the cheese. Correct seasonings, then blend 2–3 tablespoons of the sauce into the spinach and set aside. Mix the cream cheese together with the egg, mushrooms, mushroom soup and several tablespoons of the white sauce. Place a crêpe in the centre of a lightly greased baking dish, spread with spinach sauce cover with a crêpe, spread with the cream cheese mixture and continue in this way until the crêpes and fillings have been used up. Spread the remaining cheese sauce on top, sprinkle with the remaining cheese, dot with butter and bake in 180°C (350°F) oven till bubbling and golden on top.

STUFFED ARTICHOKES

Prepare a bechamel sauce with 50 g (2 oz) melted butter. Stir in 2 tablespoons flour and 2 cups milk.

Add $\frac{1}{2}$ cup grated cheddar cheese, 3 tablespoons cream and a squeeze of lemon juice.
4–6 medium sized artichokes
Boiled shrimps

Method: Cut the hard stems from the artichokes and trim the tip off each leaf with a scissors. Cook in boiling salted water to which you have added 1 teaspoon lemon juice, until the hearts are tender.

Drain well. Open out carefully and remove the thistle; keep warm. Reserve a few shrimps for garnish and fold the balance into the bechamel sauce. Season to taste with salt and pepper. Fill the artichoke centre with this filling and garnish with remaining shrimps.

TARAMASALATA

125 g Tarama (4 oz) smoked cods roe
2 thick slices white bread, soaked in water
3 cups sunflower oil (750 mℓ)
½ cup lemon juice
2 cloves crushed garlic (optional)
1 teaspoon finely grated onion

Method: Place the oil, lemon juice and onion into a liquidizer and blend. Squeeze water out of bread and add, then blend well. Add Tarama and blend again. If necessary add a little boiling water to thin down. Serve with crisps, crudites, melba toast or crackers.

WHOLEWHEAT CRÊPES FILLED WITH SALMON & CREAM CHEESE

3 eggs
1 cup milk
¼ cup water
1 cup wholewheat flour
1 tablespoon wheat germ
½ teaspoon salt
2 tablespoons melted butter or oil

Method: Beat eggs, milk and water together. Add salt, wholewheat flour and wheat germ and beat till well blended. Lastly stir in melted butter or oil. Fry on one side only in pan greased with oil. Stack one on top of another till ready to use.

Filling:
125 g thinly sliced smoked salmon or titbits (4 oz)
1 heaped tablespoon saithe
250 g (½ lb) cream cheese
125 mℓ (½ cup) sour cream
1 finely chopped onion, fried in 50 g (2 oz) butter
1 egg
1 heaped dessertspoon flour
  salt and coarsely ground black pepper to taste.

White sauce: 1 tablespoon butter. Melt and add 1 tablespoon flour. Stir in 1 cup milk, ½ cup cream and ½ tablespoon black pepper.

To assemble and serve: Place 1 dessertspoon of the cheese filling and 1 slice salmon on each crêpe. Roll up. Place in greased pyrex dish, pour over white sauce and bake in 180°C (350°F) oven for 25–30 minutes. Serve piping hot.

Special hint: For a piquant flavour, add a teaspoon of curry powder to the white sauce before pouring over crêpes.

TUNA LASAGNE

Grate ½ onion very finely and sauté in 125 g (4 oz) butter with 1 pkt (400 g) fresh sliced, mushrooms. When the liquid from the mushrooms has cooked away, add ½ cup flour and stir over heat. Slowly add 2 cups milk, stirring all the time. Add ½ cup cream and stir until smooth. Remove from heat, add 1 cup grated cheddar cheese and season to taste with paprika, salt and black pepper. Set aside.

Add 2 tins drained, flaked tuna fish to the following: Sauté 1 chopped onion and 2 cloves crushed garlic in 50 g (2 oz) butter. Stir in 1 small tin cream of tomato soup and 1 dessertspoon maizena mixed with ½ cup cold water. Add ½ teaspoon mixed herbs and ½ teaspoon dried parsley.

Boil 1 packet (250 g) green lasagne noodles in salted water with 1 tablespoon oil, until tender. Drain on clean cloth.

Butter a casserole dish and alternate layers of tuna sauce, noodles and white sauce in that order. To serve cover top with foil and bake at 180°C (350°F) until piping hot. Remove foil, sprinkle with paprika and parmesan cheese and leave in the oven a few minutes longer.

2. SOUPS

BORSCHT

6 raw beetroot, peeled and grated coarsely
10 cups water
3 teaspoons salt
¼ teaspoon pepper
 juice of 1 large lemon
½ teaspoon tartaric acid
1½ tablespoons sugar
250 mℓ sour cream (½ pint)

Method: Boil grated beetroot in water till tender, about 30–40 minutes. Add salt, pepper, lemon juice, tartaric acid and sugar. Boil a further few minutes. Refrigerate till cold then add cream. Adjust seasonings if necessary. Serve with hot boiled new potatoes.

BOUILLABAISSE

2 kilos (4 lb) filleted and cleaned mixed fish including shrimps, crayfish or langoustines, clams or mussels, red roman or stumpnose or yellowtail, sole, kingklip or/and stockfish. (Use tinned mussels or clams if fresh are unobtainable.)

Ask your fishmonger for the fish bones and heads as these are used for the stock:

4 onions finely chopped
1 large can peeled tomatoes (410 g)
½ teaspoon celery salt
1 teaspoon coarsely ground black pepper
½ teaspoon each basil, origanum, thyme and
 rosemary
3 cups fish stock
½ cup sunflower seed oil or olive oil
6 cloves crushed garlic
3 tablespoons chopped parsley
2–3 teaspoons salt
¼ teaspoon chilli powder
 pinch saffron
1 cup beer or dry white wine

Method: Prepare *fish stock* by boiling the fish bones and heads with 1 whole onion, 1 stick celery, 2 or 3 bay leaves, a few peppercorns and water to cover. Simmer partially covered, 35–45 minutes.

While the stock is cooking, sauté the chopped onions and parsley in the oil until onions are soft. Add garlic, herbs, chopped tomatoes, and simmer 10 to 15 minutes or till mushy. Add seasonings, 3 cups strained fish stock and beer or wine and when simmering lightly, add the fish, cut into bite size chunks, shellfish, clams or mussels. This is the most crucial time as you do not want to overcook the fish. Serve with garlic bread.

Rouille: A strong sauce served with bouillabaisse and onion soup.

Prepare as follows: Crush 2–4 cloves garlic with 5 mℓ (1 teaspoon) cayenne pepper and 10 mℓ (2 teaspoons) paprika. Mix with 2 tablespoons oil and 1 thin slice of bread soaked in fish or onion stock, depending on soup, and 1 tablespoon mayonnaise.

CHICKEN SOUP

3 slices shin
2 slices flank
 few chicken portions or giblets will do
6 carrots, peeled but left whole
1 whole onion
2–3 sticks celery
 few sprigs parsley
2 turnips
2–3 parsnips
3 leeks
4 teaspoons salt
1 teaspoon celery salt
 dash pepper
1 teaspoon seasoning salt
4 chicken cubes
 few drops of egg yellow or a pinch if in
 powder form

Method: Wash meat off very well. Sprinkle the flank and shin with 1 tablespoon salt, then pour over boiling water to cover and leave to stand for 10–15 minutes. Drain well.

Meanwhile place a very large saucepan $\frac{3}{4}$ filled with water, on the stove. When boiling add the meat and chicken portions or giblets and the vegetables and seasonings and simmer gently for about 5 hours.

Add egg yellow. Strain. Bring to the boil, when adding noodles or lokshen, then turn down immediately after to simmering point.

Special point: By washing the meat off well with salt and water, your soup will be very clear and never cloudy.

ACCOMPANIMENTS TO CHICKEN SOUP

1. MEAT PIES

2 cups flour
2 tablespoons vegetable fat
1 tablespoon chicken fat
1 dessertspoon sugar
1 egg
2 teaspoons baking powder
   pinch salt
   water to make into dough

Method: Sift flour, baking powder, salt and sugar. Rub in fat with fingers. Add beaten egg and enough water to make into a dough. Roll out. Cut into rounds and place 1 tablespoon meat filling on each. Press ends together to form a ridge on top and fry in oil on three sides till golden brown. Serve immediately.

Meat filling: Fry onions in oil and mince with the shin and flank from the soup. Add $\frac{1}{2}$ teaspoon salt, dash pepper, 1 teaspoon sugar and 2 tablespoons liquid from the top of the soup. Mix well together.

2. KNEIDLACH

2 eggs
$\frac{1}{2}$ teaspoon sugar
$\frac{1}{2}$ cup water
$1\frac{1}{4}$ cups matzo meal
$\frac{1}{2}$ cup melted chicken fat (melt fat first, then measure)
salt, pepper and cinnamon

Method: Beat eggs slightly. Add fat, water and seasonings and beat again. Stir in the matzo meal. Allow to stand for a few hours. Roll into balls the size of golf balls using wet hands. Boil in salted water for $\pm$ 1 hour. Boil rapidly for the first 10 minutes then turn down to low heat. Keep covered for the first 25 minutes.

3. KREPLACH

2 cups flour
$\frac{1}{2}$ teaspoon salt
2 eggs
   cold water to make into dough

Method: Sift flour and salt. Make a well in the centre and add slightly beaten eggs and water. Roll out the dough thinly on a floured board. Cut into squares, fill with meat and pinch closed. Boil in the soup $\frac{1}{2}$ hour before serving.

Meat filling: Boil 2 slices flank and 1 slice shin in soup until tender. Fry 2 sliced onions in oil until golden. Mince with meat. Season to taste with salt, pepper and $\frac{1}{2}$ teaspoon sugar.

4. MEAT BLINTZES

Method: Beat 3 eggs with 2½ cups cold water. Add 1½ cups flour sifted with pinch salt and ½ teaspoon baking powder. Grease pan with oil and fry on one side only.

Meat filling: Fry 2 chopped onions in oil and then mince with boiled shin or flank from soup. Add ½ teaspoon salt. Dash pepper, 1 teaspoon sugar and 2 tablespoons stock from top of soup.

Mix well together. Adjust seasoning. Place a spoonful of filling on each crêpe. Roll up in envelope fashion. Fry in hot oil till crisp and golden.

CREAM OF ASPARAGUS SOUP/ MUSHROOM SOUP

2 x 410 g tins asparagus cuts, drain and reserve juice (2 lb)
1 chicken cube
2 teaspoons powdered vegetable broth (use 4 teaspoons vegetable broth only if kosher)
2 cups boiling water
75 g butter (3 oz)
1 teaspoon sugar
3 tablespoons flour
1 tablespoon maizena
2 cups milk
250 mℓ cream (½ pint)
   salt and black pepper to taste

Method: Prepare stock with cube, vegetable broth and boiling water. Melt butter in a medium sized saucepan. Stir in flour and maizena. Slowly add milk, asparagus juice and stock and stir till thickened. Add sugar, salt and pepper. Lastly add asparagus chunks and cream. Sprinkle with chopped parsley to serve.

Special hint: Use 2 tins sliced mushrooms instead of asparagus cuts and proceed in exactly the same way for cream of Mushroom Soup.

CRUSTED SEAFOOD BISQUE

125 g butter (4 oz)
2–3 cups milk
1 fillet monkfish
2 Crayfish tails
1 tin baby clams
½ kilo shelled prawns (1 lb)
2 medium potatoes
   seafood spice
2 tablespoons sherry
½ cup white wine
250 mℓ cream (½ pint)
2 onions
   bay leaves, peppercorns
½ cup flour
2 cups water
   salt and black pepper
1 small tin cream of tomato soup (± 200g)
   dash cayenne pepper

Method: Simmer prawns, monkfish and crayfish in water and wine, with 1½ sliced onions, bay leaves and peppercorns, salt and black pepper for 15–20 minutes. Remove fish, strain and reserve stock. Meanwhile boil diced potatoes till very tender. Sieve and set aside. Grate the remaining onion finely and fry in butter till soft. Stir in flour and then add fish stock, juice of clams, milk and sherry and stir till smooth. Add cream and fish, cut into bite size chunks, clams and tomato soup. Stir in potato. Season to taste.

Cut out circles of puff or flaky pastry with soup bowl and bake in oven till golden brown. Top each bowl of soup with this.

For kosher requirements substitute 500 g (1 lb) kingklip for monkfish and omit prawns, crayfish and clams.

DUTCH CURRIED PEA SOUP

1 onion, sliced
1 lettuce, shredded
2 sticks celery, diced
1 clove crushed garlic
8–10 cups water
1 chicken cube
4 teaspoons powdered vegetable broth
2½ teaspoons salt
1 teaspoon curry powder
50 g (2 oz) butter or 2 tablespoons oil
2 carrots, grated
1 large potato, grated
1 kilo frozen peas (2 lb)
250 mℓ (1 cup) cream

Method: Sauté onion, lettuce, celery and garlic in butter or oil. Add carrots, potato, peas, water and seasonings. Simmer for about 2½ hours. Liquidise, return to stove and add cream. Adjust seasonings if necessary. Serve with croûtons.

For kosher requirements omit chicken cube, or alternatively, stir in 2 sachets unbeaten orley whip instead of cream.

LEBANESE CUCUMBER SOUP

2–3 English cucumbers
   salt, black pepper, dash tobasco
1¼ cups strong chicken stock
2 potatoes boiled and sieved
   few cooked prawns coarsely chopped (optional)
1 chopped hard boiled egg for garnish
1 cup tomato juice (250 mℓ)
2 cartons yoghurt (500 mℓ)
250 mℓ (½ pint) whipped cream
2 cloves crushed garlic

Method: Chop up cucumber, salt lightly and weight down with a plate for ½ hour before draining. Meanwhile in blender combine the stock, tomato juice, yoghurt, potato, cream, garlic and seasonings. Lastly fold in cucumber and prawns. Chill for at least 2–3 hours. Pour into soup tureen, garnish with egg. Serve with herbed garlic bread.

For kosher requirements omit prawns altogether.

Herbed Garlic Bread:
Soften 125 g (4 oz) butter. Mix in 4–6 cloves crushed garlic, 1 teaspoon mixed dried herbs and ½ teaspoon freshly ground black pepper. Slice a french loaf diagonally in 5 cm (2 inch) thick slices, but do not cut right through. Smear butter thickly between each slice. Wrap in foil and heat in 200°C (400°F) oven for about 20 minutes.

SOUFFLÉD FRENCH ONION SOUP

6 onions thinly sliced
½ cup oil
1 teaspoon mustard powder
1 beef bouillon cube
2 teaspoons salt
2 cloves crushed garlic
1 tablespoon flour
2 chicken cubes
   about 10 cups water
   black pepper (coarse grind)
   toasted rounds of french loaf.

Method: Slice onions thinly and sauté with crushed garlic in oil, till golden brown. Add mustard and flour and stir till smooth. Add the chicken cubes, beef cube and water as well as seasonings. Stir well and allow to simmer for 1 hour. Adjust seasonings.

Soufflé topping:
2 tablespoons flour
1¼ cups milk
2 egg whites, stiffly beaten
   salt, pepper and nutmeg

2 tablespoons butter
1 cup grated swiss or cheddar cheese

Prepare bechamel sauce by melting butter over low heat. Stir in flour and slowly add milk, stirring constantly till thick. Fold in cheese and season with salt, pepper and nutmeg.

To serve: Pour soup into bowls, top with thin toasted rounds of french bread, spoon soufflé mixture over this and place under broiler for 8–10 minutes. Serve immediately.

For kosher requirements, omit chicken cubes, use 2 onion cubes instead.

MINESTRONE

2–3 tablespoons oil
4–6 carrots diced
500 g frozen peas (1 lb)
1 clove crushed garlic
1 small tin tomato purée
2 large ripe tomatoes, skinned and chopped
4 teaspoons salt
½ teaspoon pepper
4 chicken or vegetable cubes
½ cabbage, finely shredded
2–3 slices shin
   a few marrow bones (optional)
   handful spaghetti, or use 1 tin spaghetti in tomato sauce
2 sticks celery diced
2 onions chopped
2 turnips diced
2–3 cups sugar or butter beans soaked in cold water overnight (or use drained tinned beans)
2 potatoes diced
   water to cover
   cheddar or parmesan cheese for serving. (do not serve cheese, if kosher)

Method: Heat oil in large saucepan. Add onions, garlic, celery and cabbage and fry till limp. Add all remaining vegetables, (except potatoes and spaghetti) meat and marrow bones. Three quarter fill pot with water. Cover and allow to cook over gentle heat 2–3 hours. Add tomato purée, seasonings, potato and spaghetti and allow to cook another hour or two. Serve with the cheese if desired.

WINTER SOUP

6 leeks thinly sliced
8 potatoes quartered
4 carrots thinly sliced
50 g (2 oz) butter or margarine or 2 tablespoons oil
2 chicken cubes
2 teaspoons powdered vegetable broth
   salt and pepper to taste
8–10 cups water

Method: Cook leeks till glassy in butter. Add potatoes and carrots. Add water to cover. Add seasonings. Simmer 1 hour. Liquidise, heat and serve.

3. FISH

BAKED AVOCADO STUFFED WITH LOBSTER

4 lobster tails (For an alternative use 2 tins salmon)
3 avocado pears
 lemon juice
250 mℓ (½ pint) cream or 125 mℓ (¼ pint) cream and 125 mℓ (¼ pint) milk
¼ teaspoon cayenne pepper
1 large onion diced
1 green pepper diced
 salt and coarsely ground black pepper to taste
50 g butter (2 oz)
125 g fresh sliced mushrooms (4 oz)
 grated cheddar cheese and breadcrumbs

Method: Sauté onion and green pepper in butter till slightly golden. Add mushrooms and simmer for 5 minutes. Add lobster, which has been boiled and diced, or salmon and juice, cream and milk/maizena mixture. Add seasonings and stir till thickened. Remove from heat. Cut avocados in half, remove pips and sprinkle generously with lemon juice. Spoon the lobster mixture into the avocados, sprinkle with breadcrumbs and cheese, place in a shallow baking pan filled with 2 cm (1 inch) hot water. Bake in pre-heated oven (180°C–350°F) for 20–25 minutes.

Special hint: You may use kingklip as well. In this case, cut into large cubes and sauté with the onion and green pepper.

BAKED FISH AU GRATIN

1½ kilos stock fish minced (3½ lb)
3 onions, sliced and fried in 2 tablespoons butter and 2 tablespoons oil
1 tablespoon flour
2 tablespoons matzo meal
2 eggs plus 1 yolk
2 teaspoons salt
 pepper to taste
1–2 teaspoons seafood spice
2 carrots
 approximately 1 cup cold water

Sauce:
2 small onions, chopped and fried in butter
1 small tin button mushrooms, drained
1½ cups grated cheddar cheese
1 cup cream, thick or sour
½ cup milk

Method: Mince fish with carrots and onions, adding the oil and butter that the onions have been fried in as well. Add all other ingredients, except those for the sauce, and mix very well. Adjust seasonings. Shape into balls and place in greased pyrex dish. Spoon the onions and mushrooms over the fish, sprinkle with half the cheese and pour over the milk and half the cream. Bake in 180°C (350°F) oven for three quarters of an hour. Remove from oven, sprinkle with remaining cheese and cream. Serve warm.

Special hint: These fish balls are delicious just rolled in matzo meal or cornflake crumbs and fried in oil till nicely browned.

COQUILLES ST JACQUES

1–2 kilos prawns (2–4 lb)
1 onion, finely chopped
1 small glass port wine (125 mℓ)
125 mℓ cream (½ cup)
2 egg yolks
 salt, black pepper
1 pkt fresh mushrooms, sliced and fried in oil (400 g)

Sauce:
2 tablespoons butter
½ cup flour
 milk to make medium consistency

Method: Boil the deveined prawns in salt water for 5 minutes. Shell and cut into bite size pieces. Melt a little butter in a frying pan and add onion. Cook gently until the onion is soft. Pour in the port wine and simmer gently for 2–3 minutes. Remove pan from heat and add lightly beaten egg yolks and cream. Make the bechamel sauce, and mix together with the cream sauce. Season with salt and pepper. Add mushrooms and prawns. Spoon into the shells, pipe a border of mashed potatoes and place under the griller for a few minutes to brown. Serve piping hot.

CREAMED FISH IN RICE RING

4–6 soles filleted, rolled and secured with toothpicks *or* 8–10 lobster tails, boiled and cubed *or* 1½ kilos (3 lb) kingklip cubed.
3 tablespoons butter
½ teaspoon salt, ¼ teaspoon pepper
250 mℓ (½ pint) cream
2 egg yolks
¼ cup marsala or sherry
1 tablespoon maizena, mixed to a paste with cold water
dash cayenne pepper

Method: Place butter in a medium sized frying pan and when hot sauté the fish for a few minutes. Add cream, turn down to low heat and simmer gently for 2–3 minutes. Remove fish, leaving cream in the pan. Mix together the egg yolks, wine and maizena, and add to the cream, cooking gently till thickened. Add cayenne, and then return fish to sauce to heat through. Pour into the centre of the rice ring, and serve piping hot. Can sprinkle with paprika or finely chopped parsley if so desired.

Rice ring:
2 cups rice
4 cups water
1 onion chopped
50 g (2 oz) butter
½–¾ cup grated cheddar cheese

Prepare the rice ring: Boil rice in slightly salted water till tender. Brown onion in butter, add rice and cheese, mixing well. Press into a fluted ring mould with the back of a spoon, and then invert onto your serving platter. Decorate with thin strips of green pepper and tomato, by placing down the grooves, formed by the mould.

CURRIED FISH BALLS

1½ kilos stock fish minced (3 lbs.)
3 onions, sliced and fried in 2 tablespoons butter and 2 tablespoons oil
1 tablespoon flour
2 tablespoons matzo meal
2 eggs + 1 yolk
2 teaspoons salt
pepper
2 carrots
1 teaspoon sugar
1 teaspoon seafood spice
1 cup cold water

Method: Mince fish with carrots and onion, adding the oil and butter that the onions have been fried in as well. Add all other ingredients and mix well with spoon. Add more spice if necessary. Shape into balls,* coat with matzo meal and fry in oil till golden brown.

Sauce:
¾ cup vinegar
¾ cup water
bay leaves and peppercorns
2 tablespoons tomato sauce
2 tablespoons sugar
2 tablespoons apricot jam

2 dessertspoons curry powder
   sultanas (optional)
1 tin pineapple chunks (410 g)

Method: Dissolve curry in a little water, then boil all ingredients together for 5–10 minutes. Pour over fish.

FAMILY BAKED FISH

Prepare fish as given above till *

Place in pyrex dish. Fry 2 onions in 2 tablespoons butter. Add 2 skinned and chopped tomatoes, simmer till soft. Spread over fish, and dot with tomato sauce. Pour over $\frac{1}{2}$ cup milk and bake in 180°C (350°F) oven for $\frac{3}{4}$ hour. One tin of sliced button mushrooms may be added to the fish 10 minutes before removing from oven. When baked, remove and pour over 125mℓ (quarter pint) thick cream.

FISH FLORENTINE

$\frac{1}{2}$ cup cream (125 mℓ)
$2\frac{1}{2}$ cups milk
3 tablespoons butter
3 tablespoons flour
   salt, cayenne, pepper, nutmeg
1 handful chopped spring onions
1 handful chopped fennel
60 g (2 oz) grated cheddar cheese
750 g ($1\frac{1}{2}$ lb) kingklip or other fish
2 pkts frozen chopped spinach (500 g)
   few bayleaves and pepper corns
1 onion finely chopped
1 teaspoon salt
   dash pepper

Method: Place milk, bayleaves and peppercorns in a large pan with salt and pepper and poach fish gently in milk for a few minutes. Remove fish and strain milk. Melt butter sauté onion and stir in flour, then slowly add milk, stirring all the time till thickened. Add cream and fennel.

Stir in cheese and season to taste with salt, cayenne pepper and nutmeg. Boil spinach according to directions on packet. Drain off very well and fold in a few tablespoons of the white sauce. Spread into bottom of casserole dish. Place fish fillets on top and then pour over white sauce. Sprinkle with a little paprika and additional grated cheese. Heat through in oven and place under griller to brown.

Special hint: Nice dish to make with fresh salmon.

FISH STRUDEL

125 g butter (4 oz)
125 mℓ cream ($\frac{1}{2}$ cup)
$\frac{1}{2}$ cup grated cheese
1 pkt fresh mushrooms (400 g)
2 tablespoons maizena mixed with a little milk
1 finely diced onion
   salt and pepper to taste
1 kilo (2 lb) shelled prawns or fish of your choice (e.g. kingklip)
$\frac{1}{2}$ kilo (1 lb) phyllo pastry (available from Greek speciality shops)
   breadcrumbs
   additional melted butter for phyllo.

Method: Melt butter in a saucepan and sauté the onion, then add the mushrooms and cook gently until liquid has evaporated. Add the prawns or fish and cook for a further few minutes, or till the fish is done. Add the cream, cheese, maizena mixture and cook over low heat till thickened. Season to taste. Can add a dash of lemon juice and cayenne pepper if desired. Allow mixture to cool. Brush one phyllo sheet with melted butter, sprinkle with breadcrumbs. Place another layer of phyllo on top of this, and again brush with melted butter and

sprinkle with breadcrumbs. Place another layer of phyllo on top of this, and again brush with melted butter and sprinkle with breadcrumbs. Repeat once more, then place a strip of the fish mixture, about 2 cm (1 inch) from the edge of the long side of the phyllo, fold in the sides and roll up as you would for a swiss roll. Continue making strudels in this way until you have used all the filling. You may freeze them at this stage.

To bake, place on buttered baking sheets, sprinkle with a little water and bake in a 180°C (350°F) oven for 25 minutes then switch oven off completely and leave for another 10–15 minutes so that the phyllo becomes very crispy. Cut into thick slices to serve.

Quick tip: Use filling from salmon blinis for a change.

FISH SUPREME EN PAPILOTE

1 filleted sole or 1 slice fish per person (kingklip, stock, stumpnose etc.)
2 cups cooked rice
250 g ($\frac{1}{2}$ lb) butter
2 skinned tomatoes, chopped
1 large onion, chopped
1 tin button mushrooms, drained (410 g)
$\frac{1}{2}$ kilo (1 lb) cleaned prawns or shrimps (boiled)
1 small tin cream of tomato soup
1 green pepper, chopped
2 sticks celery, chopped
$\frac{1}{2}$ teaspoon mixed herbs
$\frac{1}{2}$ teaspoon dried parsley
2 tablespoons tomato sauce
   juice of $\frac{1}{2}$ lemon
   salt, black pepper (coarse grind) seafood spice
$\frac{1}{4}$ teaspoon cayenne pepper
$\frac{1}{2}$–1 cup thick cream
4 cloves garlic

Method: Cut out 8 pieces of foil in the shape of a heart, large enough to hold one slice of fish and allowing a 5 cm (2 inch) border. Now cut out another 8 pieces of foil small enough to cover the top of the larger hearts, once the edges have been turned up. Place a few tablespoons of rice on each large heart. Season your fish with salt, pepper seafood spice, sprinkle with lemon juice and sauté in butter for ± 5 minutes. Fry your onion, green pepper and celery in half the butter until golden brown, add the tomatoes and mushrooms and cook to a mush. Stir in the tomato soup and boiled prawns, and season with salt, pepper and cayenne pepper. Place a little of this mixture on each mound of rice, then place your seasoned cooked fish on top of this and again place the balance of the tomato mixture over the fish. Sprinkle with the tomato sauce and dot with the remaining butter, then sprinkle the mixed herbs and parsley over this. Cover with foil and place on a baking sheet at the bottom of a very hot oven 225°C (450°F) for about $\frac{1}{2}$–$\frac{3}{4}$ hour. Remove from oven, cut a little foil out of the centre and place a large blob of cream in the centre of each. Serve warm.

This may also be cooked in one large heart if so desired.

Dot with the remaining butter, which has been melted with the 4 cloves of crushed garlic. Serves 8.

FRESH SALMON ANDALOUSE

Method: Place 1 cup semi-sweet wine and 1 cup cold water, 1 sliced onion, few bay leaves and peppercorns in a saucepan and bring to the boil. Add salmon cutlets and poach gently for a few minutes. Carefully remove with a slotted spoon onto foil and allow to cool thoroughly.

Peel off skin, place on lettuce leaves on

serving platter and spoon over the following sauce which has been prepared 24 hours in advance, refrigerated and allowed to thicken.

Prepare homemade mayonnaise as follows: In blender place 2 eggs, 1 teaspoon salt, dash black pepper, 2 tablespoons vinegar, 2 level teaspoons mustard powder, 2 teaspoons sugar and a dessertspoon Worcestershire sauce. Blend for a minute then slowly add $1\frac{1}{2}$–2 cups oil till thick and creamy.

Still using blender, add to the mayonnaise, a few tinned drained pimento, $\frac{1}{2}$ cup cream, 1 tablespoon tomato sauce, 1 tablespoon crushed ice, dash cayenne and paprika, 1 teaspoon brandy.

Blend for another minute. If necessary, add more salt and black pepper. Top each coated cutlet with a few strips of fresh thinly sliced green pepper or sprinkle with a little finely chopped parsley.

GRILLED PRAWNS OR LANGOUSTINES

Method: Wash and devein shellfish but do not remove shells. Place in a large earthenware bowl and sprinkle generously with garlic salt. Mix together the juice of 1 lemon, 1 cup oil, 1 teaspoon mixed herbs and about 1 teaspoon fresh or dried parsley and allow fish to marinate in this mixture for at least half an hour. If you want to add peri-peri powder at this stage, you may do so. Meanwhile crush 5–6 cloves of garlic, place in a small pot, add 250–375 g (8–12 oz) butter and heat together till butter is melted. Remove fish from marinade, place on foil on a grilling pan, then place in the oven as close to the grilling unit as possible, brushing the fish every few minutes with the garlic-butter mixture.

N.B. Before turning the oven onto grill, first preheat to 225°C (450°F).

The shellfish must be grilled on both sides before removing from oven. Make sure that they are well cooked. Place on a bed of rice and pour over the remaining butter garlic sauce. *Do not add salt* to the butter-garlic mixture or to the prawns as the garlic causes it to become sufficiently salty. Garnish with lemon wedges, sprigs of parsley, black olives and serve with garlic bread and a Greek salad.

RUSSIAN KULIBIAK

Pastry:
$1\frac{1}{2}$ cups flour
150 g butter cut into small pieces (5 oz)
$\frac{1}{4}$ teaspoon salt
1 egg yolk
1 tablespoon lemon juice
iced water

Method: Sift flour and salt into bowl. Add pieces of butter cutting in with knife. Make a well, add egg yolk and lemon juice and enough water to form a firm dough (which should be lumpy). Chill for $\frac{1}{2}$–1 hour.

Filling:
$\frac{1}{2}$ kilo (1 lb) stockfish or kingklip
$\frac{1}{2}$ kilo (1 lb) Cape salmon off bone or fresh Pink salmon
50 g (2 oz) butter
1 onion halved
1 carrot
2 celery stalks trimmed and halved
1 onion chopped
1 bouquet garni
$\frac{1}{4}$ cup water
50 g (2 oz) butter melted
4 hard boiled eggs sliced
1 teaspoon salt
$\frac{1}{2}$ teaspoon black pepper
1 tablespoon fresh chopped parsley

1 egg lightly beaten
1 tin small (225 g) sliced button mushrooms
125 mℓ ($\frac{1}{4}$ pint) cream
3 tablespoons cooked rice (optional)
$\frac{1}{2}$ teaspoon seafood spice
1 level dessertspoon maizena mixed to a paste with a little cold milk

Method: Place fish, bouquet garni, celery, carrot and onion halves into a saucepan with the water. Bring to boil, then simmer for 15 minutes approximately or until the fish flakes. Remove pan from heat, lift out fish and cool.

Meanwhile fry 1 chopped onion in butter until transparent. Add the mushrooms and sauté them for a few minutes. Add cream and maizena, stir till thickened. Remove from heat, add fish, hard boiled egg and rice. Let cool. Add seasonings.

Divide pastry into two pieces, roll out into two oblongs, place on baking sheet. Spread filling over one half leaving a 2 cm ($\frac{1}{2}$-inch) space all the way around edge of pastry. Place second piece of pastry on top, sealing edges well. Brush with beaten egg and puncture with fork. Cut two slits in the middle of dough to let steam escape. Bake at 180°C (350°F) for approximately 30 minutes or until pastry is a golden brown.

HERRING SECTION

CHOPPED HERRING – Refer to Jewish Section

DANISH HERRING

8–12 herrings
1 cup brown sugar
1$\frac{1}{2}$ cups tomato purée
$\frac{1}{3}$ cup oil
$\frac{1}{4}$ teaspoon pepper
1 teaspoon mustard
$\frac{1}{2}$ cup chopped green pepper
1$\frac{1}{2}$ cups chopped peeled granny smith apples
1$\frac{1}{2}$ cups brown vinegar
1 diced pickled cucumber
1$\frac{1}{2}$ cups diced onion

Method: Chop off heads and tails of herrings and remove stomach. Place in a large bowl of cold water and allow to soak for 18 hours. Remove skin and fillet the herrings, then cut into pieces. Mix together the brown sugar, tomato purée, oil, pepper, mustard and vinegar. Place the herring, green pepper, apples, cucumber and onion in a bowl and pour over the liquids.

HERRING IN CREAM

6 herrings soaked for 18 hours
1 large or 2 medium onions (see special hint)
250 mℓ thick cream
$\frac{3}{4}$ cup vinegar
2 dessertspoons sugar
$\frac{3}{4}$ cup mayonnaise
  bay leaves and pepper corns

Method: Skin and debone herrings and cut into 2 cm ($\frac{3}{4}$-inch) slices. Mix together cream, vinegar, sugar and mayonnaise. Place herrings, sliced onions and bay leaves and peppercorns in a glass bowl in layers alternating with the cream mixture. Allow to marinate in fridge 3–4 days before using.

Special hint: Soak whole onions overnight in strong salt water solution to remove bitterness.

HERRING SALAD

6 herrings soaked for 18 hours
250 mℓ ($\frac{1}{2}$ pint) cream
$\frac{3}{4}$ cup vinegar
1 cup mayonnaise
2 dessertspoon sugar
1 cup diced fresh cucumber
1 cup diced pickled cucumber
1 cup diced apple (granny smith)
1 cup diced cold boiled potatoes
1 cup diced cold boiled beetroot
2 bananas sliced (optional) pour over juice of $\frac{1}{2}$ lemon
1 cup chopped onions (see special hint)

Method: Skin and bone herrings, cut into 2 cm ($\frac{3}{4}$-inch) slices. Mix together cream, vinegar, mayonnaise and sugar. Place in layers, in a glass bowl, herrings, then chopped vegetables and pour over cream mixture, ending with cream mixture. Allow to marinate in fridge for 3–4 days before using.

Special hint: Soak chopped onion in vinegar for $\frac{1}{2}$ hour to remove bitterness.

GEFILTE FISH – Refer to Jewish Section

KALAMARI

2–3 pkts squid (750 g)
1 teaspoon salt
 juice of 1 lemon
1 teaspoon garlic salt
$\frac{1}{2}$ teaspoon pepper
4 cloves garlic

Batter:
1 cup flour
1 egg
$\frac{1}{2}$ cup beer
1 teaspoon salt
$\frac{1}{2}$ cup milk
25 g (1 oz) melted butter

Method: Clean squid out very well, removing eyes and insides, as well as peeling all the fine purple skin on the tentacles. Rinse very well then cut into slices to form rings and allow tentacle clusters to remain whole. Dry off well and place in an earthenware bowl. Sprinkle with garlic salt, salt, pepper, lemon juice and crushed garlic. If you have some garlic juice (obtained in a bottle) you may add a few drops of this as well. Mix all together and allow the squid to marinate in this way for a good few hours. Make the batter by sifting the flour and salt into a bowl. Make a well in the centre. Mix the milk, beer and egg yolk together and pour into the well. Stir till smooth then add the melted butter. Allow the batter to rest for at least half an hour before folding in the stiffly beaten egg white.

Heat about 2 cups oil in a large frying pan, immerse squid into the batter, allowing excess to drip off and fry till golden brown. Drain and serve on a large platter, decorated with celery curls, slices of pineapple and shrimp chips.

It is important that you do not fry the squid for too long as this causes it to become tough.

LOBSTER SOUFFLÉ IN THE SHELLS

2 tablespoons flour
2 tablespoons butter
$\frac{1}{2}$ cup milk
2 boiled lobsters
5 egg yolks, beaten
 salt and pepper
$\frac{1}{4}$ cup chopped mushrooms sautéed

6 egg whites
2 tablespoons breadcrumbs or grated cheese

Method: Melt butter in a saucepan. Add flour and stir till smooth, add the milk, stirring constantly. Cook for 10 minutes and set aside to cool.

Chop lobster meat coarsely reserving the shells, add to the white sauce. Add the yolks a little at a time, beating well after each addition. Add salt, pepper and mushrooms. Beat egg whites till stiff but not dry. Fold into lobster mixture carefully. Place lobster shells on a greased pan and fill $\frac{2}{3}$ full. Sprinkle with breadcrumbs or cheese and bake 20 minutes in 180°C (350°F) oven. Serve immediately.

LOBSTER THERMIDOR

4–6 lobster tails, boiled
50 g (2 oz) butter
4 tablespoons flour
1½ cups milk
1 cup cream
1 finely grated onion
  salt, pepper (black)
  dash tabasco
1 teaspoon mustard powder
1 egg slightly beaten
125 g (4 oz) cheddar cheese, grated
2 tablespoons sherry
1 tablespoon lemon juice
1 tin sliced mushrooms

Method: Cube lobster tails, reserve shell. Sauté onion and mushrooms in butter. Stir in flour and milk, stirring over low heat till thickened. Add cream and seasonings, egg and cheese. Fold in lobster. Return to heat for a further 5–10 minutes, spoon into shells, top with additional cheese and sprinkle with breadcrumbs. Heat through in 180°C (350°F) oven for 15–20 minutes.

PAELLA

1 jointed chicken seasoned with salt, pepper, garlic salt and ginger
1 can tomatoes or 4 ripe skinned tomatoes
2 teaspoons salt
$\frac{1}{8}$ teaspoon cayenne pepper
2 cups uncooked rice
2 onions finely chopped
$\frac{3}{4}$ kilo clams or 1 tin
1 tin peas or 1 cup frozen
1 tin pimentos, drained
450 g (1 lb) hake or kingklip
$\frac{3}{4}$ cup oil
2–3 teaspoons chicken powder or 1 cube
½ teaspoon pepper
2 cloves crushed garlic
  pinch saffron or ½ teaspoon turmeric
1 pkt prawns 250 g (½ lb)
2–3 lobster tails
1 cup frozen green beans
1 tin artichoke hearts, drained (400 g)
  few slices squid (optional)

Method: Heat the oil in a deep frying pan. Add the seasoned chicken and brown, then add the onion and garlic. When the onion is golden, add the peeled chopped tomatoes. Cook for a few minutes, then add the rice and simmer 10 minutes.

Add peas, beans and artichokes and let them cook for a while with the chicken etc. After this mixture has been cooking for a few minutes, add the sliced pimentos and the fish (cube the hake) i.e. clams, lobster, prawns, squid and season to taste, then let the whole mixture boil fast for 8–10 minutes. Reduce heat and simmer on low for another 10 minutes. Add the saffron and 2–3 cups water to the pan. When the rice is cooked and the water has been absorbed, leave the paella in the oven for 15 minutes to give it a nice golden colour. Remove from oven and serve.

Special hint: The paella may be cooked in the oven only if you prefer.

PRAWNS IN CREAM AND WINE

1–2 kilos (2–4 lbs) prawns
1 onion finely chopped
1 small glass port wine
125 mℓ ($\frac{1}{4}$ pint) cream
2 egg yolks
   salt, black pepper
1 pkt fresh mushrooms, sliced and fried in oil

White sauce:
50 g (2 oz) butter
   milk to make medium consistency
$\frac{1}{2}$ cup flour

Method: Boil the prawns in salt water for 5 minutes. Shell and cut into bite size pieces. Melt a little butter in a frying pan and add onion. Cook gently until the onion is soft. Pour in the port wine and simmer gently for 2–3 minutes. Remove pan from heat and add lightly beaten egg yolks and cream. Make the white sauce and mix together with the cream sauce. Add mushrooms and prawns.

   N.B. This dish may be made in advance, and if necessary, frozen. However when it is reheated, it must not be allowed to boil otherwise it will curdle.

PRAWNS LISBOA

Method: Marinate $2\frac{1}{2}$ kilos (5 lbs) cleaned prawns in lemon juice from one lemon, 1 teaspoon garlic salt and $\frac{1}{2}$ cup oil and leave to stand for at least half an hour. Drain, then fry in butter or oil for 3–5 minutes. Place on a bed of rice in a casserole dish and pour over the following sauce:

   Chop 1 onion finely and fry in 125 g (4 oz) butter with 4 cloves crushed garlic. Add 1 skinned and chopped tomato and allow to simmer till sauce is pink and no pieces of tomato remain. Add 1–2 teaspoons salt, 1 teaspoon peri-peri powder, $\frac{1}{8}$ teaspoon cayenne pepper, $\frac{1}{2}$ cup white wine, $\frac{1}{2}$ cup water, 1 rounded teaspoon flour mixed to a paste with cold water, 1 tablespoon chutney, 1 dessertspoon lemon juice and 2 level teaspoons sugar. Allow to simmer gently for 5 minutes. Lastly stir in $\frac{1}{2}$ cup sweet cream. Pour over prawns.

   N.B. For the above recipe the prawns may be left with or without the shells, whichever is preferred.

SALMON OR SEAFOOD CRÊPES

Crêpe batter:
3 eggs
$1\frac{1}{2}$ cups flour
$2\frac{1}{2}$ cups cold water
$\frac{1}{2}$ teaspoon baking powder
   pinch salt

Method: Beat all ingredients together till smooth. Strain. If too thick, add a little more water. Fry in a small oiled pan till crisp and golden, stack one on top of the other as they cool.

Filling:
2 tins salmon or tuna drained
125 g (4 oz) fresh mushrooms or 1 tin creamed mushrooms
1 large onion chopped
1 green pepper seeded and diced
250 mℓ ($\frac{1}{2}$ pint) cream or 125 mℓ ($\frac{1}{4}$ pint) cream and 125 mℓ ($\frac{1}{4}$ pint) milk
2 dessertspoons maizena mixed with half a cup milk
   dash cayenne pepper
   salt and black pepper to taste
50 g (2 oz) butter
1 dessertspoon lemon juice

Method: Sauté onion and green pepper in butter till slightly golden. Add washed sliced mushrooms or creamed mushrooms and simmer for 5 minutes. Add salmon and juice, cream and milk/maizena mixture. Add seasonings and lemon juice and stir till thickened.

Place a spoonful of filling on each crêpe, roll up, envelope fashion enclosing sides, and place in greased pyrex dish. Make a white sauce by melting 50 g (2 oz) butter. Stir in 2 tablespoons flour and then slowly add 2–2½ cups milk. Stir in ½ cup grated cheddar cheese, season with salt and black pepper. Spoon over crepes and bake 180°C (350°F) oven till hot and bubbling (about 20 minutes).

Special hint: Use tuna fish instead of salmon for a more economical dish.

For a more exotic dish use a mixture of boiled prawns, lobster, clams, etc.

SALMON IN WINE SAUCE

4–6 salmon cutlets
1 cup semi sweet white wine
1 cup cold water
1 onion chopped, 1 onion sliced
  bay leaves, peppercorns, salt, black pepper
½ packet fresh mushrooms – sliced
1 tablespoon sherry
250 mℓ (1 cup) cream
½ cup grated cheddar cheese
125 g (¼ lb) butter
2 tablespoons flour
½ teaspoon mustard powder

To garnish: 1–2 sprigs mint, a few maraschino cherries and walnuts

Method: Pour the wine and water into a saucepan. Add the sliced onion, bay leaves and peppercorns and bring to the boil. Add the salmon cutlets and poach gently for a few minutes. Carefully remove salmon and place in a buttered pyrex dish. Strain the stock and reserve. Fry the chopped onion in butter till glassy. Add the mushrooms and sauté till lightly browned. Stir in the flour and mustard powder. Add the fish stock slowly, stirring constantly till thickened. Add sherry, salt, black pepper and cream. Allow to simmer a few minutes. If the sauce is too thick, thin down with milk.

Pour the sauce over the salmon cutlets, sprinkle with cheese and pats of butter. Garnish with cherries and walnuts. Heat in oven till sauce bubbles. Remove, decorate with mint sprigs and serve piping hot.

SEAFOOD CASSEROLE EN CROÛTE

For pastry:
2 cups flour
250 g (½ lb) butter
½ cup boiling water
  pinch salt

Method: Grate butter into bowl. Add boiling water, stir with fork quickly till mushy, then add salt and flour. Wrap in waxproof paper and chill overnight. Roll out into one rectangular piece and cut out into the shape of large fish using a cardboard guide. Cut the remaining dough into strips 1–2 cm (½–1 inch) wide and place all round the fish, building up the sides as for patties and brushing with beaten egg whites inbetween. Bake in hot oven, till puffy, then turn down and brown about 20–30 minutes.

Seafood filling:
500 g kingklip (1 lb) or 500 g stockfish (1 lb)
250 g (½ lb) prawns (shelled and deveined)
1 sliced onion
1 cup white wine
1 cup water
  bay leaves, peppercorns

Method: Boil the fish in the wine and water with the seasonings till cooked, about 5–10 minutes. Drain and flake the fish removing bones and skin.

Make the sauce as follows:
125 g (4 oz) butter
½ finely grated onion
2 cups milk
1 tin cream of mushroom soup (385 g)
1 tablespoon lemon juice
½ cup flour
1 cup grated cheddar cheese
½ teaspoon paprika
1 slightly beaten egg
   salt, black pepper

Method: Melt butter in frying pan, add onion and sauté lightly. Stir in flour and slowly add the milk. Add cheese, mushroom soup, lemon juice, paprika, salt and pepper to taste and then stir in slightly beaten egg. Fold fish into this sauce. Spoon into pastry shell and heat in 180°C (350°F) oven. Garnish with lemon wedges and parsley.
  Special hint: Can use pastry as given for spinach and feta cheese flan.

SPAGHETTI WITH CLAM SAUCE

½ packet spaghetti (500 g)
1 packet frozen clam meats if available otherwise tinned
1 onion, chopped
4 cloves crushed garlic
4 tablespoons butter or olive oil
2 large tomatoes skinned and chopped
1 tablespoon chopped parsley
  sliced black olives
  salt, freshly ground black pepper, origanum

Method: Boil spaghetti in salt water for 20–25 minutes. Cream 125 g (4 oz) butter, then add ½ cup finely diced or minced parsley. Toss with the spaghetti. Make clam sauce: – Sauté onion and garlic in butter or olive oil. Add tomatoes and cook till soft. Add clams and cook for 5 minutes (or if clams are frozen, cook till done). Add chopped parsley, seasonings and sliced black olives. Pour over spaghetti, toss lightly before serving.
  Special hint: Vary this dish by using a selection of seafoods, such as shrimps, prawns, lobster and kingklip or mussels.

STUFFED TROUT AMANDINE

Fresh trout (depending on no. of persons)
125 g (¼ lb) butter
1 tablespoon oil
  milk, flour, salt and pepper
  clean trout and season and stuff with the following –
2 tablespoons fresh breadcrumbs
  salt, black pepper
1 tablespoon butter in which ½ chopped onion has been sautéed
50 g (2 oz) grated cheese
1 tablespoon cream

Method: Fry onion in butter and add all other ingredients. After trout have been stuffed and seasoned, dip in milk, then flour and sauté in 125 g (¼ lb) butter and oil till brown. In another pot, cook 125 g (¼ lb) butter and a handful blanched almonds till brown, add juice of ½ lemon and pour over trout. Serve with boiled new potatoes, sprinkled with parsley and a French salad.

STUFFED TROUT WITH LEMON HERB SAUCE

4 fresh trout

Method: Wash fish well with water and remove slime by rubbing the skin with the cut side of a lemon. Trim fins and tail with scissors and remove inside bone with a sharp knife, by pushing the flesh away from bone with fingers. Season with salt, pepper, seafood spice and lemon juice. Place stuffing inside, securing the trout with tooth-picks. Dip in cold milk and then coat with flour. Fry on both sides in a lot of butter. Pour over the sauce and serve.

Sauce: Melt 125 g (4-5 oz) butter, ½ finely chopped lemon. Stir in 1 teaspoon mixed herbs, 1 teaspoon fresh or dried parsley, 2-3 tablespoons cream and season with ½ teaspoon salt and ½ teaspoon lemon pepper.

Stuffing: Sauté 1 chopped onion in 60 g (3 oz) butter. Add 6 large fresh mushrooms and simmer until liquid is reduced. Season with salt and black pepper and ½ teaspoon dried parsley. Stir in 4 tablespoons wholewheat breadcrumbs, 1 peeled and grated granny smith apple, and ¼-½ cup coarsely chopped pecan nuts and 1 cup cooked brown rice. Bind with a little cream if necessary.

SWEET & SOUR PRAWNS

For Kosher requirements, fillets of soles, cubed kingklip or cubed chicken breasts may be used for this dish, in exactly the same way.

1 kilo (2 lb) cleaned prawns
2 tablespoons soya sauce
½ teaspoon salt
 dash pepper
 juice of ½ lemon
1 teaspoon garlic salt

Method: Combine the soya sauce, lemon juice and seasonings in a bowl and marinate the prawns in this for a few hours or overnight if preferred.

Batter: Mix together till smooth – 3 cups self-raising flour and 2¼ cups cold water.

Drain excess marinade off prawns, drain well on absorbent paper, coat with flour then mix into the batter. Drop by teaspoonsful into hot oil about 5 cm (2 inches) deep and fry till golden brown. Drain on brown or absorbent paper. Place on a bed of rice and pour over the following sauce.

Sauce: Boil together 1¼ cups vinegar, 1 cup water, ⅔ cup tomato sauce, ½ cup sugar, juice of 1 tin pineapple chunks. Thicken with 1 tablespoon maizena mixed to a paste with a little water. Set aside. Sauté lightly in a little oil slices of celery, cucumber, onion, green pepper, water chestnuts, pineapple chunks, bamboo shoots or bean sprouts, until limp. Drain off excess oil and add to sauce.

TROPICAL PRAWN JAMBALAYA

 prawns, monkfish, lobster or kingklip – boiled
1 large chopped onion
1 tin drained button mushrooms
125 g (4 oz) butter
1½ cups rice boiled with 1 teaspoon butter
250 mℓ (½ pint) cream
½ cup white wine
1 teaspoon salt
½ teaspoon black pepper
½ teaspoon nutmeg
1 tin (410 g) peas, drained
1 tin (410 g) pineapple chunks, drained
1 tin (410 g) peach slices, drained
1 tin (410 g) red cherries, drained
1 teaspoon mixed herbs
 melon & spanspek slices for decoration

Method: Sauté onion in butter. Add fish and mushrooms and cook a further 5–7 minutes. Stir in cream and wine, mixed herbs and seasonings. Mix together the cooked rice and fish mixture, and add peas, pineapple, peaches and cherries. Place on a large ovenware platter or paella dish. Cover with foil and heat through in 180°C (350°F) oven for 20–30 minutes. Decorate with spanspek and melon slices.

VELVYT FISH MOULD À LA NEWBURG

Fish cream:
250 g (½ lb) stockfish
250 g (½ lb) kingklip
2 eggs beaten
125 mℓ (½ cup) cream
1 onion, finely diced and sautéed in butter

Roux:
¾ cup milk
50 g (2 oz) butter
½ cup flour
  salt, pepper, seafood spice

Sauce:
50 g (2 oz) butter
½ teaspoon paprika
1 tablespoon flour
½ glass sherry
¾ cup fish stock or milk
  approximately 1 doz prawns or cubed lobster
½ cup (¼ pint) cream

Method: Make the roux by bringing the milk and butter to the boil. Add the flour all at once and stir until smooth. Season and allow to cool. Place raw minced fish and roux in mixmaster bowl and beat until smooth. Stir in beaten eggs, sautéed onion and cream. Adjust seasonings. Pour into a buttered mould, cover with greased foil, then place in a shallow pan with water in 180°C (350°F) oven for approximately 40 minutes or until firm to the touch. Prepare the *sauce* by melting the butter, add paprika and cook 1 minute. Stir in flour and blend in stock or milk. Allow sauce to boil. Boil shelled prawns in sherry and add to sauce with the cream. To serve, turn mould onto a platter and spoon over sauce. Garnish with sprigs of parsley.

WHOLE BAKED FISH PORTUGAISE

1 line fish preferably stumpnose
(50 g) 2 oz butter
¼ cup oil
1 large tomato diced
1 stick celery diced
  salt and pepper
  juice of 1 lemon
1 onion chopped
1 green pepper, chopped (optional)
1 heaped teaspoon seafood spice
½ teaspoon celery salt
1 tablespoon soya sauce

Method: Have your fishmonger remove eyes of fish and scrape off all the scales. Season inside and out with salt, pepper and seafood spice and sprinkle with lemon juice. Fry the onion, green pepper and celery in butter and oil till golden brown, add tomato and simmer a few minutes longer. Add celery salt and soya sauce. Place half the vegetable mixture on a large sheet of aluminium foil, place fish on top and cover with remaining vegetable mixture. Fold the foil to cover the fish completely. Place on a baking tray or in a roasting pan and bake in a 200°C (400°F) oven for ¾ of an hour to an hour, depending on the size of the fish. Do not allow the fish to overbake, it must be juicy. Open the foil halfway through the cooking period to allow the fish to brown.

Remove from oven, place on a bed of rice, and tear the foil away from underneath the fish, allowing the juices to saturate the rice. Insert black olives for eyes and serve.

Special hint: Kabeljou is also delicious and economical.

WHOLE KABELJOU MAYONNAISE

Method: Line a roasting pan with a double layer of aluminium foil. Season cleaned fish with salt, pepper, seafood spice and sprinkle with juice of 1 lemon inside and out.

Place in roasting pan, dot with 125 g (4 oz) butter and 2–3 tablespoons oil. Cover over with the foil and bake on the bottom shelf of a 180°C (350°F) oven for about 40 minutes – 1 hour depending on the size of the fish. A very big fish could take $1\frac{1}{2}$ hours, but do be careful not to overcook.

Allow to cool completely before removing from pan.

Place on a large platter lined with lettuce. Cover with mayonnaise and decorate using olives for eyes and strips and slices of pickled cucumber, tomato, anchovies, radish roses, celery curls and slices of lemon.

Special tip: Test with a fork and if flesh flakes easily, it is cooked.

4.
POULTRY

APRICOT GLAZED BABY CHICKENS

Method: Split chickens down back, season with salt, pepper, garlic salt, ginger and seasoning salt. Place on grilling rack over roasting pan, skin side down, sprinkle with the juice of 1 lemon and brush with oil on both sides. Place in a 200°C (400°F) oven, middle shelf till golden brown about 30–35 minutes.

Mix together $\frac{1}{2}$ cup hot chutney, $\frac{1}{2}$ cup apricot juice and $\frac{1}{2}$ tin puréed apricots, 2 tablespoons lemon juice and 1 teaspoon prepared mustard. Brush over the chickens. Sprinkle with slivered almonds and return to oven as before till crisped and well browned – about 10 minutes.

Serve on a bed of saffron rice and garnish with the remaining apricot halves.

BARBECUED CHICKEN

Method: Cut two chickens into serving portions and season with salt, pepper, garlic salt and seasoning salt. Sprinkle with flour and brown in oil. Place in a casserole dish and pour over the following sauce.

Chop 2 onions and fry in oil till golden brown. Add 2 large skinned diced tomatoes and simmer for 5 minutes. Add 1 chicken cube, 1 cup water, 1 cup tomato sauce, $\frac{1}{2}$ cup Worcestershire sauce, 1 tablespoon soya sauce, $\frac{1}{2}$ cup hot chutney and 1 teaspoon sugar. Simmer for 2–3 minutes.

Bake covered in a 180°C (300°F) oven for $1\frac{1}{2}$–2 hours. Serve on rice.

CHICKEN À LA KING

Method: Boil 2 chickens in water to cover with 2 whole onions, 2 whole carrots, salt and pepper. Reserve stock.

Cut the chicken into bite size pieces, removing the skin and bones. Fry 2 chopped onions, 1 chopped green pepper, 1 stalk chopped celery and 1 packet (fresh) sliced mushrooms or 1 tin mushrooms (no juice) in 4 tablespoons oil till soft and golden brown. Add $\frac{1}{2}$ cup flour and stir till smooth. Add enough stock to make a fairly thick sauce. Season with salt, black pepper, and paprika. Add chicken and serve piping hot over a bed of rice. Sprinkle with cayenne pepper if desired. Good with French salad.

CHICKEN PAPRIKA

Method: Fry chicken in oil till golden brown. Remove and set aside. Fry 2 chopped onions in same oil. Add chicken portions, 1 teaspoon salt, 4 tablespoons paprika, 2 chicken cubes, and 3 or 4 cups boiling water. Allow to simmer till tender. Few minutes before serving add 250 mℓ ($\frac{1}{2}$ pint) sour cream mixed with 2 heaped teaspoons maizena. Serve on noodles or rice.

CHICKEN BREASTS IN CREAM & CIDER

Method: 8 chicken breasts, remove bone, butterfly, beat with mallet then halve each portion. Season with salt and coarsely ground black pepper. Place in heavy pan with 75 g (3 oz) butter or margarine and brown chicken. Turn down heat, add bouquet garni, 1 small finely diced onion, 2 peeled and diced granny smith or ohenimuri apples, 1 tablespoon brandy and 1 cup apple cider.

Simmer covered over low heat for 35 minutes. Discard bouquet garni, remove chicken and keep warm. Turn up heat and to juices in pan add 250 mℓ ($\frac{1}{2}$ pint) cream or 2 sachets orley whip with 1 teaspoon maizena

mixed to a paste with a little cold water. Stir till thickened then pour over chicken.

Garnish with apple rings sliced and sautéed in butter, then sprinkled lightly with cinnamon or nutmeg and 1–2 tablespoons toasted flaked almonds. Serve with rice and salad.

CHICKEN CASSEROLE

2 chickens cut into portions
  salt, pepper, garlic salt and flour
2 onions, chopped
2 sticks celery, diced
400 g fresh mushrooms (1 lb)
1 carrot diced
1 cup peas
2 tomatoes, skinned and diced
1 tablespoon soya sauce
1 chicken cube
1 cup water
½ teaspoon celery salt
1 teaspoon sugar
½ cup hot chutney
½ cup tomato sauce

Method: Season chicken portions with garlic salt, salt and pepper and sprinkle with flour. Brown in oil and place in casserole dish. Prepare sauce by frying onion, celery and carrot till golden brown. Add tomatoes and mushrooms and cook a further 7–10 minutes. Add peas, water, chutney, tomato sauce, seasonings. Simmer 2–3 minutes. Pour over chicken and bake covered in a slow oven 150°C (300°F) for 1½–2 hours.

CHICKEN MARYLAND

6 chicken breasts
  salt, pepper, garlic salt, ginger, seasoning salt – about ½ teaspoon of each
  flour

2 eggs beaten with ¾ cup water
  breadcrumbs, or cornflake crumbs
2–3 cups oil
1 tin pineapple rings drained (410 g)
3 bananas halved and sprinkled with lemon juice
1 tin creamed sweetcorn (410 g)
1 bottle maraschino cherries

Method: Wash off chicken breasts, removing all the little bones, except the main breastbone. Pull the latter bone, upwards, away from the meat to resemble a cutlet. Dry the meat well, then season and place each cutlet between two sheets of waxproof paper and beat with a mallet till breast is fairly flat. Dip in flour, then beaten egg and water, then breadcrumbs, pressing them well into the meat, leave in the fridge till required. Heat oil in a large frying pan and fry the chicken on medium low heat till crisp and golden brown. Drain on brown paper and place in warming oven. Pour the *sweetcorn* into a bowl, stir in 1 egg, 3 heaped tablespoons flour, 1 teaspoon baking powder, salt and pepper. Mix well then drop by spoonfuls into the oil and fry till golden brown. Drain on brown paper, and keep warm.

Make a *batter* for the *pineapple* and *bananas* as follows:

Sift together 1 cup flour and 1 teaspoon salt, ½ teaspoon baking powder. Make a well in the centre and add 1 egg yolk which has been mixed with 1 cup milk (or water) then stir in 25 g (1 oz) melted butter or margarine. Lastly fold in 1 stiffly beaten egg white. Partly dip the pineapple and banana into the batter and fry till golden brown. To serve, place the chicken in the centre of a large plate, surround with assorted fritters and garnish with cherries and parsley if desired.

If you prefer a *sauce* with your meat, try this for your *Chicken Maryland*.

Melt 25 g (1 oz) margarine, or 2 tablespoons oil, stir in 2 tablespoons flour. Add chicken or beefstock made with 2 cups boiling water and $1\frac{1}{2}$ chicken or beef cubes, and stir till smooth. Stir in one third of a cup Marsala or Madeira wine and season with salt and black pepper.

CHICKEN PIES

Quick puff pastry:
250 g butter or veg fat ($\frac{1}{2}$ lb)
$\frac{1}{2}$ cup boiling water
2 cups flour
  pinch salt

Method: Grate fat into bowl. Stir in boiling water. Add salt and flour. Wrap in waxproof paper, and chill overnight. Roll out, cut into rounds and place in oiled patty tins.

For Kosher requirements make the puff pastry as previously described using a vegetable fat instead of butter. Prepare the chicken by placing $\frac{1}{2}$ cup oil in a pot with 1 large chopped onion, 1–2 sliced carrots, 2 cloves, finely chopped garlic, 1–2 sticks chopped celery, and the chicken seasoned with salt, pepper, garlic salt, ginger, seasoning salt, 2 bay leaves, a few peppercorns and 1 teaspoon chicken powder. Brown all the vegetables and chicken a little, then add about 1 cup water and allow to simmer on medium low heat for 1 hour. Add 1–2 cubed potatoes, 1 cup peas, 1 packet freshly sliced mushrooms and continue to simmer for another $\frac{1}{2}$ hour adding more water, if necessary. Remove chicken, discarding skin and bones and flake. Remove the bay leaves and peppercorns from the pot. Return flaked chicken to the pot and mix with the vegetables. Thicken with 1 tablespoon maizena mixed to a paste with cold water. Place the combined chicken and vegetable mixture in the patty shells. Place strips or rounds of pastry over chicken mixture, brush with beaten egg and sprinkle with sesame seed. Bake 225°C (450°F) oven till golden brown.

Variation: Can substitute veal for chicken.

CHICKEN WITH KUMQUATS AND MANDARINS

Method: Season chicken with salt, pepper garlic salt, ginger and seasoning salt. Pour over $\frac{1}{2}$ cup oil and roast uncovered in 180°C (350°F) oven till golden brown, about 1–$1\frac{1}{2}$ hours. Cut into portions, place in casserole dish and pour over the following sauce.

Drain off all but 1 tablespoon fat from roasting pan. Add 1 cup water, 1 cup orange juice, 1 teaspoon syrup, 1 teaspoon sugar, 1 dessertspoon soya sauce, $\frac{1}{2}$ teaspoon salt and a dash of pepper.

Thicken with 1 tablespoon maizena and 1 teaspoon gravy powder mixed to a paste with cold water. Cook till thickened, strain and add 250 g ($\frac{1}{2}$ lb) kumquats and 1 tin drained mandarin segments. Bake uncovered in a slow oven 150°C (300°F) for 45 minutes. Garnish with toasted slivered almonds.

CHUTNEY CHICKEN WITH BANANAS

1 packet chicken portions
1 teaspoon salt
2 teaspoons lemon juice
4 level teaspoons curry powder
2 level teaspoons cinnamon
2 tablespoons honey
1 teaspoon French American mustard
1 dessertspoon oil
$\frac{1}{4}$–$\frac{1}{2}$ cup hot chutney

Method: Rub chicken portions with oil. Combine salt, curry, cinnamon and rub over each portion. Allow to stand for

15 minutes. Combine honey, lemon juice, chutney and mustard and pour over chicken. Allow to marinate 1–2 hours, then bake covered at 180°C (350°F) for ½ hour, then place on braai. Braai unpeeled bananas until skins are black. Unpeel and sprinkle with salt and pepper. *If you wish to oven cook it only*, bake for 1 hour covered and a further ½ hour uncovered. Placed peeled, halved bananas, which have been soaked in lemon juice, in between the chicken portions for the last ½ hour.

DUCK BIGARADE

2 ducks seasoned with salt, pepper, garlic salt, ginger and seasoning salt
6 oranges, peel, removing all pith and slice reserving juice
1 cup orange juice
4 tablespoons sugar
3 tablespoons vinegar
3 cups chicken stock (boiling water mixed with 1 chicken cube)
2 tablespoons lemon juice
1 tablespoon soya sauce
1 tablespoon tomato sauce
½ cup curacao or any orange flavoured liqueur
1 teaspoon salt
dash pepper
1 dessertspoon maizena
1 teaspoon gravy powder
rind of 1 orange

Method: Slice the orange rind very thinly into strips and boil in a little water for a few minutes, then drain well, to remove bitterness. Place seasoned ducks on wire rack over roasting pan and place in a 180°C (350°F) oven for 1¼ hours, till golden brown. Remove from oven, cool and cut into quarters or portions, if you prefer, and place in casserole dish (large and shallow). Do not place one piece on top of the other — it must be in a single layer.

Meanwhile prepare the sauce. Place sugar and vinegar in a saucepan to caramelise. Do not allow to burn. Remove from heat and add the chicken stock, orange juice, (from sliced oranges as well) lemon juice, orange rind, soya sauce, tomato sauce, orange liqueur, salt and pepper, maizena and gravy powder which have been mixed with a little cold water to a paste. Return to stove and cook till thickened, stirring constantly.

Arrange sliced oranges on top of duck, pour over sauce and bake in a slow oven 150°C (300°F) for 45–60 minutes or till tender, basting occasionally.

FRIED CHICKEN

2 chickens, cut into portions
½ cup oil
½ cup lemon juice
2 teaspoons salt
3–4 cloves crushed garlic
1 teaspoon black pepper, coarse grind
1 teaspoon origanum
Flour
3 eggs, slightly beaten
oil for frying

Method: Combine the oil, lemon juice, garlic, herbs and seasonings. Marinate the chicken in the mixture for 2 hours at room temperature. Drain well. Roll chicken in flour then dip in egg.

Heat oil till very hot, add chicken and fry till well browned and tender. Drain and keep hot whilst preparing the balance.

GLAZED BANANA STUFFED CHICKEN

Method: Heat 2 tablespoons oil in pan. Add 2 cloves garlic. Cook 15 seconds, remove and discard. Add 1½ cups freshly made breadcrumbs and sauté till crisp and brown. Add 2 tablespoons lemon juice, 1 teaspoon finely grated lemon rind, 2 teaspoons brown sugar, 1½ tablespoons rum, ½ teaspoon nutmeg, ¼ teaspoon cayenne pepper, ¾ teaspoon salt, ½–1 teaspoon coarsely ground black pepper. Set aside. Dice 3 ripe bananas and mix with 1 tablespoon lemon juice. Mix all together very thoroughly. Place banana stuffing in chicken cavity. Season the chicken well with salt, pepper, garlic salt, seasoning salt and ginger. Pour over 1 cup oil and roast uncovered 180°C (350°F) oven for 1½–2 hours.

Make a gravy by pouring off fat from pan. Add 2 cups water, 1 teaspoon gravy powder, ½ chicken cube, 2 teaspoons maizena, salt and pepper and stir over heat till thickened. Strain.

Glaze chicken with:
¼ cup honey
½ cup chutney
 juice of 1 lemon or ¼ cup
½ packet flaked almonds

Brush on both sides and brown on lightly oiled foil under griller

Quick tip: The glaze is nice on a plain grilled chicken as well.

MARINATED GRILLED CHICKEN

2 spring chickens
¾ cup oil
1 tablespoon finely chopped or dried parsley
2 teaspoons salt
1 teaspoon garlic salt
1 teaspoon mustard powder
 juice of 1 large lemon or 2 smaller lemons
4 cloves crushed garlic
1 teaspoon black pepper (coarse grind)
1 teaspoon mixed herbs or origanum

Method: Split chickens down the back. Combine remaining ingredients to make a marinade. Marinate chickens in this mixture from 1 hour to overnight. Drain off marinade and reserve. Place on grilling tray over roasting pan. Place in 200°C (400°F) oven, bottom shelf and cook for 1–1¼ hours, turning and basting frequently with the remaining marinade.

Special Hint: This chicken is particularly good cooked in a rotisserie.

ORIENTAL DUCK

1–2 ducks
 salt and pepper
1 teaspoon garlic salt
2 onions whole
1 large tin pineapple chunks, reserve juice
1 cup orange juice
2 tablespoons ginger liqueur
2 tablespoons brandy
2 tablespoons pineapple liqueur
1 teaspoon ginger
1 heaped teaspoon gravy powder
2 tablespoons maizena
1 chicken cube
3 tablespoons tomato sauce
2 tablespoons soya sauce
 preserved ginger
¾ cup preserved ginger syrup
1 tablespoon sugar

Method: Season ducks with salt, pepper, ginger and garlic salt and place 1 whole onion in each. Place on roasting rack and roast till golden brown for 1–1¼ hours. Cool and cut into serving portions, then arrange in casserole dish. Pour fat off roasting pan and make sauce as follows:

Sauce: Pour two cups water into pan. Dissolve gravy powder and maizena in cold water and add to pan with chicken cube, tomato sauce, soya sauce, ginger syrup, orange juice, pineapple juice, sugar, little salt and pepper, ginger liqueur, pineapple liqueur and brandy. Stir till mixture boils. Strain and pour over ducks. Chop up several pieces of ginger and add to duck with pineapple chunks. Bake uncovered in a slow oven for ¾ hour basting occasionally and turning duck if necessary.

This dish may be prepared in the morning and left to marinate, till ready to bake.

ROAST TURKEY

Clean Turkey thoroughly. Mix together:
2 teaspoons salt
1 teaspoon pepper
½ teaspoon seasoning salt
½ teaspoon garlic salt
½ teaspoon ginger
½ teaspoon paprika

Method: Rub well into the skin of the turkey, as well as under the breast skin and inside the cavity. Squeeze the juice of ½ a lemon in the cavity only and place a whole peeled onion inside as well. Place in a roasting pan and pour 1 cup oil over. Roast uncovered in the bottom of a moderate oven, basting occasionally and taking special care not to prick the skin of the turkey. Roast for 1½ hours – depending on size of turkey. It is not necessary to roast even a very large bird for more than 2 hours, unless of course it is stuffed.

Gravy: Pour off fat from the roasting pan. Stir into the pan about 1 cup water, 2 teaspoons maizena, 2 teaspoons gravy powder, ½ chicken cube, salt and pepper to taste, cook until thickened, then strain.

Quick tip: 10 or 15 minutes before removing from the oven, pour over the turkey the juice of 1 or 2 oranges, depending on size of bird.

SPICY CHICKEN CASSEROLE

1–2 packets chicken portions
1½ teaspoon salt
½ teaspoon cayenne pepper
2 tablespoons Worcestershire sauce
1 tablespoon soya sauce
2 tablespoons vinegar
1 teaspoon mustard powder
2 large green peppers
2 large onions
1 packet fresh mushrooms, sliced (400 g)
2 large tomatoes, skinned
1 teaspoon mixed herbs
1 chicken cube
1 cup water
 oil for frying

Method: Season chicken with salt, pepper and garlic salt. Sprinkle lightly with flour then brown chicken in oil. Remove from pan and place in casserole dish. Fry mushrooms, coarsely chopped onions and green peppers in the same oil till limp. Add chopped tomatoes and cook another 10–15 minutes. Add all seasonings and water. Pour over chicken and bake in oven in covered dish for ¾ hour. Remove cover and allow chicken to cook uncovered for another 15–20 minutes. Serve with chicken liver rissoto and a French salad.

Special hint: This dish is equally good substituting veal chops, for the chicken.

SPRING ROLLS

1 cooked chicken, skinned and diced or
 leftover chicken
1 tin button mushrooms, drained and sliced
1 onion diced
1 tin bamboo shoots or bean sprouts
6 water chestnuts (optional)
½ cup fine noodles, cooked
1 teaspoon salt

½ teaspoon ginger
dash pepper
½ teaspoon sugar
¼ cup chopped spring onions
2 tablespoons oil
rice paper
1 beaten egg

Method: Place oil in frying pan. Heat and add onion, mushrooms, bean sprouts, spring onion and water chestnuts and fry till wilted. Add chicken, noodles, seasoning and fry another 2–3 minutes. If the mixture does not bind, add 1 dessertspoon maizena, mixed to a paste with ½ cup water, and cook again for a few minutes. Place a spoonful of filling on rice paper and roll up lengthwise. Seal with beaten egg. Dip each roll in batter and deep fry in oil till golden brown. Serve with sweet and sour sauce.

Batter: Mix together 3 cups self-raising flour with 2½ cups cold water.

Sweet and sour sauce:
2 tins pineapple chunks
1 finely chopped green pepper
1 small onion, finely chopped
2½ tablespoons sugar
1 tablespoon tomato sauce
juice of 1 lemon
2 tablespoons soya sauce
dash of Worcestershire sauce
½ teaspoon ground ginger
1 tablespoon vinegar
1 dessertspoon maizena mixed with 1 cup cold water
salt and pepper to taste

Method: Fry green pepper and onion in a little oil till soft, then add the pineapple, lemon juice, sugar, soya sauce, tomato sauce, Worcestershire sauce, maizena and water and stir constantly till thickened. Season to taste with salt and pepper. If desired, you may add julienne strips of cucumber skin, fresh pineapple and celery.

Quick tip: You may use leftover diced beef as well in place of chicken.

Makes approximately 2 dozen.

STUFFED CHICKEN ALMONDINE

10–12 chicken portions, deboned
salt, pepper, garlic salt, ginger, seasoning salt
250 g fresh sliced mushrooms (½ lb)
1 chicken cube
2½ cups water
1 teaspoon mixed herbs
¼ cup oil
1 tablespoon flour
3 cloves crushed garlic
1 large finely chopped onion
¾ cup medium dry red wine
1 dessertspoon tomato paste
2 tablespoons toasted flaked almonds

Method: Debone chicken portions by scraping the flesh away from the bones, using a sharp knife, and cutting the skin only when absolutely essential. The inside thigh and wing bone will have to be snipped all the way down with a scissors and then pushed away from the bone. Season lightly with salt, pepper, garlic salt and ginger. Place a spoonful of stuffing, recipe below, on the inside of each portion, then form a bundle, enclosing with the use of the skin and ensuring that each portion is well rounded. Place *very close* together (this ensures that the stuffing does not come out) in a large casserole or pyrex dish. Pour over the following sauce –

Sauce: Sauté the onion and garlic in oil till lightly browned. Add sliced mushrooms, and cook until liquid evaporates. Stir in flour, then add wine, crushed chicken cube, water, tomato paste and mixed herbs.

Season to taste with salt and black or white pepper. Simmer 2–3 minutes. Pour over chicken. Sprinkle with almonds. Cover with foil and bake in 180°C (350°F) oven for 1 hour, then uncover and bake till nicely browned but not dry.

Stuffing: Crumble the inside of 1 loaf of white or wholewheat bread, one or two days old. Add 4 tablespoons oats, 1 tablespoon flour, ½ teaspoon mixed herbs, ½ teaspoon thyme, ½ teaspoon origanum, 1 teaspoon dried parsley. Sauté 1 large chopped onion in 4 tablespoons chicken fat and add this to the breadcrumb mixture together with 2 peeled and grated granny smith apples. Mix all together. Season with salt and pepper.

Special hint: I collect the fat from the chickens, dice it and use it for the stuffing, by frying with the onions, about 3–4 large pieces. This really makes all the difference.

TROPICAL DUCK

1–2 ducks
2 whole onions
   salt, pepper, ginger, garlic salt
1 tin red or black cherries
1 tin mandarin segments
1 tin lychees
   juice of 1 or 2 oranges
2 tablespoons cherry brandy
2 tablespoons brandy
1 teaspoon gravy powder
2 teaspoons maizena
½ chicken cube
3 tablespoons tomato sauce
2 tablespoons soya sauce
2–3 tablespoons sugar

Method: Season ducks with salt, pepper, ginger and garlic salt and place 1 whole onion in each cavity. Place on roasting rack over roasting pan and place in a 200°C (400°F) oven (bottom shelf) till golden brown, about 1 hour, turning over once half way through the cooking time. Remove from oven and when cool enough, cut into portions, then arrange in a casserole dish, in a single layer. Pour the drippings from the duck out of the roasting pan and make the sauce as follows –

Sauce: Pour 2 cups water into the roaster. Dissolve gravy powder and maizena in cold water and add to pan with chicken cube, tomato sauce, soya sauce, syrup from cherries only, orange juice, sugar, salt and pepper to taste, cherry brandy or liqueur and brandy. Stir constantly till mixture boils, scraping the bottom of the pan as you do so. Taste and adjust seasonings or sugar if necessary. Strain, and pour over the duck portions. Bake, uncovered, in a slow oven for ¾–1 hour, basting occasionally and turning the portions.

Remove from oven, arrange the cherries, mandarin segments and lychees on top and return to the oven for a further 10 minutes, to heat the fruit.

This dish may be prepared in the morning and baked just before required.

UPSIDE DOWN CHICKEN PIE

Pastry: Sift together 2 cups flour, 2 teaspoons baking powder, 1 dessertspoon sugar and a pinch of salt. Grate in 125 g (4 oz) margarine. Add one beaten egg and enough water to make into a dough.

To prepare chicken: Place 1 chicken in a large pot with 2 chopped onions, 2 chopped carrots, ¼ cup oil, 2 cloves garlic, salt, pepper, ginger, seasoning salt, garlic salt, bay leaves and peppercorns. Allow to brown slowly, then add 1 cup water and let cook slowly till tender. When the chicken is ready, add 1 cup peas and one tin drained and sliced mushrooms.

Cut the chicken into serving portions and place in a baking dish that has been lined with see through cooking foil. Arrange the chicken pieces skin side down. Now arrange the peas, mushrooms and carrots inbetween the pieces of chicken. Cover with the dough. Cut a few slits in the dough to allow the steam to escape. Bake in a 200°C (400°F) oven until the crust is golden brown. To serve turn upside down onto serving plate, and decorate with sprigs of parsley. Add a little more water to the pot in which the chicken was braised and thicken with maizena, as this will be the gravy which you will serve with the chicken pie. If necessary season with more salt and pepper.

Special hint: Can also skin and dice chicken and place in wedges with vegetables.

5. MEAT SECTION
1. Beef
2. Lamb
3. Veal

1. BEEF

BEEF OLIVES OR VEAL BIRDS

6 slices tenderised steak or veal schnitzels
2 onions
½ cup cream if desired
2 sticks celery
2 cloves garlic
2 chopped carrots
    bay leaves, peppercorns, salt, pepper, garlic salt, ginger
1 cup chicken stock
½ cup white wine

Stuffing: Take the inside of half a loaf of white, wholewheat or rye bread one or two days old, and crumb it. Add about 3 or 4 tablespoons oatmeal and 1 tablespoon flour as well as ½ teaspoon mixed dried herbs, ½ teaspoon thyme, ½ teaspoon sage, ¼ teaspoon origanum and rosemary if you have it and 1 teaspoon parsley fresh or dried. Now fry 1 chopped onion in fat or butter till soft and add to breadcrumbs, grate 2 green peeled apples and add as well with salt and pepper (about ½ teaspoon). Mix all together. Place some in each beef olive or veal bird then roll up. Secure with toothpicks. Season with salt, pepper, garlic salt and ginger.

Method: Brown veal birds in ½ cup oil or 125 g (¼ lb) butter. Remove from pot and brown the chopped onions, celery, garlic and carrots. Put the veal birds back in pot and add 2 bay leaves and a few peppercorns, 1 cup chicken stock and ½ cup wine. Simmer for 1–1½ hours. Before serving add 1 tin sliced and drained mushrooms and if desired ½ cup cream. Serve on noodles or rice with a French salad.

BRISKET WITH PRUNES

Ask your butcher for a piece of fresh brisket 2–3 kg (5–7 lb) *Cut off the bone.* Place in a pot with 5 or 6 cups water. Add one onion halved, one carrot quartered and the following –
1 teaspoon ginger
2 teaspoons salt
½ chicken cube
½ teaspoon seasoning salt
½ teaspoon garlic salt
¼ teaspoon pepper

Method: Simmer covered for about 3 hours until almost tender. Add about 1 dozen prunes, juice of one lemon and 3–4 tablespoons syrup. Simmer again until liquid is reduced and the meat is brown and tender. Spoon off the excess fat and thicken the gravy with 1 tablespoon gravy powder mixed with ½ cup cold water.

    N.B. Add par-boiled halved potatoes ½ hour before serving.

    Serve on a meat platter surrounded with potatoes and prunes.

CAVIAR TOPPED BEEF STROGANOFF

1 kg (2 lb) cubed topside steak
2 large onions chopped
1 packet fresh sliced mushrooms (400 g)
2 tablespoons Worcestershire sauce
¼ cup red wine
2 tablespoons butter or oil
2 tablespoons maizena
2 beef cubes
2 teaspoons salt
1½ cups water

¼ teaspoon pepper
1 teaspoon prepared mustard
1 teaspoon paprika
¼ teaspoon cayenne pepper
250 mℓ (1 cup) sour cream
1 jar caviar

Method: Heat the butter or oil in a large saucepan and brown meat and onion. Add mushrooms and cook a few minutes. Stir in Worcestershire sauce, and beef cubes. Add water, wine and seasoning. Cook over gentle heat (covered) for about 1½–2 hours, or until meat is tender. Mix maizena and mustard together with a little cold water and add, stirring till thickened. Stir in cream and adjust seasonings to taste. Serve on rice or noodles and sprinkle each serving with caviar. Serve with a French salad.

N.B.: For kosher requirements substitute 2 sachets orley whip and juice of ½ lemon for sour cream.

FILLET EN BOITE NO. 1

Method: Take a whole fillet, season with salt, pepper, garlic salt and rub in with 1 teaspoon mustard powder. Slice two onions and place over fillet, wrap in foil and leave in fridge overnight. This is not absolutely necessary but it does tenderise the meat and improve the flavour.

Roast in 1 cup oil for ½–¾ hour in a very hot oven, 225°C (450°F).

Sauce: Fry 2 chopped onions and 400 g (1 lb) fresh sliced mushrooms in oil or butter till lightly browned. Stir in 1 dessertspoon flour, ½ teaspoon mustard powder. Add 250 mℓ (½ pint) sour cream, 1 tablespoon prepared mustard, 3 tablespoons sherry, and 1 egg yolk. *Do not allow to boil* as it will curdle. Cook only till thickened. Season with salt and black pepper (coarse grind) to taste. Pour over fillet and serve.

Special hint: If sauce does curdle, beat with egg beater to rectify.

For kosher requirements use scotch fillet and substitute 2 sachets unbeaten orley whip with 1 teaspoon lemon juice for sour cream.

FILLET EN BOITE NO. 2

Method: Take a whole fillet, season with salt, pepper, garlic salt, ginger and rub in with 1 teaspoon mustard powder. Slice two onions and place over fillet, wrap in foil and leave in refrigerator overnight. Alternatively, you may season thick slices of fillet steak with salt and black pepper and grill with very little oil, then pour over the sauce.

Sauce:
1 onion chopped
1 tablespoon vinegar
1 dessertspoon dry mustard
1 teaspoon sugar
1 egg yolk
2 tablespoons finely chopped pickled cucumber
250 mℓ (1 cup) thick cream or 1 sachet orley whip
1 dessertspoon sherry
1 tin button mushrooms, drained
1 tablespoon flour
¾ teaspoon salt
¾ cup water

Method: Fry the chopped onion in a little oil till golden brown, add mushrooms and fry a further few minutes. Mix the flour, mustard, sugar, salt and vinegar till smooth and add to the pan, stir till blended. Beat the egg yolk slightly and add the water, then stir into the mustard mixture. Simmer gently for 1–2 minutes, then stir in sherry, cream or orly whip and cucumber. *Do not allow this sauce to boil*, otherwise it will curdle.

FILLET BEARNAISE

Method: Season thick slices of fillet steak with salt, pepper and barbeque spice. Fry in a hot pan with a little oil till cooked to your desire. (Serve with sauce bearnaise.) Serve with grilled mushrooms and herbed tomatoes.

Bearnaise sauce:
4 egg yolks
250 g ($\frac{1}{2}$ lb) butter
$\frac{1}{4}$ teaspoon salt
   dash cayenne pepper
1 tablespoon water
2 tablespoons tarragon vinegar
2 crushed peppercorns
1 teaspoon chopped parsley
$\frac{1}{2}$ cup dry white wine
1 tablespoon chopped spring onions

Method: Combine the spring onions, parsley and peppercorns with the vinegar and white wine in a saucepan. Cook until liquid is reduced to about $\frac{1}{2}$ cup.

Beat egg yolks very well and slowly add the liquid to the yolks, beating all the time. Place in double boiler and beat with a wire whisk till mixture is light and fluffy. Add butter gradually, beating all the time till mixture is thick. Season to taste with salt and pepper.

GARLIC STEAK WITH ANCHOVY SAUCE/ CHASSEUR SAUCE

Method: Crush 3–4 cloves garlic and mix with 2 teaspoons celery salt, $\frac{1}{2}$ teaspoon mixed herbs, $\frac{1}{2}$ teaspoon dried parsley, 8 tablespoons oil, 4 tablespoons soya sauce, 4 tablespoons lemon juice, 2 teaspoons coarsely ground black pepper, $\frac{1}{4}$ cup chopped spring onions. Cut an additional 2–3 cloves garlic in slivers and insert into meat, either fillet or scotch fillet, then pour over the sauce and allow the meat to marinate for a few hours or overnight. The fillet may then be roasted in the oven with $1\frac{1}{2}$ cups oil on 200°C (400°F) for $\frac{3}{4}$ of an hour, or if preferred on top of the stove in a large pot uncovered. The *scotch fillet* must be roasted in a 200°C (400°F) oven with $1\frac{1}{2}$ cups oil for about 50 minutes, uncovered, on the bottom shelf of the oven.

Garlic anchovy sauce: Fry 2 chopped onions and 3 cloves chopped garlic in 4 tablespoons oil till lightly browned. Add 4 skinned chopped tomatoes and allow to simmer 10 minutes. Add 1 tin finely chopped anchovies, 1 tablespoon chopped parsley, $\frac{1}{2}$ cup white wine, $\frac{1}{2}$ teaspoon coarsely ground black pepper, 1 teaspoon dried mixed herbs and 1 tablespoon capers (optional).

Thicken with 1 teaspoon gravy powder mixed to a paste with cold water and allow to simmer for 15–20 minutes.

Chasseur sauce: Fry 2 chopped onions and 2 cloves chopped garlic in 4 tablespoons oil till lightly browned. Stir in 1 tablespoon flour. Add $\frac{1}{2}$ chicken cube dissolved in $1\frac{1}{2}$ cups water with 1 heaped teaspoon gravy powder and 1 teaspoon maizena. Stir till smooth. Add $\frac{1}{2}$ cup white wine, 1 tablespoon tomato purée, freshly ground pepper, $\frac{3}{4}$ teaspoon salt, good pinch origanum and 1 tin sliced and drained button mushrooms. If sauce is too thick, add more water.

ITALIAN LIVER

750 g ($1\frac{1}{2}$ lb) ox or calves liver
2 tablespoons flour
1 chopped onion
1 chopped green pepper
125 g (4 oz) chopped mushrooms
3 tablespoons oil

3 large skinned tomatoes, diced
1 clove crushed garlic
1½ teaspoons salt
⅛ teaspoon pepper
3 cups cooked rice or spaghetti

Method: Dip liver into boiling water, let stand 5 minutes. Drain. Cut into cubes, and dredge with flour. Brown liver, onion and green pepper in oil. Add mushrooms, tomatoes, garlic and seasonings. Simmer 25 minutes. Serve over rice or spaghetti.

MARINATED HAWAIIAN FILLET OF BEEF

1 whole fillet or 2 kilo (4–5 lb) piece of scotch fillet
½ cup oil
¼ cup lemon juice
¼ cup soya sauce
2 cloves crushed garlic
1 teaspoon coarsely ground black pepper
¼ cup chopped spring onions
1 teaspoon celery salt
1 tin (410 g) pineapple rings
8–10 maraschino cherries
   mozzarella cheese
   few sprigs parsley or mint

Method: Mix together the oil, lemon juice, soya sauce, garlic, black pepper, spring onions and celery salt. Pour over beef and allow to marinate for at least 3 hours or overnight. Place in 200°C (400°F) oven, uncovered, in roasting pan with the marinade and roast for 35–45 minutes, depending on the size of the beef and whether you use fillet or scotch fillet, the latter will take about 50 minutes and the fillet 35–40 minutes. Baste occasionally and turn over halfway through the cooking period.

When cooked, place on serving platter or board covered with foil, and cover with slices of cheese, top with the pineapple rings and place a cherry in the centre of each pineapple ring. Place under the griller for a few minutes, or till the cheese has melted. Garnish with sprigs of parsley or mint and serve immediately.

HAMBURGERS

To prepare the mince meat for hamburgers:
1 kilo (2 lb) mince meat
1 bread roll 2–3 days old or 2 dessertspoons matzo meal
1 medium onion
½ teaspoon pepper
1 teaspoon chicken soup powder or 1 cube
1 ripe tomato
1 small granny smith apple, peeled
2 teaspoons salt
½ teaspoon ginger, dash garlic salt
½ cup cold water

Method: Grate roll, tomato, onion, apple, and add to meat. Add water and spices and mix well with fork. Form into patties and fry in oil till nicely browned and cooked through.

CURRY MEAT BALLS

1 kilo (2 lb) mince meat
Prepare mince as for hamburgers.

Sauce: Fry 1 onion in 2–3 tablespoons oil until glassy, add 1 chopped tomato, ½ sour chopped apple and 1 cup water and simmer for 10 minutes. Add mince balls which have been browned in oil and let simmer for about two hours, then add 1–2 tablespoons vinegar, a dessertspoon apricot jam, 1 teaspoon salt, 1½ tablespoons curry powder, 1 dessertspoon flour, which has been mixed to a paste with cold water and simmer for a further 15 minutes. Serve with rice and sambals.

Sambals: Cut two tomatoes in small pieces, 1 green pepper and 1 small onion chopped. Mix with $\frac{1}{2}$ cup vinegar, $\frac{1}{2}$ teaspoon salt, 1 teaspoon sugar, dash pepper.

Slice 2–3 bananas, pour over juice of 1 lemon.

Sliced mango when in season.

Sliced cucumber, sprinkled with dill and pour over 250 mℓ ($\frac{1}{2}$ pint) yoghurt.

Chutney, dessicated coconut.

MINCE MEAT LOAF

Prepare mince meat as for hamburgers, form into loaf with hands on foil lined roasting pan. Arrange thick slices of tomato and onions on top of loaf and thick slices of potato around, pour over 2–3 tablespoons fat or oil and bake for one hour in moderate oven.

AMERICAN GROUND BEEF TURNOVERS

Prepare mince as follows:
1 kilo (2 lb) mincemeat
1 medium sized onion
1 ripe tomato
$\frac{1}{2}$ teaspoon ginger
$\frac{1}{2}$ teaspoon garlic salt
$\frac{1}{2}$ teaspoon seasoning salt
1 chicken cube dissolved in $\frac{1}{4}$ cup boiling water, then fill cup with cold water
1 stale roll
1 sour apple, peeled
2 teaspoons salt
$\frac{1}{2}$ teaspoon pepper
1 teaspoon sugar

Method: Grate roll, tomato, onion and apple on the coarse side of the grater. Mix into the mincemeat with the stock, and seasonings. When you have mixed very well, pat into large flat rounds onto a slightly oiled sheet of aluminium foil. Spread each round with a thin film of mustard, then place 1 teaspoon each of finely chopped pickled cucumber and onion on one half of each round. Dot with tomato sauce, then fold over in half and seal well with fingers so that the filling is completely enclosed. Heat 2–3 tablespoons oil in a frying pan till very hot, add beef turnovers, lower heat to medium and even low if necessary, adjusting the temperature throughout the cooking period, and fry till nicely browned and cooked through. Serve with baked potato and salad.

Special hint: Ideally one should use a non-stick pan for this. However, if and when using an ordinary pan, remove from heat for a few minutes when meat sticks and it will come loose.

CABBAGE BLINTZES

1 kilo (2 lb) mincemeat, not too lean
1 bread roll grated (2–3 days old)
1 medium onion, grated
1 ripe tomato skinned and grated
1 granny smith apple, grated
2 teaspoons salt
1 teaspoon garlic salt
$\frac{1}{2}$ teaspoon barbecue spice
$\frac{1}{2}$ teaspoon ground ginger
$\frac{1}{2}$ teaspoon pepper
$\frac{1}{2}$ chicken cube
1 large cabbage
   approximately 1 cup cold water

Sauce:
2 skinned tomatoes grated
1–2 raw beetroot grated
   juice of 1 lemon
2 tablespoons tomato sauce
1 chicken cube
2 tablespoons syrup
1–2 tablespoons sugar

salt and pepper to taste
1 cup water
1 dessertspoon maizena, mixed with a little cold water

Method: Prepare the mince, by mixing together all the ingredients very well. Soften the cabbage leaves in boiling water, removing the hard vein from the surface with a sharp knife. Roll the mince into balls, and place each one in a cabbage leaf and roll up, as you would a blintze. Place in a large saucepan. Mix together ingredients for sauce, except maizena, and pour over cabbage blintzes. Simmer covered over low heat for about $1\frac{1}{2}$ hours. Add maizena to meat in saucepan. Transfer meat and gravy to a large casserole dish, in a single layer, and place in a 180°C (350°F) oven to brown, for about $\frac{1}{2}$ hour.

LASAGNE

1 pkt Lasagne noodles (250 g)
$\frac{1}{2}$ kilo (1 lb) ground beef
3 cloves garlic
2 onions
1 teaspoon mustard powder
250 g ($\frac{1}{2}$ lb) mushrooms
1 tin peeled tomatoes (396 g)
1 tin tomato purée
1 teaspoon mixed herbs
$\frac{1}{2}$ teaspoon origanum
3 tablespoons Worcestershire sauce
1 tablespoon vinegar
$\frac{1}{2}$ teaspoon salt
1–2 bay leaves
   mozzarella cheese or parmesan cheese

Bechamel sauce:
4 tablespoons oil or butter
1 cup flour
2 chicken cubes dissolved in 4 cups boiling water, or use 4 cups milk

Method: Boil noodles in salt water with 1 tablespoon oil for 20–25 minutes. Remove with slotted spoon and place on clean cloth.

Brown onions and garlic (chopped) in oil, then add meat and brown. Add peeled tomatoes, purée, mixed herbs, origanum, mustard, Worcestershire sauce, bay leaves and vinegar. Add fresh sliced button mushrooms. Simmer for $\pm 2\frac{1}{2}$ hours

Make bechamel sauce, by heating oil or butter, stir in flour then stock till thick and smooth, over low heat. Place a layer of meat sauce in greased pyrex dish, cover with noodles, then bechamel sauce. Repeat once more. Bake in 180°C (350°F) oven for 30 minutes. Place mozzarella or parmesan cheese on top and place under griller to brown. Serve with French salad.

SAUERBRATEN BEEF RING

1 kilo (2 lb) mincemeat
1 stale roll grated
1 sour apple, peeled and grated
1 tomato grated
1 teaspoon salt
$\frac{1}{2}$ teaspoon pepper
$\frac{1}{2}$ teaspoon ginger
$\frac{1}{2}$ teaspoon seasoning salt
$\frac{1}{2}$ teaspoon garlic salt
1 teaspoon sugar
1 chicken cube dissolved in $\frac{1}{4}$ cup boiling water, then fill with cold water

Sauce:
$\frac{1}{2}$ pkt crushed ginger snaps
2 cups boiling water mixed with 2 beef or chicken cubes
$\frac{1}{2}$ cup brown sugar
$\frac{1}{4}$ cup lemon juice
   handful sultanas, optional

Method: Prepare mince by mixing all ingredients and seasonings well together. Adjust seasonings if necessary. Place in a round tin with hole in the middle which has been well oiled. Bake in 180°C (350°F) oven for three quarters of an hour. Meanwhile prepare sauce by placing all ingredients in a saucepan and cook on low for 10–15 minutes, stirring constantly. Turn meat out onto serving platter, pour half sauce over and return to oven for 20 minutes. Serve with remaining sauce. Fill centre with peas or mixed vegetables.

Special hint: A non-stick bundt tin is ideal for this.

MONKEY GLAND STEAK

Method: Use rump steak or tenderised steak, seasoned with salt, pepper. Grill in a pan using a little oil, rare, medium or well done, whichever your preference and keep warm in warming draw.

Pour over the following sauce.

Chop 2 onions and fry in oil till golden brown. Add 2 large skinned, diced tomatoes and cook to a mush. Add 1 crumbled chicken cube, 1 cup water, 1 cup tomato sauce, $\frac{1}{2}$ cup Worcestershire sauce, 1 tablespoon soya sauce, $\frac{1}{2}$ cup hot chutney and 1 teaspoon sugar, salt and pepper to taste. Simmer to boiling point. Pour over steak and serve immediately.

Sprinkle with chopped parsley for garnish.

OXTAIL WITH BAKED BEANS

Method: Wash 1 or two oxtails very well with hot water and scrape off some of the fat. Place in a large saucepan with water to cover and 1 tablespoon salt and boil for half an hour. Remove and discard the water. This is just to clean the oxtail very well. Chop two onions, 2 sticks celery, 2 carrots, 2 skinned and diced tomatoes and place in a large saucepan with $\frac{1}{2}$ cup oil and brown lightly. Add the oxtail, 2 teaspoons salt, $\frac{1}{2}$ teaspoon pepper, 1 teaspoon seasoning salt, 1 teaspoon garlic salt, $\frac{1}{2}$ teaspoon ginger and 2–3 cups water and allow to simmer on low for 5–6 hours or as long as it takes for the oxtail to become tender. Add more water during the cooking process if necessary, $\frac{1}{2}$ an hour before serving add 1 tin baked beans in tomato sauce. Serve on rice or mashed potatoes.

PEPPER STEAK

fillet or sirloin steaks
4 tablespoons coarsely crushed peppercorns
salt
4 tablespoons oil or butter
1 tablespoon brandy
$\frac{1}{4}$ cup sherry
250 ml ($\frac{1}{2}$ pint) cream or 2 sachets orley whip
1 level teaspoon gravy powder mixed with $\frac{1}{2}$ cup water

Method: Heat oil or butter in frying pan. Sprinkle steaks with salt and press peppercorns well into the meat. Place steaks in a very hot pan and then turn the heat down to medium and cook *once only* on each side, do not keep turning the steak over and over as this causes the meat to become dry. The steak is pink in the middle when the juice begins to penetrate the surface of the steak after it has been turned. Remove the steaks to a heated platter and stir the sherry and brandy into the pan, scraping the bottom and sides of the pan. Now stir in the cream, which has been mixed with the gravy powder and water. Pour over the steak, sprinkle with chopped parsley and serve immediately. Baked potatoes and French salad with green goddess salad dressing are excellent accompaniments.

ROAST SCOTCH FILLET WITH HERB SAUCE

Prepare the meat by washing it well and seasoning as follows – ± amounts.

1½ teaspoon salt
½ teaspoon ginger
¾ teaspoon garlic salt
½ teaspoon white pepper
½ teaspoon seasoning salt
½ teaspoon mono sodium glutamate

Method: Rub the entire surface with 2 teaspoons mustard powder. Quarter or halve 3–4 cloves of garlic and put some under the fat of the meat and the remainder in slits made in the meat with a sharp knife. Wrap in aluminium foil and leave overnight in fridge. Roast uncovered with 1 cup oil poured over, at about 200°C (400°F) on bottom-most shelf of oven for about 1 hour, depending on size.

Sauce: may be made in advance and re-heated.
1 pkt black mushrooms (400 g)
250 mℓ (½ pint) sour cream/orley whip
1 level teaspoon mustard powder
½ teaspoon dried parsley
   butter or oil
1 teaspoon flour
2 tablespoons sherry
1 dessertspoon brandy
½ teaspoon mixed herbs
   black pepper, garlic salt, salt

Method: Sauté mushrooms in butter/oil until soft. Add salt, black pepper, garlic salt and herbs. Blend flour and mustard with sherry and brandy and add to mushrooms. Stir until thickened. Add cream and cook a few minutes more.
   N.B. If you are using the orley-whip add 1 teaspoon lemon juice to sour it.

TACOS

Pita
4 cups flour, 2 cups luke warm water
2 teaspoons dried yeast
2 teaspoons oil
2 teaspoons salt

Method: Place the yeast in a shallow bowl. Pour over warm water, allow to stand for 10–15 minutes. Place unsifted flour in a large bowl and make a well in the centre. Stir the oil and salt into the yeast and then pour into the well and stir till all the flour has been mixed in. Knead on a lightly floured board till smooth, about 5 minutes. Cover with a cloth and allow to stand in a warm place until doubled in bulk, or leave overnight. Punch down. Divide into portions about the size of tennis balls. Roll out about 2 cms thick and place on a floured baking tray. Cover and allow to stand for a further 15–30 minutes. Bake in 225°C (450°F) oven for 12–15 minutes.
   N.B. Pappadums (Indian curry biscuits) may be used instead of the Pita.

Meat:
1 kilo cubed bolo, chuck or cubed steak
1 can red indian beans or red kidney beans
1 can baked beans in chilli sauce
1 large green pepper, seeded and diced
2 large tomatoes, skinned and diced
2 onions chopped
2 cloves crushed garlic
1 tablespoon maizena
1 teaspoon origanum
¼ cup oil
1 beef or chicken cube
½ teaspoon cayenne pepper
1 teaspoon chilli powder
1 teaspoon mustard powder
2 tablespoons Worcestershire sauce
2 tablespoons vinegar
1½ teaspoons salt
2 cups water

Method: Brown beef in hot oil. Remove from pot, then brown onions and peppers, adding more oil if necessary. Return beef to pot, and then add garlic, tomatoes, spices and herbs and simmer for about $\frac{1}{2}$ hour. Add water and cook covered until beef is tender, about $\frac{1}{2}$–1 hour. Add drained red kidney beans and beans in chilli sauce and thicken with maizena mixed to a paste with a little cold water. Simmer a further 10 minutes, and adjust seasonings if neccesary.

Gaucamale sauce: Combine 2 cups sieved avocado with salt and pepper to taste. Add 2 cloves crushed garlic, 1 teaspoon lemon juice, 1 dessertspoon vinegar and $\frac{1}{2}$ cup mayonnaise.

1 large shredded lettuce, parmesan cheese.

To serve: Place halved Pita or Pappadum on plate. Sprinkle with a little shredded lettuce. Spoon a generous helping of meat over. Top with 1–2 tablespoons Gaucamale and finally sprinkle parmesan cheese on top.

Special hint: If meat is too hot for your liking, use baked beans in tomato sauce, instead of chilli beans.

TONGUE IN APRICOT SAUCE

Method: 1 pickled tongue boiled till soft with bay leaves, 2 cloves garlic, peppercorns, carrots and sliced onion, reserve stock.

Slice and place in casserole dish. Pour over following sauce.

Combine in a saucepan the juice of 1 tin apricots, 1 teaspoon gravy powder and 1 dessertspoon maizena, mixed to a paste with water, $1\frac{1}{2}$–2 cups stock from boiled tongue, 2 tablespoons soya sauce, $\frac{1}{4}$ cup tomato sauce, 1 chicken cube, 2 tablespoons brown sugar, 1–2 tablespoons apricot liqueur, 1 tablespoon brandy, salt and pepper to taste. Let simmer till thickened. Pour over tongue and bake uncovered in a slow oven for about $1\frac{1}{2}$ hours. Arrange apricots over tongue and bake another 15 minutes or till apricots are tinged with brown. Serve with rice and green peas.

This dish may also be made with cherries in which case you would substitute cherries in place of apricots and use cherry liqueur instead of apricot liqueur, otherwise it is exactly the same.

TOURNEDOS ROSSINI

Butter or oil
4 thick slices fillet steak
$1\frac{1}{2}$ teaspoons dried rosemary or origanum
$1\frac{1}{2}$ teaspoons dried parsley
1 teaspoon maizena
125 mℓ/$\frac{1}{2}$ cup sour cream or 1 sachet orly whip
salt and black pepper (coarse grind)
$\frac{1}{4}$ cup brandy
1 dessertspoon soya sauce
1 teaspoon gravy powder
$\frac{1}{4}$ cup milk or water
chicken liver pâté, ready made. (See liver pâté roll)

Method: Heat oil or butter in frying pan. Season steaks with salt and pepper and grill over medium heat about 5 minutes on each side, increasing heat if necessary. Add 1 tablespoon additional oil or butter to pan. When melted add brandy, allow to warm. Ignite and blaze. Remove meat and keep warm. Add cream, mushrooms, soya sauce and herbs. Simmer 2 minutes. Mix maizena and gravy powder with milk or water. Stir in and cook till thickened, adjust seasoning if necessary.

Spread each steak thickly with liver pâté, pour over sauce and serve immediately. Baked potatoes or creamed spinach in tomatoes are nice accompaniments.

Serves 4.

WELLINGTON BOOT

1 whole fillet
1 cup oil
  salt, pepper, garlic salt, seasoning salt, ginger
2 onions chopped
1 pkt fresh mushrooms, sliced (400 g)
2–3 cloves crushed garlic
250 g chicken livers (8 oz)
½ teaspoon each origanum and rosemary
  quick puff pastry, recipe given below

Method: Wipe fillet and season with salt, pepper, garlic salt, seasoning salt and ginger. Pour oil into a roasting pan and allow to get very hot in 225°C (450°F) oven. Place the fillet in the pan and roast for 35 minutes. Turn halfway through roasting period. Remove from oven and allow to cool completely.

Roll out the pastry so that it is big enough to encase the whole fillet. Place the filling given below, in a thick strip down the centre, place the fillet on top and cut the pastry at 2 cm (1 inch) intervals in strips at a slant all the way down on both sides. Plait these alternately over the top of the fillet, place on a baking tray and bake on centre shelf of a 225°C (450°F) oven till pastry is golden brown, about 35–40 minutes. Serve with a gravy made in the roasting pan.

Filling for Wellington Boot:

Method: Fry onions in oil till golden brown, add mushrooms and cook till liquid has evaporated. Boil livers in water seasoned with salt and pepper for a few minutes, then dice and add to the pan, with crushed garlic and herbs. Thicken the mixture with 1 teaspoon maizena mixed to a paste with a little cold water, and 1 teaspoon gravy powder, and season to taste. Cool thoroughly before using.

QUICK PUFF PASTRY

250 g butter (½ lb) margarine or vegetable fat
½ cup boiling water
2 cups flour
  pinch of salt

Method: Grate fat into bowl. Add boiling water. Stir quickly with fork till mushy, then add salt and flour. Place in waxproof paper and chill overnight. Bake in hot oven 225°C (450°F) and then turn down.

2. LAMB

BARBEQUE LAMB

Marinade for a leg, ribs or chops, may also be used for steak.

½ cup oil
¾ cup vinegar
1 cup water
½ cup tomato sauce
½ teaspoon black pepper
1 large onion grated
2 cloves crushed garlic
3 teaspoons Worcestershire sauce
2 dessertspoons lemon juice
2 teaspoons mustard powder
1 teaspoon chilli powder
  few bay leaves
1 teaspoon salt
5 teaspoons sugar
½ teaspoon marjoram

½ teaspoon thyme
½ teaspoon origanum
½ teaspoon dried parsley

Method: Mix together in a saucepan oil, vinegar, water, tomato sauce, lemon juice, mustard, pepper, chilli powder, garlic salt and onion. Stir until boiling. Stir in herbs and allow to simmer for 7–10 minutes. Wash the meat well. Dry thoroughly and place in roasting pan or earthenware pot. Pour over half the marinade and leave at least 2 hours, but preferably overnight. Use the remaining marinade to brush the meat whilst braaiing. A leg of lamb cooked on a spit will take at least 2–2½ hours.

FRUITED LAMB IN CURRY SAUCE

Method: Season a leg of lamb (for kosher requirements, use a crown of lamb) with 2 teaspoons salt, ½ teaspoon pepper, 1½ teaspoons garlic salt, 1 teaspoon ginger and a little seasoning salt and then rub with 2 level dessertspoons curry powder. Pour over ¼ cup oil and roast uncovered for ¾ hour in a 180°C (350°F) oven (bottom shelf). Drain fat from pan. Combine the juice of 2 x 439 g apricots and 2 x 439 g pineapple chunks with 1 tin (200 g) apricot juice, and half the fruit as well as 2 cloves crushed garlic. Pour over the lamb, cover and return to oven for another 2 hours. Mix 1 tablespoon maizena to a paste with a little cold water and add this to the pan to thicken the juices. Use the remaining fruit on skewers and alternate with maraschino cherries for colour. Place in oven to heat through. Place meat on serving platter, pour over fruit sauce then insert fruited skewers into the lamb and use mint leaves for garnish as well. When serving present each guest with a fruited skewer for their meat.

LAMB CHOPS PARMIGIANA

1 medium sized eggplant, peeled, sliced thin and salted
oil for frying
1 kilo lamb or veal chops (2 lb)
6 fresh tomatoes skinned
2 large onions, finely chopped
1 cup flour seasoned with 1 teaspoon salt, ½ teaspoon pepper and 1 teaspoon garlic salt
2 cloves crushed garlic
mozzarella cheese and ½ cup parmesan cheese, optional

Method: Sprinkle the eggplant slices generously with salt and let stand for ½ hour. Drain well dip in plain flour and fry in oil until tender. Drain on absorbent paper. Cut tomato in thick slices and add to the pan with the onion and garlic and simmer for five minutes. Place the eggplant slices in the bottom of a large shallow baking dish and cover with the tomato mixture. Dredge the chops in the seasoned flour and sauté in oil till golden brown on both sides. Arrange the chops on top of the vegetables. Cover with slices of mozzarella cheese, optional. Pour the sauce, given below, over the dish and then sprinkle the entire surface with the parmesan or breadcrumbs. Bake for 30 minutes at 190°C (375°F). If not sufficiently brown, place under broiler for a few minutes.

Sauce:
2 tablespoons oil
1 tablespoon flour
⅔ cup red wine
1 cup chicken stock
1 tablespoon tomato purée

Heat oil in a pan, blend in the flour, and then slowly stir in the tomato paste, stock and wine. Simmer until smooth and slightly thickened.

LAMB CURRY WITH YOGHURT

Stewing lamb depending on the number of persons.

2 sticks celery
2 cloves garlic crushed
2 onions chopped
2 carrots chopped
2 tomatoes, skinned and chopped
2 granny smith or cooking apples, peeled and cut into small pieces
1 tin curried vegetables (410 g)
2–3 brinjals which have been sliced then sprinkled with a lot of salt and left to stand for ½ hour
4 baby marrows sliced
2 chicken cubes
2–3 potatoes, quartered
1–2 teaspoons salt
½ teaspoon ginger
3 tablespoons apricot jam
1 level dessertspoon curry powder, mixed to a paste with cold water
1 tablespoon vinegar
1–2 cups yoghurt

Method: Wash meat off well. Pour oil, about 1 cup, into a pot and brown the meat. When all the meat has been browned, remove from pot and set aside. Place onions, celery, garlic, apples and carrots in pot and cook till lightly browned. Return meat to pot, add tomatoes, seasonings, except curry, water to just cover and cook gently for ½ hour. Add brinjals, baby marrows, potatoes and cook again for another ½ hour. Add tinned curried vegetables, apricot jam and vinegar, as well as the salt. Stir in curry mixture and simmer till thickened. Just before serving stir in 1–2 cups yoghurt, depending on taste.

Serve with the following:
Fresh cucumber sliced and mixed with dill and yoghurt.
Dice tomatoes, onions and greenpepper mixed together.
Bananas sliced and sprinkled with lemon juice.
Slices of paw paw and mangoes, when in season.
Dessicated coconut.
Chutney.
Pappadums.

BARBEQUE RIBS

1½–2 kilos (3–4 lb) of ribs, either lamb, veal or baby beef. Roast lamb ribs in oven to remove fat, if using immediately, otherwise leave to marinate in sauce as for a braai.

1 large onion chopped
¼ cup oil
1 cup tomato sauce
½ cup water
1 chicken cube
¼ cup Worcestershire sauce
2 cloves crushed garlic
¼ cup soya sauce
¼ cup vinegar
2 tablespoons syrup or honey
2 teaspoons tabasco
2 teaspoons salt
1 teaspoon mustard powder

Method for marinade: Brown onion and garlic slightly in oil. Add remaining ingredients. Simmer 15 minutes.

Method for cooking: Place spareribs in roasting pan, cover with barbeque marinade and roast in a slow oven 150°C (300°F) about 2–2½ hours or till tender. Place under griller and grill till nicely browned and crisp on edges. Serve with baked potatoes and a French salad.

MOUSSAKA

Boil as much stewing lamb as you wish, and if desired some chops as well. Mince, discarding fat and bones.

Slice 4–5 egg plants, sprinkle thickly with salt and allow to stand 20 minutes then rinse off well.

2 tomatoes skinned and diced
1 tablespoon flour
1 teaspoon salt
¼ teaspoon pepper
1 teaspoon mixed herbs
1 teaspoon mustard powder
3 cloves chopped garlic
1 tin tomato purée
1 tablespoon vinegar
2 tablespoons Worcestershire sauce
½ cup oil
2 onions diced

Method: Heat oil in large saucepan. Sauté onion and garlic. Add tomatoes and cook for about 5 minutes. Stir in lamb, mustard powder, salt, pepper, vinegar, Worcestershire sauce, mixed herbs and tomato purée. Cover and simmer over low heat for approximately 1 hour placing an asbestos mat under the pot to prevent burning. Stir occasionally. Lastly stir in flour.

Coat the eggplant with flour, (this prevents it absorbing too much oil), and fry in a little oil till tender, then arrange in the bottom of an ovenware dish. Spoon the lamb mixture over this.

Make a white sauce: with 125 g (4 oz) margarine or ½ cup oil. Stir in 2 heaped tablespoons flour. Dissolve 3 chicken cubes in 3 cups boiling water, then stir this into the roux, using more water if you find the sauce is too thick. Season to taste with salt and black pepper. Spoon sauce over lamb, sprinkle with paprika and bake for ½ hour in 180°C (350°F) oven, middle shelf.

Special hint: Can use beef mince as well.

ROAST LAMB AND POTATOES WITH MINT SAUCE

1 leg of lamb weighing approximately 2 kilos (4–5 lb)
4–6 cloves garlic, cut into slivers
1 onion, cut into pieces
2 teaspoons salt
1 teaspoon lamb seasoning
1 teaspoon black pepper
1 dessertspoon rosemary
1 teaspoon freshly chopped or dried parsley
½ cup oil
½ cup lemon juice

Method: Wash meat off well. Make incisions all over meat and insert pieces of garlic and onion deep into the leg.

Mix together all remaining ingredients and rub well into the lamb, pouring the balance over.

Roast uncovered (bottom shelf) in 200°C (400°F) oven for 1¾–2 hours.

Parboil peeled potatoes for 20 minutes and halfway through the cooking period place all around the lamb, turning and basting at intervals. Serve with fennel and carrots as additional vegetables or just with a red kidney bean salad.

Prepare mint sauce: Chop a few sprigs of mint very finely and mix with ½ cup oil, 1 cup brown vinegar, 1 teaspoon sugar and a dash of salt and pepper.

ROMAN LAMB

Method: Cut three cloves garlic into slivers and place them in slits in the leg of lamb. Season the lamb with a teaspoon salt, 1 teaspoon origanum and 1 teaspoon rosemary. Pour over ½ cup oil and place in 200°C (400°F) oven for 1 hour. Chop up 3 onions and fry in oil till lightly browned, then mix with the following sauce:

1 can tomato purée
1 teaspoon paprika
1 teaspoon salt
2 tablespoons vinegar
1 can water
½ teaspoon cayenne pepper
2 tablespoons Worcestershire sauce
½ cup brown sugar

Pour this mixture over lamb in the roasting pan, then cover with lid and cook in a very slow oven 120°C (250°F) for 2½ to 3 hours. Baste occasionally and serve with the sauce in which it has been cooked. If necessary, thicken this gravy with 1 dessertspoon maizena mixed to a paste with water.

Special hint: Use the same sauce with browned lamb chops, or ribs – delicious.

LAMB IN PHYLLO

6 Loin chops or large pieces of lamb cut from leg, seasoned well with salt, pepper, garlic salt and rosemary
3 large tomatoes (skinned and chopped)
½ cup oil
125 g frozen peas (4 oz)
250 g phyllo pastry (8 oz)
3 cloves crushed garlic
2 sticks diced celery
1 grated carrot
salt and pepper
6 potatoes, cubed and parboiled
1 cup breadcrumbs
3 onions sliced
1–2 tablespoons finely chopped parsley
½ teaspoon origanum
garlic salt

Method: Heat ¼ cup oil in frying pan over high heat. Brown meat. Remove and set aside. Sauté onion, garlic, for a few minutes. Add carrots and celery. Add more oil if necessary. Add tomatoes and simmer until a mush. Stir in peas, potatoes, parsley, origanum and seasonings. Brush two phyllo sheets lightly with oil, sprinkle in between each sheet lightly with breadcrumbs. Place one sheet on top of the other, fold in half and again brush with oil. (This will be enough for one person only.) Place a dessertspoonful of the vegetables on the edge of the pastry, place lamb on top of vegetables, top with more vegetables. Fold over sides to enclose filling and roll up like a swiss roll. Place parcels on an oiled baking sheet, brush parcels lightly with oil and bake at 180°C (350°F) for about 1 hour. (Pastry should be very flaky and crispy.)

3. VEAL

POTATO STUFFED BREAST OF VEAL

Have the butcher cut a pocket in a breast of veal weighing approximately 1½ kilos (3 lb) or use a deboned leg of veal.
season with 1½ teaspoons salt, ½ teaspoon pepper
1 teaspoon garlic salt, 1 teaspoon seasoning salt
1 teaspoon ginger
2 carrots, sliced
2 onions, diced
4–6 cloves garlic, crushed
few bay leaves and peppercorns
1 cup oil

Stuffing:
125 g, washed and sliced mushrooms (4 oz)
4 large potatoes, coarsely grated
1 finely diced onion, sautéed in a little oil or fat
1 teaspoon salt
pepper to taste
1 tablespoon flour (heaped), 3 tablespoons matzo meal
1 egg, lightly beaten
1 teaspoon caraway seeds

Method: Combine all ingredients, for stuffing and fill the pocket of the breast of veal, then sew up well or secure with skewers. Place the seasoned veal in a roasting pan with the carrot, onions, garlic, bay leaves and peppercorns, cover and roast in a slow oven 160°C (325°F) for about 2 hours, uncover and allow to brown. When done, remove meat from pan, keep warm, then add water to the pan mixed with 1 teaspoon gravy powder, 1 teaspoon maizena, $\frac{1}{2}$ chicken cube, salt and pepper and cook till thickened. Strain and serve with the veal.

Special hint: You may also use veal schintzels, fill with stuffing, roll up, secure with toothpicks. Brown in oil in saucepan, then season and add vegetables as above but cook on top of stove on very low heat, adding water, a little at a time.

VEAL GOULASH

Preferably make this dish the day before required.

oil for frying
2 large onions finely chopped
2–3 cloves garlic, crushed
1 teaspoon salt
1 kilo or (2 lbs) veal (cubed)
1½ teaspoons caraway seeds
1½–2 tablespoons paprika
1–1½ mixed herbs
fresh ground black pepper
1 red pepper ⎱ Sliced into rings
1 green pepper ⎰
1 x 400 g can tomatoes
1 chicken cube ⎱ Combine to
½ cup water (125 mℓ) ⎰ make stock
1 teaspoon sugar
1 tablespoon tomato purée or paste
1 packet mushrooms (250 g), washed and sliced
1 carton sour cream (250 mℓ)

Method: Sauté onions and garlic in about $\frac{1}{2}$–$\frac{3}{4}$ cup oil. Fry gently for 5 minutes. Add veal and fry briskly until browned on all sides. Stir in herbs, caraway seeds, paprika, black pepper, salt to taste, cook for 2 minutes, stirring constantly.

Add peppers, tomatoes and stock. Place in a casserole dish, cover and place in a slow oven for approximately 2–2½ hours at 150°C or (300°F). Add mushrooms for the last 30 minutes. Before serving adjust seasonings. Pour over sour cream, serve with buttered noodles.

1 dessertspoon maizena mixed to a paste with a little cold water may be added the same time as the mushrooms for a slightly thicker sauce.

For kosher requirements: substitute 2 sachets unwhipped orley whip and 1 teaspoon lemon juice in place of sour cream.

6. VEGETABLES

BAKED POTATO WITH CAVIAR

4 large baking potatoes
 butter
 salt, freshly ground pepper
½ cup sour cream
1 x 50 g jar black caviar
 lemon juice

Method: Wash and scrub potatoes and rub them with a generous amount of butter. Puncture top of each potato with a sharp knife to make a steam vent. Bake in a 180°C (350°F) oven for about 1 hour or till tender. When done, remove from oven, slice open tops, and punch the ends to expose the inside. Cover with soft butter and churn into the interior of the potato. Season with salt and pepper and spoon a generous layer of sour cream on top. Make a trough down the centre and fill with caviar. Sprinkle caviar with a few drops of lemon juice and serve immediately.

CHICKEN LIVER RISOTTO

½ cup oil
1 medium sized onion, finely chopped
125 g sliced mushrooms (4 oz)
1⅓ cups rice washed and soaked in water for 30 minutes, then drained
2½ cups boiling chicken stock
1 small tin tomato purée
8–10 chicken livers, cut into small pieces
2 tablespoons chopped parsley

Method: In a large saucepan heat half oil. Add onion and cook till soft but not brown. Add mushrooms and cook another 3 minutes. Add rice and cook for 2 minutes, stirring constantly. Add stock and purée and cook uncovered over high heat for 15 seconds. Cover the saucepan, reduce heat to low and simmer gently for 20 minutes, till rice is tender and liquid absorbed. Meanwhile cook the chicken livers in the remaining oil for about 10 minutes. When the rice is cooked, stir in the chicken livers and parsley.

CRUMBED ASPARAGUS

1 can asparagus
1 egg diluted with 2 tablespoons water
 paprika
 salt
 oil for frying
 breadcrumbs or cream crackers crushed

Method: Drain asparagus and dip in beaten egg. Roll in cracker crumbs, dip in egg again. Fry in deep fat, drain on paper towelling. Sprinkle with salt and paprika.

FRIED FENNEL

4 fennel bulbs, cut into quarters
1–2 cloves garlic, diced
2 tablespoons finely chopped parsley
75 g (3 oz) butter

Method: Wash fennel thoroughly. Boil for 10 minutes in salted water. Drain thoroughly and set aside.
  Place butter in pan till golden. Add fennel and cook covered over medium heat for 15–20 minutes. Add chopped parsley and garlic and cook a further 2–3 minutes.
  Special hint: can be made with broccoli instead of fennel.

FRIED MUSHROOMS

 button mushrooms, washed well and dried

1 egg
flour seasoned with salt, pepper and garlic salt
breadcrumbs
oil for frying

Method: Toss mushrooms in seasoned flour, dip into beaten egg, then coat with breadcrumbs. Fry in deep oil till golden brown.

Special hint: Parboiled cauliflowerettes can be cooked in the same way.

POTATO GNOCCHI

Method: Boil 10 large potatoes in their jackets in salted water till tender. Peel and sieve whilst hot, then place on lightly floured board. Make a well in the centre and add 2 eggs, salt and pepper.

Mix in and then knead adding a little more flour so that the mixture is easy to handle. Roll into sausages, cut into 2,5 cm (1 inch) cubes. Holding a fork in a horizontal position facing you, press each cube against the tynes with your thumb towards the end of the fork so that the Gnocchi curves. Place on a floured cloth whilst preparing the balance.

Boil in salted and oiled water; when they surface remove with a slotted spoon and place in a greased pyrex dish.

Pour over any one of the sauces given below, then bake in a 180° C (350°) oven till hot and bubbling. Sprinkle with parmesan cheese after removing from oven.

Tomato sauce: Sauté 1 chopped onion, 2 cloves crushed garlic, 2 sticks diced celery and 2 grated carrots in a little oil and butter,* add 4–6 skinned diced tomatoes; simmer to a mush. Lastly add 100 g ($\frac{1}{2}$ tin) tomato paste, salt and pepper to taste, 1 chicken cube, 1 teaspoon basil and 1 teaspoon mixed herbs. Simmer another few minutes. Adding a little water if sauce becomes too thick.

Bolognaise sauce: Prepare sauce as above till.* Then add 500 g (1 lb) mincemeat and cook till brown. Continue as above adding tomatoes etc.

Cheese sauce: Melt 50 g (2 oz) butter in a saucepan. Fold in 250 g grated cheddar or parmesan cheese and 125 mℓ ($\frac{1}{2}$ cup) thick or sour cream. (Season to taste with salt, pepper and nutmeg.) After removing from oven, sprinkle with chopped parsley.

POTATO LATKES

6 medium potatoes grated
1 small onion grated
1 small sweet potato grated
$\frac{1}{2}$ cup flour
1 teaspoon baking powder
2 eggs
1 teaspoon salt
dash pepper

Method: Throw excess juice off the grated potatoes and onion. Add remaining ingredients. Drop by spoonfuls into hot oil and fry till crisp and golden. Drain well on absorbent paper. Serve with cinnamon and sugar.

Special hint: Beating the egg whites stiffly, and folding in last, makes them more crisp.

CRISPY FRIED ONION RINGS

Method: Slice onions thinly. Boil for a few minutes. Drain off well. Dip in flour then in mixture of 1 cup self raising flour mixed with cold water to make thick batter. Fry in hot oil.

POTATO NESTS

Method: 2 potatoes – yield 4, (sliced very thinly). Fry in 3 tablespoons oil till tender and sticky, 3–4 minutes. Press into oiled, floured, patty tins. Bake at 225°C (450°F) for 20 minutes. Fill with peas or mixed vegetables.

POTATO PUDDING

6 potatoes finely grated
1 onion finely grated
2 tablespoons chicken fat
1 teaspoon baking powder
½ teaspoon sugar
1 teaspoon salt
¼ teaspoon pepper
2 eggs
2 tablespoons flour

Method: Mix all the ingredients together, excluding the egg whites, which must be stiffly beaten and added last. Pour into a greased pyrex dish. Pour a little oil on top. Bake 45 minutes in a moderate oven.

Special hint: This is a very small pudding, so bake in 18–20 cm (7 or 8-inch) round pyrex, otherwise double recipe.

PUMPKIN FRITTERS

2 cups cooked pumpkin, cool and mash
½ cup flour
2 teaspoons baking powder
¼ cup sugar
½ teaspoon salt
2 eggs
 oil for frying

Method: Mix all ingredients together. Drop by spoonfuls into hot oil and fry till crisp and golden. Drain well on absorbent paper. Serve with cinnamon and sugar.

RATATOUILLE

1–2 chopped onions
4 cloves garlic
½ cup oil
2–3 skinned tomatoes
1 green pepper diced (optional)
6 sliced baby marrows
3 large brinjals, peeled and sliced
1 cup green beans
1 chicken cube
1 packet fresh mushrooms (125 g) optional
 salt, pepper and garlic salt to taste

Method: Fry onion, garlic and green pepper in oil till golden. Add tomatoes, sliced mushrooms, baby marrows, brinjals and beans. Allow to simmer till tender, adding water if necessary. Season with chicken cube, salt, pepper and garlic salt and simmer another 10 minutes.

RED CABBAGE

1 red cabbage roughly shredded
2 sour apples, peeled and sliced
6 cloves
 juice of one lemon
½ cup brown sugar
1 cup water
½ teaspoon salt, dash pepper
2 tablespoons oil

Method: Wash cabbage and drain. Heat oil in saucepan. Add cabbage and cook till limp. Add all other ingredients. Simmer for 1–2 hours. Thicken with 1 dessertspoon maizena mixed to a paste with a little water. Adjust seasonings if necessary.

Special hint: Nice accompaniment to duck.

STUFFED ONIONS

4 medium sized onions
2 tablespoons fresh breadcrumbs
  salt and black pepper (mill grind)
1 tablespoon melted butter
1 tablespoon cream
½ cup grated cheese

Method: Cook onions in boiling salt water 15–20 minutes. Cook and drain. Scoop out centres and chop finely, mix with breadcrumbs, melted butter, cream and half the grated cheese. Season with salt and pepper. Fill the onion shells with this mixture, place in an ovenproof dish, pat small knobs of butter on top, sprinkle with remaining cheese. At this stage you may pour over a white sauce, if desired, then sprinkle with paprika and bake in 200°C (400°F) oven for 20–30 minutes.

BAKED BUTTERNUT

Method: Slice butternut lengthways in half, scoop out pips and fill hollows with diced onion, green pepper and mushrooms which have been sautéed in butter and seasoned with salt and pepper. Put 2 halves together again, wrap in foil and bake in hot oven 200°C (400°F) for 1–2 hours or till tender.

VEGETARIAN LASAGNE

Pasta: Sift 1½ cups flour into mixmaster bowl. Make a well in the centre and add 2 eggs. Add 1 rounded dessertspoon frozen or fresh chopped spinach. Knead with a dough hook till smooth. Roll pasta out till paper thin on lightly floured board. Cut into strips 15 x 5 cm (6 x 2 inches)

Method: 12 brinjals – cut into rounds and sprinkle with salt. Leave to stand for ½ hour. Drain, rinse and sauté in oil till soft and brown. 1¼ kilo mushrooms (5–6 packets). Wash off well. Fry in oil or butter till limp, with 4 cloves crushed garlic, salt and black pepper. Add ½ cup sherry. Simmer 20 minutes. Slice 3–4 large onions in rings. Sauté in oil till soft and golden brown. Add ½ cup sherry, 4 grated carrots, 1 kilo (2 lb) tin whole peeled tomatoes, salt and pepper. Simmer 1–1½ hours. Prepare white sauce by melting 125 g (4 oz) butter. Stir in 1½ cups flour, then slowly add 8 cups milk. Stir in 250 g (8 oz) grated cheddar cheese and salt and pepper to taste. Prepare lasagne pasta by boiling in salted water till tender. Drain with slotted spoon and place on a clean cloth.

Place all the vegetables, pasta and white sauce in layers in a greased pyrex dish. Sprinkle with parmesan cheese and bake in medium oven, till hot and bubbling.

7. SALADS & DRESSINGS

ARTICHOKE SALAD

2 tins artichoke hearts
1 tin green beans
1 tin asparagus cuts
1–2 tins button mushrooms
1 tin black olives (Calamata)
1 finely chopped green pepper
1 finely chopped onion
1 tablespoon chopped parsley

Method: Drain the tinned vegetables and pour over the following dressing: Combine, 1 teaspoon salt, $\frac{1}{2}$ teaspoon coarsely ground black pepper, $\frac{1}{2}$ cup oil, 2 cloves garlic crushed, $\frac{1}{2}$ cup vinegar.

BANANA WALDORF SALAD

6 red skinned apples, diced
2 green skinned apples, diced
4–6 bananas sliced
 juice of 1 lemon
4 sticks celery diced
100 g (1 packet) walnuts, chopped coarsely
1 cup sultanas
1 tin pineapple chunks, drain, reserve juice (285 g)
1 cup mayonnaise
1 teaspoon curry powder
2 tablespoons honey

Method: Sprinkle diced apples and bananas with lemon juice to prevent discolouring. Place apples, bananas, pineapple, celery, walnuts and sultanas in layers in a salad bowl, finishing with the latter two.
 Mix together the mayonnaise, curry, honey and $\frac{3}{4}$ cup of the pineapple juice. Pour over salad and mix well. Serve on lettuce leaves or in a glass bowl.

CABBAGE/PINEAPPLE SALAD

Method: Shred cabbage and soak in salt water for a few hours. Drain well and mix with 2 grated carrots and 1 diced pineapple. Sprinkle with 1 teaspoon salt, $\frac{1}{2}$ teaspoon pepper, juice of 1 lemon, 1 teaspoon sugar, few drops tabasco, then mix in and pour over 1 cup mayonnaise.

CABBAGE SALAD WITH PIQUANT SOUR CREAM DRESSING

Method: Shred 1 cabbage finely and soak in salt water for a few hours. Drain well, place in salad bowl and pour over the following dressing:
 Mix together: 250 mℓ ($\frac{1}{2}$ pint) sour cream, 1 tablespoon finely grated onion, 1 teaspoon salt, 1 teaspoon sugar, few drops tabasco, 1 tablespoon prepared white horseradish, $\frac{1}{2}$ teaspoon paprika.
 Can sprinkle with caraway seed if desired.
 Special hint: You may use 1 cup mayonnaise instead of sour cream.

CUCUMBER AND YOGHURT SALAD

4 English cucumbers, thinly sliced
1 tablespoon chopped fresh dill or a teaspoon dried
$\frac{1}{4}$ cup chopped spring onions
250 mℓ sour cream (1 cup)
250 mℓ plain yoghurt (1 cup)
$\frac{3}{4}$ cup buttermilk
1 teaspoon paprika
 few drops garlic juice
1 teaspoon black pepper coarse grind
$\frac{1}{2}$ teaspoon salt
 few drops tobasco

Method: Sprinkle cucumbers lightly with 1 teaspoon salt, and allow to stand overnight with a plate pressed on top. Drain excess liquid from cucumbers. Mix together all remaining ingredients for dressing. Place a layer of cucumbers in your salad bowl, spoon over enough dressing to cover, and continue in layers till all ingredients have been used. Garnish with chopped mint or parsley.

FRENCH SALAD

Method: Combine the following vegetables: 1 large lettuce, thoroughly washed and torn into pieces. Radishes halved or sliced, 1 English cucumber peeled and sliced, green pepper rings, 1 tin drained black olives, 2–3 firm tomatoes – sliced, cherry tomatoes are also nice, avocado pear, sliced and sprinkled well with lemon juice, pickled cucumber slices (optional), pickled onions (optional), sliced baby marrow, fresh sliced mushrooms.

Surround the bowl with sliced pineapple and garnish with quarters of hard boiled egg and onion rings. You may also add a few cubes of feta cheese on top. Sprinkle with dried herbs.

Special hint: Serve with side dishes of garlic croûtons, crisply fried and chopped bacon and grated or diced hard-boiled egg. Chinese sprouts are a lovely addition when obtainable. There are a few different varieties.

For a special occasion, brush rim of glass bowl with slightly beaten egg white, then dip in finely chopped parsley. A nice idea is to place, different bowls of salad dressings (e.g. french, avocado, roquefort) in a large tray or container and surround with crushed ice.

PALM HEART & ARTICHOKE SALAD

1 tin palm hearts
1 tin baby corn cobs (available from Chinese or speciality shops)
fresh sliced mushrooms
1 lettuce torn into pieces
1 tin drained artichoke hearts

Method: Toss all ingredients together and pour over the following dressing:

4 tablespoons oil
2 tablespoons vinegar
$\frac{1}{2}$ teaspoon coarsely ground black pepper
2 teaspoons salt
1 teaspoon garlic salt
2 teaspoons mustard powder

RED KIDNEY BEAN SALAD

1 tin red kidney beans
1 cup diced cucumber
1 cup diced celery
$\frac{1}{2}$ cup diced green pepper
$\frac{1}{2}$ cup chopped spring onions
$\frac{1}{2}$ teaspoon salt
dash coarsely ground black pepper
$\frac{1}{2}$ cup French dressing or mayonnaise

Method: Toss all vegetables together and pour over dressing. Garnish with celery curls.

SPINACH SALAD

6 large spinach leaves, torn into pieces
8 slices crisply fried bacon, diced
125 g fresh sliced mushrooms, washed and sprinkled with lemon juice
1 large tomato sliced thinly
$\frac{1}{4}$ cup chopped spring onions
1 cup roquefort dressing

Method: Toss all vegetables and bacon together. Pour over dressing.

For kosher requirements use maken and French dressing.

SUMPTUOUS SALAD

8 cups mixed salad greens (lettuce, cucumber, celery, spring onions, etc)
2 cups cauliflowerettes broken into bits
1 carrot diced
1 cup shredded red cabbage
1 green pepper finely chopped

Method: Toss all ingredients together and pour over French or roquefort dressing.

TOMATOES AND GREEN PEPPERS STUFFED WITH POTATO SALAD

4 tomatoes halves
4 green peppers halved
1 cup mayonnaise
1 tablespoon vinegar
1 teaspoon mustard powder
1 finely diced green pepper
1 finely diced red pepper
   a few chopped spring onions
1–1½ teaspoons salt
   pinch pepper
½ teaspoon sugar
6 medium potatoes

Method: Scoop out pulp of tomatoes and drain upside-down on absorbent paper. Remove seeds from peppers. Boil potatoes in their jackets in salt water until tender. Cool, peel and cut into cubes. In a large bowl combine potato with chopped peppers. Mix together the mayonnaise, vinegar, salt, sugar, mustard, pepper and spring onions. Spoon over the potatoes lightly. Fill tomatoes and green peppers with potato salad and sprinkle with crushed crisps and paprika.

DRESSINGS

AVOCADO CREAM CHEESE DRESSING

2 avocados sieved or mashed
2 dessertspoons lemon juice
125 g (4 oz) cream cheese
250 mℓ yoghurt (1 cup)
125 mℓ (½ cup) cream optional
2 teaspoons anchovy sauce or paste
   salt to taste
   coarsely ground black pepper to taste
   few drops tabasco
½ cup vinegar, add more if needed.

Method: Blend all ingredients together till smooth. Pour over French salad.

FRENCH DRESSING

1 full teaspoon salt
1 teaspoon garlic salt
1 teaspoon mustard powder
1 teaspoon sugar
½ teaspoon seasoning salt
½ teaspoon coarsely ground black pepper
1 teaspoon French salad dressing (if available)
4 cloves crushed garlic optional
   few drops tabasco
½ teaspoon origanum
1 cup vinegar
1 cup oil, ½ cup water

Method: Combine the above in a a bottle. Shake very well. This is sufficient for 3–4 salads, and may be stored in the fridge.

CREAMY FRENCH DRESSING

Method: Add ½ cup cream to 1½ cups French dressing.

GREEN GODDESS SALAD DRESSING

1 cup mayonnaise
½ cup sour cream
¼ cup chopped parsley
2 tablespoons chopped spring onions
2 tablespoons anchovy paste
3 tablespoons tarragon vinegar
1 teaspoon Worcestershire sauce
   dash dry mustard powder
1 clove garlic, crushed
¼ teaspoon pepper

Method: Combine all ingredients. Chill and allow flavours to blend and dressing to thicken – about 2 hours. This will keep in refrigerator for two weeks.

POPPY SEED DRESSING

Method: Mix 1 cup French dressing with 1 cup mayonnaise and 2 tablespoons poppy seed. Beat with rotary beater till blended. Good with any salad.

ROQUEFORT DRESSING

125 g roquefort cheese (4 oz)
1 cup mayonnaise
2 cloves crushed garlic
1 tablespoon anchovy sauce or paste
125 mℓ sour cream (½ cup)
¼ cup vinegar
1 tablespoon lemon juice
¼ teaspoon salt
½ teaspoon coarsely ground black pepper

1 tablespoon finely chopped parsley
1 tablespoon finely chopped spring onion

Method: Place all ingredients except parsley and spring onion in blender. Buzz till smooth. Add parsley and spring onion if desired.

THOUSAND ISLAND DRESSING

1 cup mayonnaise
½ cup tomato sauce
1 teaspoon Worcestershire sauce
   dash cayenne pepper
1 teaspoon vinegar
½ teaspoon sugar
   salt and pepper to taste

Method: Combine above ingredients.

MAYONNAISE

4 eggs
4 tablespoons vinegar
2 teaspoons salt
   dash pepper (black)
3 cups oil (750 mℓ)
2 level teaspoons mustard powder
1 teaspoon Worcestershire sauce
4 teaspoons sugar

Method: Using a food processor, or blender, blend eggs, vinegar, salt, pepper, mustard, Worcestershire sauce and sugar very well. Slowly add 1 bottle (750 mℓ) oil till thick and creamy.

8. DESSERTS
1. Hot
2. Cold

SPECIAL HINTS:

Gelatine is very easy to use if you dissolve it first in 1–2 tablespoons cold water and then stir in ¼ cup boiling water and mix it thoroughly until the liquid is clear and *no crystals* can be seen. However, if it is still not thoroughly dissolved place the cup or bowl into a larger bowl of boiling water and stir till clear.

Always dissolve your gelatine in this way regardless of what the recipe specifies, as the little extra cold and boiling water is not going to make the slightest difference to the recipe.

Egg Yolk Custards: It is very difficult, especially for an inexperienced cook, to feel the difference when an egg yolk custard thickens, but if you allow it to boil, the custard will curdle and taste floury.

Just imagine placing an egg yolk in boiling water. It will immediately, begin to set. Bearing in mind that this is all that is really required, as long as the temperature is sufficiently high, but just below boiling, your custard will be fine, and will thicken considerably more as it cools and sets. However, you should still be able to *feel* the difference in texture.

1. HOT

BAKED ALASKA

Use either a bought swiss roll or make your own
1 tin pineapple rings (drained) and soaked in Kirsch
1 litre ice-cream
3 egg whites
¾ cup castor sugar

Method: Cut swiss roll into fairly thick slices and sprinkle each slice with a little brandy or Kirsch and place on a wooden board that has been covered with foil. Place a pineapple ring on each round and top with a scoop of ice-cream. Make a stiff meringue with the egg whites and sugar. Completely cover the swiss roll, fruit and ice-cream with the meringue. Top with a cherry and bake in 250°C (500°F) oven for 3–5 minutes. To serve, heat some brandy to boiling point, set alight and pour over alaska.

BOGATSA

4 cups milk
2 eggs
1 teaspoon grated lemon or orange rind
½ cup semolina or Cream of Wheat
⅔ cup sugar
Phyllo pastry (½ kilo) – 1 lb
Melted butter

Method: Line a rectangular pyrex dish with 8–10 layers of Phyllo pastry, brushing with melted butter between each layer and bringing the first two or three layers up the sides of the dish as well.

Filling: Boil the milk with half the sugar. Add the semolina in a slow stream from high up. Boil stirring all the time with a wooden spoon over a low heat till very thick. Allow to cool, stirring occasionally to prevent a skin forming on the top. Add 1 teaspoon finely grated lemon or orange rind. Separate the eggs, and beat the yolks with the remaining sugar till light and creamy. Fold this and the stiffly beaten egg whites into the semolina mixture. Pour into the pyrex dish over the Phyllo pastry. Cover with another 10 layers of Phyllo, brushing in between with melted butter. Trim edges and allow to set in fridge for a while before cutting right through the top layers of Phyllo into little squares, making sure that the custard doesn't ooze through the top. You may now freeze till required or bake in 180°C (350°F) oven for 1 hour, then turn oven off completely and leave for another 30 minutes. Serve with cinnamon and sugar.

CAFÉ BRULOT
(A delicious after dinner coffee)

1 tablespoon whole allspice
1 lemon rind, cut into thin slivers
1 orange rind, cut into thin slivers
1 whole cinnamon stick
¼ cup brandy
3 cups Expresso or double strength hot coffee

Method: In top of chafing dish place allspice, lemon rind, orange rind and cinnamon stick. Place the sugar and brandy in ladle or bowl and heat. Set the brandy afire and pour over the spice mixture. Light the flame under the chafing dish and using the ladle or a large spoon, keep pouring the brandy over the other ingredients until the sugar dissolves. When dissolved, immediately add the coffee, which should be freshly made and about 50% stronger than usual. Keep ladling for a few moments to mix the coffee, then serve in demitasse cups. Serves 6. Place dollop of whipped cream on top.

CHEESE BLINTZES – Refer "Jewish Section".

CRÊPES CALYPSO

Batter:
1 cup flour
4 eggs
2 cups milk
   pinch salt
   oil for frying

Method: Beat all the ingredients together till smooth. Heat oil in a small pan and pour in a thin layer of batter. Fry quickly till crisp and golden. Remove onto a clean cloth and when cool, stack one on top of the other. Keep warm in warming oven. Fill with drained pineapple chunks, which have been marinated in rum and pineapple liqueur. To serve, pour over hot chocolate sauce and sprinkle with flaked toasted almonds.

Sauce:
75 g (3 oz) butter
250 mℓ (½ pint) cream
100 g (4 oz) chocolate
1 teaspoon vanilla

Method: Melt chocolate and butter in double boiler, stir in cream and vanilla.

CRÊPE DELIGHT

Prepare batter for "Crêpes Calypso" as given above.

Filling: One sponge cake cut into fingers. Soak in the following custard till it has all been absorbed:

4 egg yolks
2 dessertspoons sugar
2 cups milk, scalded
1 teaspoon vanilla or 1 dessertspoon orange liqueur

Method: Beat egg yolks and sugar till light and creamy. Add scalded milk beating all the time as you do so. Place in a double boiler and cook stirring constantly till very slightly thickened. Remove from heat; add vanilla or liqueur.

Place a finger of custard soaked cake on each crêpe and roll up. Place in greased pyrex dish and pour over the following sauce:

Sauce:
½ cup brown sugar
½ cup water
 juice of 2 oranges
 juice of 1 lemon
1 tablespoon butter
2 tablespoons brandy
2 tablespoons each of two fruity flavoured
 liqueurs

Method: Boil all ingredients for sauce together. Add 1 punnet fresh sliced strawberries and allow to simmer for 2–3 minutes. Mix 1 dessertspoon maizena to a paste with a little cold water and thicken the above sauce with this. Remove from heat and stir in 1 dessertspoon red (strawberry or raspberry) jelly. Bake the crêpes in a 200°C (400°F) oven for 20–25 minutes or till hot or bubbling. Serve piping hot with whipped cream.

Special Hint: Any fruit of your choice could be used for the above topping. You could also substitute boudoir biscuits for the sponge cake.

DELICIOUS NOODLE PUDDING

Method: Boil 250 g (½ lb) thick ribbon noodles in salt water for about 15–20 minutes till soft. Drain and mix in 2 tablespoons melted butter 125 mℓ (¼ pint) cream, ¾ cup sugar, 1 tablespoon syrup, 4 tablespoons cream cheese, and ½ teaspoon cinnamon. Beat 2 eggs and 1 cup milk, mix together with noodles. Pour into buttered pyrex dish and bake 180°C (350°F) oven for ¾ hour.

FLAMING CRÊPES MONTMORENCY

2 cups flour
1 tablespoon sugar
 pinch salt
2 eggs and 2 yolks
1 cup milk
1 cup beer
3 tablespoons oil
2 tablespoons brandy

Method: Beat the eggs and sugar. Add the milk, beer, oil and brandy. Add the sifted dry ingredients and beat till smooth. Pour the mixture through a strainer and leave to stand for an hour or so. If the mixture is too thick, add more milk or beer. Grease a little pan with oil and fry on one side only, stacking one on top of the other when cool.

Filling:
1–2 bottles of cherry pie filling. Make a thin custard with 2 dessertspoons custard powder and 2 cups milk or more. Sweeten with 2 tablespoons sugar. Place a dessertspoon each of cherry pie filling and custard in each crêpe, then fold up in envelope fashion. Place in a pyrex dish and pour over the following sauce:

Sauce:
1 cup brown sugar
60 g butter (2 oz)
 juice and rind of 1 lemon
1 cup orange juice
 rind of 1 orange
2 tablespoons each of a few fruity flavoured
 liqueurs

Method: Melt butter, add brown sugar, add all other ingredients except the liqueurs, and cook gently till sugar has dissolved. Lastly, stir in liqueurs. To serve, bake in a hot oven till sauce is bubbling. Heat ½ cup brandy to boiling point. Ignite and pour over crêpes. Delicious served with whipped cream, ice-cream or creme bruleé spooned over them!

For kosher requirements: Use 2 cups beer for crêpes, omit cutard filling and omit butter from sauce.

FLAMING STRAWBERRY CRÊPES

1 cup flour
4 eggs
  oil for frying
½ ℓ milk (2 cups)
  pinch salt

Method: Beat all the ingredients together till smooth. Heat oil in a small pan and pour in a thin layer of batter. Fry quickly till crisp and golden. Remove onto a clean cloth and when cool, stack one on top of the other.

Filling:
Use either the tinned strawberry pie filling or make a strawberry filling as follows:

3 punnets strawberries halved
¾ cup sugar
¼ packet red jelly (2 dessertspoons)
¼ cup water
2 dessertspoons maizena to a paste with cold
  water.

Method: Bring the sugar and water to the boil. When the sugar has dissolved, add strawberries and allow to simmer for a few minutes. Add jelly and maizena and simmer till thickened. Allow to cool thoroughly.

Sauce:
1 cup sugar
50 g (2 oz) butter
  juice and rind of 1 lemon
1 cup orange juice
  rind of 1 orange
1 liqueur glass of 2 or 3 fruity flavoured
  liqueurs.

Method: Place all the above ingredients in a saucepan and bring to the boil.

To Serve: Warm the filling, roll the crêpes with the hot mixture inside then place on a buttered ovenware platter, platter, sprinkle with a few tablespoons brown sugar and place under the griller to caramelize. Pour sauce over and flame with ½ cup brandy, which has been brought to the boil and then lit.

Special Hint: Use rhubarb, in exactly the same way, when strawberries are not in season. Tinned apricots are also nice to use.

FRUIT COBBLER

¼ cup brown sugar
1 teaspoon cinnamon
¾ packet crushed ginger nuts
  stewed apples
  satsuma plums, tinned or fresh
2 pears, peeled and sliced
3 sliced bananas
  peaches, or any stewing fruits in season

Method: Mix fruit, cinnamon and sugar together. Place in ovenware dish. Top with crushed biscuits and bake in 180°C (350°F) oven for 30–40 minutes. Serve hot with whipped cream or custard.

KAISERSCHMARREN

½ cup raisins or sultanas
3 eggs separated
½ cup milk
2 tablespoons brandy
2 tablespoons sugar
½ cup (125 mℓ) cream
1 cup flour, sifted

Method: Soak raisins or sultanas in brandy for about 1 hour. Meanwhile prepare batter by beating the egg yolks and sugar till light and fluffy. Add flour, alternately with milk and cream, then lastly fold in stiffly beaten egg whites.

Heat 1 tablespoon oil in a small frying pan. Spoon in sufficient batter to cover the bottom of the pan. Cook till golden on both sides. Turn out onto a clean cloth and when cool, stack one on top of the other till required. Repeat until all the batter has been used up. Using a fork, tear the pancakes into small pieces.

Melt 175 g (6 oz) butter in a large frying pan. Add ½ cup sugar, ½ teaspoon cinnamon, sultanas and brandy. Do not allow sugar to melt. Add pancake pieces, coat quickly with the sauce, dust with icing sugar and serve.

N.B.: It is imperative that you do not allow the sugar to dissolve.

Special hint: Traditionally it is served in pieces, but I always feel it is a pity to do this, so I serve them whole and still coat with the sauce as directed above. It is also nice to substitute 1 tin, 410 g, drained fruit for the sultanas.

ORANGE BAKED ALASKA

Prepare your own sponge as follows or use a bought one.

Sponge Cake:
2 eggs
¾ cup sugar
75 g (3 oz) butter
½ cup milk and water mixed
1 cup flour
1 heaped teaspoon baking powder

Method: Beat eggs and sugar till light and creamy. Add sifted dry ingredients. Melt butter in milk and bring to the boil. Add to mixture, bake in greased and floured 23 cm (9-inch) diameter tin in a 190°C (375°F) oven for 20–25 minutes. Peel and slice 4 oranges or use a tin of drained mandarin segments and soak for a few hours in 3 tablespoons Grand Marnier.

Orange Ice-cream Bombe
410 g condensed milk (1 lb)
1 egg
½ cup orange juice
½ cup lemon juice
  finely grated rind of 1 orange
500 mℓ (1 pint) whipped cream

Method: Beat egg and condensed milk together stir in orange juice, lemon juice and orange rind and lastly fold in whipped cream. Place in pyrex bowl in freezer for 1½–2 hours. Remove from freezer and beat 1–2 minutes. Pour into mould which has been rinsed out with ½ cup cold water and 2 tablespoons oil, return to freezer and re-freeze until solid.

Prepare meringue just before serving as follows:

4 egg whites
1 cup castor sugar

Method: Beat egg whites till soft peaks, then gradually beat in sugar till very stiff and shiny.

To Assemble: Place sponge on ovenware platter or use a wooden board covered with foil. Place macerated orange slices on top of sponge and sprinkle with the juice and liqueur. Unmould ice-cream bombe on top of this and then cover the ice-cream and sponge with the meringue. Bake in a preheated 225°C (450°F) oven for 3–5 minutes or till lightly browned. To serve, heat $\frac{1}{2}$ cup brandy to boiling point, set alight and flambe alaska!

Special Hint: A lovely granadilla ice-cream can be made in the same way by using 1 cup fresh granadillas and, of course, omitting orange juice and rind, and lemon juice.

AUNTIE ROSIE'S GLAZED XMAS PUDDING

Mix together in a large mixing bowl:

2 heaped cups freshly made breadcrumbs
1 heaped cup flour
$\frac{1}{2}$ teaspoon salt
1 cup sugar
2 teaspoons baking powder
1 teaspoon cinnamon
$\frac{1}{2}$ teaspoon mixed spice
$\frac{1}{2}$ teaspoon ginger
1 tablespoon ground almonds (optional)
Grate in: 250 g ($\frac{1}{2}$ lb) vegetable fat, then rub in well with your fingers.
Add: 500 g (1 lb) mixed fruit
    1 small grated carrot
In a separate bowl, beat 2 eggs slightly, then stir in 1 tablespoon brandy, 1 dessertspoon syrup, 1 dessertspoon apricot jam or marmalade and 1–2 tablespoons orange juice or water. Pour this mixture over the fruit mixture and mix well.

Prepare the glaze as follows: Mix together 1 cup sugar, 1 cup boiling water and $\frac{1}{2}$ cup semi-sweet white wine. Stir till sugar is dissolved.

Pour this mixture into greased steaming pots, spoon pudding mixture into this. Close pots and steam for 4 hours. On the day that you wish to use this pudding it must be steamed for a further 2 hours. Remember, the longer you steam the pudding, the nicer it is. Turn out onto serving platter and serve with ice-cream.

N.B. This pudding may be used over pesach if you substitute Matzo meal for the breadcrumbs and use self-raising flour or cake meal instead of flour. Omit baking powder.

ORANGE FLAVOURED CHEESE BLINTZES

Method: Beat 3 eggs with $2\frac{1}{2}$ cups cold water. Add $1\frac{1}{2}$ cups flour sifted with a pinch salt. Add $\frac{1}{2}$ teaspoon baking powder. Stir in $\frac{1}{2}$ teaspoon finely grated orange rind. If necessary add more milk or water. Consistency should be that of thin cream. Grease pan with oil and fry on one side only. Stack one on top of another on a clean cloth until ready to use.

Filling:
500 g (1 lb) cream cheese
1 egg, sugar to taste
2 dessertspoons Van der Hum
    dash of cinnamon
$1\frac{1}{2}$ tablespoons maizena
125 mℓ ($\frac{1}{4}$ pint) or more cream (whipped)
1 tablespoon orange juice
$\frac{1}{2}$ teaspoon finely grated orange rind

Method: Mix together by hand until smooth. Place a dessertspoon of filling in each crêpe. Roll up and place in greased pyrex dish. Dot with 1 tablespoon butter. Pour over a few tablespoons of cream. Bake in 180°C (350°F) oven for about 50 minutes. Remove from oven, sprinkle with cinnamon and sugar, flame with $\frac{1}{2}$ cup boiling Van der Hum and serve piping hot with a dollop of cream on each portion.

PEACH & CHERRY FLAMBÉ

1 tin peach halves
1 tin red cherries
 juice and rind of 1 orange
2 liqueur glasses of any fruity liqueurs
½ cup brandy
1 dessertspoon maizena
2 tablespoons butter
½ cup brown sugar
 juice of ½ lemon

Method: Drain peaches and cherries. Dissolve maizena in juices and place in chafing dish with butter, sugar, orange rind and juice, lemon juice and liqueurs and simmer on low for about 20–30 minutes. Add fruit and simmer another 10 minutes. Heat the brandy to boiling point. Flame and pour over. Serve spooned over vanilla ice-cream.

RICE PUDDING

Method: Mix 2–3 tablespoons cooked rice, with 1 tablespoon butter. Put in pyrex dish and pour over custard mixture, made as follows: Beat 3 eggs with 3 dessertspoons sugar and ½ teaspoon vanilla then pour over 3 cups scalded milk. Bake 180°C (350°F) in a dish of hot water for approximately ½–¾ hour or until set. Sprinkle top with cinnamon or nutmeg.

VARENIKY

2 cups flour
2 eggs
¼ cup cold water
 pinch salt
2 tins pitted cherries
250 mℓ (½ pint) sour cream or smetna

Method: Sift flour and salt, add slightly beaten eggs. Mix well and then knead into a dough with the water. Drain cherries. Place the juice in a saucepan and thicken on stove with 1 tablespoon maizena, mixed to a paste with a little cold water. Roll out pastry very thinly and cut into circles with a tumbler or pastry cutter. Place a few cherries onto each circle of pastry, fold, press the edges together and place in a large pan of boiling water with 1 tablespoon oil to cook for 10–15 minutes or till tender.

Remove with slotted spoon. Place in a greased pyrex dish. Pour over thickened cherry juice. Bake in the oven about 10 minutes. Remove, pour over sour cream and serve immediately.

If desired, serve with cinnamon and sugar.

Special hint: Can add a few tablespoons sugar to the thickened cherry juice.

APPLE MERINGUE

Method: Peel, core and slice 6–8 granny smith apples. Place in a saucepan with ½ cup water. Simmer until soft. Add ½–¾ cup sugar and ½ teaspoon vanilla essence. Mix well and put into a pyrex dish. Beat 4 egg whites stiffly then gradually work in 8 tablespoons castor sugar. Add ½ teaspoon lemon essence. Bake in a slow oven 125°C (250°F) until the top is as hard as meringue 3–4 hours. Serve hot or cold with whipped cream.

Special hint: 4 egg whites = ½ cup.

2. COLD

BANANA CUSTARD PUDDING DESSERT

½ cup sugar
⅓ cup maizena
3 eggs, separated
 pinch salt
2 cups milk
1 teaspoon vanilla
1 packet tennis biscuits, crushed & mixed with 50 g (2 oz) melted butter
4 medium size bananas sliced & dipped in lemon juice

Method: Blend ¼ cup sugar, maizena and salt together in top of double boiler. Add ½ cup milk and stir till smooth. Add remaining milk and cook in double boiler till thick. Beat egg yolks well and add hot custard very slowly, beating all the time. Return to double boiler and cook 2 minutes. Remove from heat and add vanilla. Preheat oven to 180°C (350°F). Line bottom of pyrex dish with ½ biscuits. Arrange sliced bananas on top. Pour ½ custard over bananas and make another layer repeating according to size of dish. Beat egg whites till stiff, add remaining sugar gradually. Spread meringue over custard. Bake 10–15 minutes. Serve hot or cold.

BRANDIED SAUCE FOR ICE-CREAM

1 cup brown sugar
½ cup water
1 cup marmalade
1 teaspoon grated lemon rind
 rind of 1 orange
½ cup sugar
1 cup strawberry jam
1 cup chopped walnuts
2 tablespoons lemon juice
1 cup brandy

Method: Place sugars and water in a saucepan and bring to the boil, stirring constantly. Reduce heat and simmer for 5 minutes. Add remaining ingredients, mix well and continue simmering for another 5 minutes. Cool the sauce, pour into a ball jar and allow to "ripen" in refrigerator for 2 weeks.

Special hint: Add 1 kilo (2 lb) fresh apricots as well, when in season with pips removed.

BUTTER CRUNCH ICE-CREAM RING

1 cup light brown sugar
1½ tablespoons syrup
⅓ cup milk
3 tablespoons butter
4 cups cornflakes
 vanilla and/or chocolate ice-cream (2 ℓ)
 Tubed chocolate sauce

Method: In a small saucepan, combine brown sugar, syrup, milk and butter. Cook over medium heat, stirring until a little dropped in cold water, forms a soft ball. Remove from heat. Meanwhile grease a large bowl well with butter. Add syrup mixture, then cornflakes and mix till cornflakes are completely coated with syrup.

Pack cornflake mixture into a well buttered 20 cm (7 or 8-inch) diameter ring mould. Allow to set at room temperature. Form ice-creams into balls. Freeze till ready to serve.

To serve: Turn ring out onto serving platter. Fill with ice-cream balls and garnish with whole strawberries. Serve with chocolate sauce.

CASSATA ICE-CREAM BOMBE

Line a mould with a 5 cm (2-inch) thick layer of vanilla or chocolate ice-cream. Allow to set in freezer.

Mix together the inner filling as follows:
1 ℓ softened vanilla ice-cream
1 cup chopped sultanas
1 cup chopped cake mix (sultanas, raisins, currants and candied peel)
½ packet broken marie biscuits
1 x 100 g slab bitter chocolate coarsely chopped (4 oz)
250 g (8 oz) glace cherries, red & green quartered
1 cup chopped pecan nuts (100 g)

Method: Spoon into the vanilla or chocolate shell. Press down well. Freeze until required. Unmould and decorate by drizzling ready made chocolate sauce (in a tube) over the bombe.
  Special hint: Rinse the mould out with ½ cup cold water mixed with 1 tablespoon oil.

CHOCOLATE MOUSSE

1 teaspoon gelatine
100 g bitter chocolate (4 oz)
4 eggs, separated
1 teaspoon vanilla
¼ cup cold water
¼ cup boiling water
⅓ cup sugar
250 mℓ (1 cup) cream or 2 sachets orley whip

Method: Dissolve gelatine in cold water. Add boiling water and stir till mixture is very clear and no crystals can be seen.
  Melt chocolate in double boiler, *without stirring*, then add vanilla and gelatine. Beat egg yolks and sugar till thick and creamy. Add chocolate/gelatine mixture beating all the while as you do so.
  Fold in stiffly beaten egg whites. Lastly fold in stiffly beaten cream. Pour into glass bowl and set in fridge. Decorate with swirls of cream topped with chocolate curls.

CHOCOLATE BOWL SURPRISE

Method: Cover a round pyrex dish with a layer of heavy duty aluminium foil. Melt 400 g (1 lb) of bitter chocolate in a double boiler. Coat the foil, in the shape of the bowl, with half the chocolate. Crush 1 packet plain or chocolate marie biscuits and press a thick layer onto the choc. Allow to harden in fridge and repeat this process once more, using the remaining chocolate and biscuits. Use some of the melted chocolate for making chocolate leaves for garnish. When the chocolate has hardened, remove the bowl and peel the foil away from the inside of the chocolate. Fill with black forest parfait as given below.

Black forest parfait:
  Vanilla ice-cream
3 tablespoons Kirsch
1 can black or red cherries
  sweetened whipped cream
  coarsely grated dark chocolate or use flaky bars

Method: Drain cherries and soak in Kirsch about 1 hour. Place juice in a saucepan and thicken with 1 dessertspoon maizena mixed to a paste with a little cold water. Cool thoroughly then mix together with cherries and Kirsch. Place scoops of ice-cream in the bottom of the chocolate bowl. Spoon over cherry mixture. Top with swirls of whipped cream, sprinkle with flaky and decorate with chocolate leaves, if desired.

CHOCOLATE CAKE CASSATA

Chocolate sponge:
6 eggs, separated
¾ cup sugar
2 tablespoons cocoa
2 tablespoons maizena

Method: Beat yolks with sugar till light and creamy. Add sifted cocoa and maizena. Lastly fold in stiffly beaten egg whites. Bake in a greased and floured swiss roll tin in 210°C (425°F) oven for 10 minutes. Turn out onto a clean cloth and cut off the ends, so that you have a large square. Cut the square diagonally across so that you have four triangular pieces. Place these triangles of cake into an earthenware pudding basin (approximately 1 ℓ capacity). Sprinkle with ¼ cup cointreau and ¼ cup brandy (optional).

Filling: Place 12 quartered marshmallows in a double boiler with 2 tablespoons milk and cook until marshmallows have dissolved. Allow to cool and then fold into 500 mℓ (1 pint) stiffly beaten cream. Fold in 1 cup chopped fresh or tinned cherries, 100 grams (4 oz) coarsely chopped bitter chocolate and 100 g (4 oz) coarsely diced pecan nuts.

Pour this mixture into pudding basin which has been lined with cake and then top with the remaining pieces of cake left over.

Allow to set in fridge overnight. Unmould onto serving platter, pipe rosettes of cream round the base and along the lines of the cake. Place a few cherries on top to form a flower and decorate further with chocolate leaves.

For Kosher requirements use 2 sachets orly whip and 1 tablespoon icing sugar. Omit marshmallow mixture and use 1 teaspoon Aga aga instead.

CHOCOLATE CHARLOTTE SUISSE

Make chocolate swiss roll as follows:
1 cup castor sugar
1 cup flour
½ cup cocoa
4 eggs, separated
½ cup boiling water – melt 1 tablespoon butter in this or use oil.
1 teaspoon vanilla
1½ teaspoons baking powder

Method: Cream yolks and sugar very well. Add water and melted butter oil mixture and vanilla. Add sifted flour, cocoa and baking powder. Lastly fold in stiffly beaten egg whites. Bake in greased and floured swiss roll tin, 190°C (375°F) oven for 8–10 minutes. Turn out onto damp cloth which has been sprinkled with sugar, and roll up. Allow to cool. Unroll gently, fill with 250 mℓ (½ pint) whipped cream or orley whip, then re-roll. Line a 22–25 cm (9 or 10-inch) springform tin with wax paper, cut swiss roll into slices and place round the side of the tin. Fill with the following chocolate mousse, then top with additional swiss roll slices (when inverted this will be your base).

Chocolate mousse:
3 eggs, separated
250 mℓ (½ pint) whipped cream or orley whip
¼ cup boiling water
1 teaspoon gelatine dissolved in 2 tablespoons cold water
110 g (4 oz) bitter chocolate
2½ tablespoons sugar
1½ tablespoons butter

Method: Beat egg yolks and sugar till light and fluffy. Place chocolate, water and butter in double boiler. (For Kosher requirements omit butter and add 1 tablespoon brandy.) Cook till melted and smooth. Add an additional tablespoon of boiling water to the gelatine, mix well then stir into double boiler with the chocolate and cook till gelatine has dissolved. Gradually add the hot chocolate mixture to the egg yolks, beating all the time, as you do so. Cool to room temperature, then fold in whipped cream. Lastly fold in stiffly beaten egg whites. Pour into tin lined with swiss roll and allow to set in refrigerator overnight. Unmould onto serving platter and decorate with whipped cream and strawberries when in season or use chocolate leaves, which are made by melting bitter chocolate in a double boiler, *without stirring* and then coating the back of rose leaves or lemon leaves fairly thickly with the melted chocolate and allow to set in fridge, then peel off the leaves.

CHOCOLATE MOSAIC DESSERT

2 teaspoons gelatine
100 g bitter chocolate (4 oz)
¼ cup hot water
1 teaspoon vanilla
1 tablespoon cold water
⅓ cup sugar
4 eggs separated
250 mℓ cream (½ pint) whipped
3 packets Boudoir biscuits, dipped in mixture of milk and brandy or water and brandy

Method: Soften gelatine in cold water. Melt chocolate in double boiler. Add hot water to gelatine and stir till smooth then stir into chocolate. Remove from stove. Beat the egg yolks with sugar till thick and creamy. Add chocolate mixture and vanilla. Fold in stiffly beaten egg whites. Lastly fold in cream. Line a loose-bottomed tin with waxproof paper. Cover the bottom with a layer of biscuits, then half the chocolate mixture, another layer of biscuits, then remaining chocolate mixture and top with more biscuits. Chill 12–24 hours. Unmould and decorate with cream rosettes and shavings of chocolate.

COUER À LA CREME

750 g (6 oz) cream cheese
2 tablespoons water
3 egg whites
  pinch salt
½ cup sugar
250 mℓ (½ pint) sweet whipped cream
1 teaspoon vanilla
125 mℓ (¼ pint) thin cream

Method: Mix whipped cream thoroughly with cream cheese. Place sugar and water in saucepan and allow to boil for a few minutes till the sugar has completely dissolved. Beat into cream cheese and add vanilla. Beat egg whites with salt till stiff and fold in. Line a heart shaped tin with a double layer of muslin or cheesecloth. Pour mixture in, fold cheesecloth over the top. Cover with foil. Place weight on top and leave in fridge 24 hours. Turn out onto serving platter. Remove cheesecloth. Cover with 2–3 tablespoons thin cream. Beat the balance of the cream till thick and pipe rosettes round the top edge of the heart. Decorate with strawberries, apricots, plums, gooseberries or fruits in season.

Strawberry sauce to serve in season: Sprinkle 1 tray fresh strawberries with a few tablespoons castor sugar. Leave to stand till juice forms at the bottom. Liquidise, heat and thicken with 1 dessertspoon maizena and 1 tablespoon brandy.

CREME BRULLÉ

2 cups cream (500 mℓ)
2 dessertspoons sugar
5 egg yolks

1 teaspoon vanilla
brown sugar

Method: Scald cream in the top of a double boiler. Beat egg yolks and sugar till thick and creamy. Add vanilla and slowly add scalded cream, beating all the while as you do so. Return *half* of this mixture into the top of the double boiler and cook, stirring all the time with a wooden spoon until the mixture thickens. Do not over cook as it will curdle. Pour into a 22 cm (9-inch) round pyrex or ovenware container. Cook the remaining mixture in the same manner and pour into the serving dish as well. Cool and allow to set in the fridge, preferable overnight.

Cover the custard completely with about 4–5 tablespoons brown sugar, place in a large tin and surround with ice cubes. Place right under the oven broiler until the sugar caramelises, watching it very carefully as you do so as the sugar burns very easily. Cool, return to refrigerator and serve when required.

CREME CARAMEL

Method: Melt ¾ cup sugar over low heat in a heavy saucepan, then pour into pyrex dish. Beat 3 eggs and 1 yolk with 2 tablespoons sugar and 1 teaspoon vanilla, just till blended, using a hand beater. Scald 3 cups milk (must be just under boiling point) and then pour, very slowly into the egg mixture, beating all the time. Pour over *cooled* caramelised sugar and place the pyrex dish in a large baking tin, which has been half filled with hot water, *not boiling water*. Bake in a 120°C (250°F) oven for 1 hour, then turn oven down to 110°C (225°F) and leave for another 30 minutes or until set. Cool and keep in fridge till required. To serve, loosen edges with knife and invert onto serving platter.

Special hint: Line baking tin with a treble thickness of newspaper before pouring in the boiling water. This prevents the custard from curdling.

CRUNCH CRUST ICE-CREAM BOMBE

1 large slab bitter chocolate (100 g)
75 g (3 oz) butter
4 cups rice crispies
16 marshmallows

Method: Melt butter, chocolate, marshmallows in saucepan till dissolved. Remove from heat and add rice crispies. Mix well, grease and line springform tin with butter and see through foil. Line tin with mixture. Chill in fridge till ready to fill.

Make chocolate ice-cream as follows:
1 large slab bitter chocolate (100 g)
2 cups milk
2 tablespoons brandy
1 tablespoon vanilla
1¼ cups sugar
4 tablespoons flour
1 tablespoon cocoa, heaped
⅛ teaspoon salt
2 eggs slightly beaten
4 cups cream

Method: Heat chocolate and 1½ cups milk over boiling water until chocolate has melted. Beat with egg beater till blended. Combine sugar, cocoa, flour and salt with ½ cup milk till smooth. Add chocolate mixture gradually then return to double boiler and cook until thickened stirring constantly. Continue to cook another 5 minutes stirring occasionally. Beat eggs in mixmaster, add chocolate mixture slowly, beating vigorously. Return to double boiler and cook 2 minutes longer, stirring constantly. Cool. Add whipped cream, vanilla and brandy. Pour into crust and freeze. Unmould to serve.

Special hint: You may fill the shell with bought ice-cream if preferred.

EASY COFFEE ICE-CREAM

3 eggs separated
1 tin sweetened condensed milk (400 g)
2 cups whipped cream (500 mℓ)
2 heaped teaspoons instant coffee powder
1 tablespoon brandy
1 teaspoon vanilla

Method: Beat the egg yolks well with the condensed milk. Fold in the whipped cream and then stiffly beaten egg whites. Dissolve the coffee in a little boiling water, then add to the mixture as well as the brandy and vanilla. Pour into a container and freeze, or pour into a mould, which also looks far more attractive. Unmould and drizzle with tubed chocolate sauce.

ENGLISH TRIFLE

1 sponge cake, home baked or bought
   apricot jam
$\frac{1}{2}$ cup sherry
$\frac{1}{2}$ cup brandy
4 egg yolks
2 dessertspoons sugar
1 cup cream (250 mℓ)
1 teaspoon vanilla
1 cup milk
1 heaped tablespoon maizena
For decoration: Maraschino cherries, blanched almonds, 1 cup cream, whipped

Method: Cut sponge cake into fingers and spread with apricot jam. Scald the cream and the milk. Beat the egg yolks with the sugar till light and fluffy, then add maizena and vanilla and beat again till blended. Slowly add the scalded mixture to the egg yolks, beating all the time. Pour this mixture into a double boiler and cook till thick, stirring all the time with a wooden spoon. Allow to cool.

Place half the sponge cake into a deep glass bowl, sprinkle with half the sherry and brandy, then cover with half the custard and top with half the whipped cream. A little icing sugar may be added to the whipped cream if desired. Repeat the process, using the rest of the ingredients, and decorate with cherries and almonds.

Remember that the whole beauty of an English trifle is the egg yolk custard – so please don't substitute with custard powder, it just isn't the same.

FLOATING ISLAND

6 egg whites
$\frac{3}{4}$ cup sugar
1 teaspoon vanilla

Method: Beat the egg whites until they form soft peaks, then add the sugar a tablespoon at a time, and continue beating till stiff and glossy. Add the vanilla.

Meanwhile make a caramel syrup, by melting $\frac{3}{4}$ cup sugar in a saucepan (as for creme caramel) and coat a pyrex dish with the caramel syrup. When the caramel has set, fill with the meringue and bake in a slow oven, 140°C (275°F), for 20–30 minutes, or until set. Cool, and unmould into a glass bowl. Gently pour in your custard sauce, until the meringue rises and floats.

Custard sauce:
4 egg yolks
1 dessertspoon maizena
1 cup cream (250 mℓ)
2 dessertspoons sugar
1 teaspoon vanilla
$1\frac{1}{2}$ cups milk

Method: Scald the cream and the milk in the top of a double boiler. Beat the egg yolks and sugar till light and creamy, then add maizena and vanilla and beat till blended. Slowly add the scalded mixture to the egg yolks, beating all the time as you do so. Return this mixture to the double boiler and cook till thickened, stirring all the time with a wooden spoon. Use as directed.

GATEAU ST HONORE

Using any good biscuit dough, roll out a round 22 cm (9-inch) in diameter and bake till golden brown. This forms the base of the Gateau.

Choux puffs:
125 g butter (4 oz)
1 cup water
1 heaped cup flour
4 eggs

Method: Bring butter and water to boil. Quickly stir in flour till mixture leaves the sides of the pan. Beat in eggs, one at a time, beating very well after each addition. Drop teaspoonful onto a greased and floured baking sheet and bake 180°C (350°F) oven 15–20 minutes, then turn oven off and leave another 10 minutes to dry out.

Custard filling: Beat 2 vanilla instant puddings with 2 cups cream and $1\frac{1}{2}$ cups milk till thick. Stir in 2 dessertspoons brandy.

You may use the custard filling for the Bee Sting cake if you wish to use a confectioners custard.

Syrup:
2 cups sugar
1 cup water
 good pinch cream of tartar

Method: Allow to boil on medium heat till light caramel colour. Remove from stove, place on wooden board and work quickly before it hardens.

To assemble: Split the puffs open with a sharp knife and insert 1 dessertspoon custard filling in each. If desired, 1 teaspoon of whipped cream can be added as well. Using the syrup to stick the puffs onto the base and to each other, build up into a pyramid shape. Now make another lot of syrup and using a spoon spin threads round and round in a circular motion until the Gateau looks like a beehive. The same syrup is used for making *friandises*. Just remember to wash your fruit the night before and never pull the stem out of grapes or the tops of strawberries as these serve to seal the fruit so that no juices escape and your friandises will remain crisp. Allow them to set on an oiled biscuit tray and serve in individual paper cups.

Suggested fruits for friandises:
Naartjie segments, with the pith removed
 and left to dry
Pitted prunes with a whole almond inserted
 in the middle
Brazil or peanuts stuck on a tooth pick with
 a glacé cherry
Grapes and strawberries when in season
Marzipan balls with a blanched almond
 pressed into the middle

GINGER MOUSSE

2 teaspoons gelatine
$\frac{1}{4}$ cup cold water
$\frac{1}{2}$ cup boiling water
4 eggs separated
$\frac{1}{3}$ cup castor sugar
$\frac{1}{2}$ cup chopped preserved ginger
$\frac{1}{2}$ cup ginger syrup
2 tablespoons ginger liqueur (optional)
250 mℓ ($\frac{1}{2}$ pint) whipped cream
 extra whipped cream for decoration

Method: Dissolve gelatine by mixing first with cold water then add boiling water and stir till completely dissolved, i.e. there must be no crystals.

Beat egg yolks and sugar till thick and creamy. Add gelatine, liqueur, ginger and syrup. Beat egg whites very stiffly and fold in. Allow to set partially in fridge then fold in whipped cream.

GRANITA DE CAFÉ

1 cup water
1 tablespoon sugar
12 artificial sweeteners
2 cups very strong coffee

Method: Combine water, sugar and sweetener in a pot and bring to boil. Boil 5 minutes and remove from heat. Stir in coffee and pour into ice-cube trays that have dividers removed. Freeze 3–4 hours, stirring every 30 minutes or do not stir and allow to freeze solid, then crush. Serve in frosted glasses with fresh slightly whipped cream.

GRANADILLA PUDDING

1 lemon jelly
1 cup fresh granadillas
1 tin condensed milk (500 g)
3 cups boiling water

Method: Dissolve jelly in boiling water. Allow to cool thoroughly. Stir in granadillas and condensed milk. Set in fridge overnight.

HALVA PUDDING

2 sachets orley whip or 500 mℓ (1 pint) cream
6 eggs, separated
$\frac{2}{3}$ cup sugar
250 g (8 oz) halva, preferably with nuts

Method: Beat egg yolks with sugar till light and fluffy. Whip orley whip or cream till stiff and fold into egg yolks. Beat egg whites stiffly and fold in. Lastly add flaked halva. Pour into mould which has been rinsed out with 1 tablespoon oil and half a cup water mixed together, allow to set in freezer for at least 18 hours. Unmould onto serving platter, decorate with chocolate sauce drizzled over, or flakes of halva.

LEMON CREAM

4 eggs
1 cup sugar
$\frac{1}{2}$ cup lemon juice
$\frac{1}{2}$ cup orange squash undiluted
500 mℓ ($\frac{1}{2}$ pint) cream
3 level teaspoons gelatine
1 cup boiling water

Method: Beat egg yolks and sugar. Add juices and gelatine, see special hint. Beat egg whites and fold in. Allow to set partially in refrigerator, then fold in the whipped cream.

Special hint: Always dissolve gelatine in **a** little cold water first, about 1 tablespoon, then stir in $\frac{1}{2}$ cup boiling water and stir till thoroughly dissolved. This additional water will not affect the texture of any recipe.

MINTED MERINGUE SANDWICH

6 egg whites
  pinch cream of tartar
$1\frac{1}{2}$ cups sugar
1 level dessertspoon sifted maizena
  few drops peppermint essence
  few drops green colouring – $\frac{3}{4}$–1 teaspoon

Method: Beat the egg whites stiffly with cream of tartar. Gradually beat in 1 cup sugar till very stiff and shiny then fold in the remaining $\frac{1}{2}$ cup sugar, maizena, essence and colouring. Pipe or spread into 2 rounds about 22–30 cm (9–12-inch) diameter, on see-thru or aluminium foil or triple thickness waxproof paper, placed on a baking sheet. Preheat oven to 200°C (400°F), turn down to 125°C (250°F) and bake for $1\frac{1}{2}$ hours. When cool, sandwich together with the following:

24 quartered white marshmallows, 2 tablespoons creme de menthe, 2 tablespoons creme de cacao, few drops green colouring.

Place these ingredients in a double boiler and cook until marshmallows are completely dissolved. Cool thoroughly, then fold this mixture into 250 mℓ ($\frac{1}{2}$ pint) whipped cream. Decorate by drizzling chocolate sauce or whipped cream over the top, and sprinkle with crushed peppermint crisp.

Special hint: Another lovely filling is to place 12 marshmallows, $\frac{1}{4}$ cup milk and 100 g (4 oz) bitter chocolate in a double boiler. When marshmallows have dissolved, allow mixture to cool and fold into 250 mℓ ($\frac{1}{2}$ pint) whipped cream.

MUD PIE

175 g butter (6 oz)
1 teaspoon vanilla
2 tablespoons cocoa
$\frac{3}{4}$ cup sugar
$1\frac{1}{4}$ cups flour
$\frac{1}{4}$ cup crushed cornflakes

Method: Cream butter and sugar, add vanilla, then blend in sifted flour and cocoa. Lastly stir in cornflakes. Press into a greased and floured 22 cm (9-inch) diameter pie dish, very thinly. Bake blind for 10–15 minutes in a 180°C (350°F) oven, then remove beans and bake a further 5–10 minutes. Allow to cool completely, then fill with $1\frac{1}{2}$ litres (3 pints) chocolate ice-cream, place in freezer whilst preparing fudge topping.

Fudge topping:
$\frac{1}{4}$ cup milk
50 g butter (2 oz)
1 tablespoon syrup
$1\frac{1}{2}$ cups sugar
$\frac{1}{2}$ teaspoon vanilla
200 g (8 oz) condensed milk
  pinch salt

Method: Rinse pot and place in it the milk, butter, sugar, syrup and salt. When butter has melted add the condensed milk. Bring to the boil and continue to boil and stir for another 15 minutes. Carefully add vanilla. Cool to luke warm then beat for a few minutes with an electric beater before pouring into a foil lined 22 cm (9-inch) diameter cake tin. Allow to set, then invert over ice-cream. Peel off foil. Decorate with whipped cream and chocolate curls.

NUT MERINGUE TORTE

Method: Beat 8 egg whites (1 cup) with a pinch of salt, in the mixmaster until they hold soft peaks. Add $1\frac{3}{4}$ cups sugar, 2 tablespoons at a time, beating after each addition, until stiff and shiny. Stir in 2 teaspoons vanilla and 1 teaspoon vinegar. Toast 2 packets, 200 g nibbed almonds till golden brown and when cool, fold into meringue mixture. Line the bottoms of 2 buttered 22 cm (9-inch) cake tins with wax paper and butter the paper.

Divide the meringue between the pans and bake in a 170°C (325°F) oven for 40 minutes. Remove the meringue from the pans, and place on a baking sheet in the oven for a further 15 minutes. Remove the paper and cool.

Beat 500 mℓ (2 cups) cream, till stiff and fold in 2 tablespoons apricot liqueur and 2 tablespoons smooth melted apricot jam. Fold in 1 tin drained, diced apricots (410 g). Place on meringue layer on a serving platter, top with the cream filling. Place the remaining layer on top and decorate with whipped cream rosettes, hazelnuts and drizzle over chocolate sauce.

PAVLOVA

A Pavlova differs from a meringue in that it should be crisp on the outside but has a thick marshmallow texture inside.

8 egg whites (1 cup)
2 cups sugar
1 teaspoon vinegar
1 level dessertspoon sifted maizena
2 teaspoons vanilla

Method: Beat whites with a pinch of salt till frothy. Gradually add sugar and vanilla and beat until stiff. Add vinegar and beat again for a few minutes. Lastly fold in sifted maizena. Pile onto an ovenware platter and shape building up the sides and hollowing out the centre. Preheat oven to 200°C (400°F), turn down to 125°C (250°F) and place Pavlova in oven. Bake for 20 minutes, then turn oven off and leave for another 20 minutes. Allow to cool and fill with whipped cream and strawberries or tinned cherries.

Hint: If you wish to make an ordinary meringue then preheat oven to 200°C (400°F). Turn down to 125°C (250°F) and bake for $1\frac{1}{2}$ hours undisturbed.

PRALINE SOUFFLÉ

Soufflé:
4 eggs
2 tablespoons honey
$\frac{1}{3}$ cup castor sugar
1 cup cream ($\frac{1}{2}$ pint)
1 dessertspoon gelatine
$\frac{1}{2}$ cup cold water

Praline:
$\frac{1}{2}$ cup chopped almonds
$\frac{1}{2}$ cup sugar

Method: First prepare the praline by placing the sugar and almonds in a saucepan and stir until the sugar has dissolved. Turn mixture onto an oiled tin and crush finely when cold.

Place egg yolks, sugar and honey in mixmaster and beat until thick. Whip cream stiffly and fold into mixture. Soak the gelatine in cold water and then gradually dissolve over heat. Add to mixture. Whisk egg whites stiffly and fold with $\frac{1}{2}$ the praline into the soufflé.

Pour into a soufflé dish and leave to set. Decorate with the remaining praline.

3 TIERED BAVARIAN CREAM

4 eggs
4 tablespoons sugar
2 dessertspoons gelatine
2 teaspoons vanilla
2 cups milk
2 dessertspoons cocoa
2 cups cream (1 pint)

Method: Beat egg yolks with sugar till light and fluffy. Add boiling milk, place in double boiler till thickens. Remove from stove and add gelatine, which has been dissolved in 2 dessertspoons cold water. Add vanilla and allow to cool. Fold in stiffly beaten egg whites and whipped cream. Divide mixture into three, add cocoa to one portion, cochineal to the other and green colouring to the last or leave

white if desired. Pour into a mould, which has been rinsed out with oil and water. N.B. this is the first mixture. Allow to set then top with the second mixture. Allow to set again, and proceed in the same manner with remaining mixture.

Allow to set in fridge overnight. Unmould onto platter and decorate with whipped cream and cherries or strawberries when in season.

TURKISH ORANGES

8 large oranges
2 cups sugar
2 cloves
1½ cups water
3 tablespoons brandy
½ cup grand marnier
½ cup curacao

Method: Peel oranges, removing all the pith. Take ½ the peel and remove all the pith then slice into paper thin slivers and place in a saucepan of cold water. Bring to boil and simmer 3–4 minutes. Drain. Slice oranges and hold together with toothpicks. Place in serving dish and arrange peel on top.

Prepare caramel: Mix sugar and water in a saucepan, add cloves and cook till a light caramel colour. Remove from heat and stir in 3 tablespoons boiling water. Cook till caramel has dissolved, stirring constantly. Remove from heat, add brandy and liqueur and spoon over oranges. Chill 4–6 hours, turning oranges from time to time. Serve with brandy snaps and fresh running cream.

ZABAGLIONE

8 egg yolks
8 dessertspoons marsala
8 dessertspoons sugar
½ teaspoon lemon rind (optional)

Method: Beat egg yolks and sugar till light and creamy. Add marsala and lemon rind and beat again. Place in the top of a double boiler and stir constantly with a wooden spoon till thick.

Remove from heat and beat again till smooth and shiny.

Pour into individual dessert bowls. Garnish with whipped cream, grated chocolate and serve with wafers.

9. CAKES

Baking tips:
Always use well rounded measurements of flour and level sugar measurements. Too much sugar is the main cause of cakes falling.

Even though the metric measurements are not exactly the same as imperial, I still regard $\frac{1}{2}$ lb of butter for example, as 250 g and a $\frac{1}{4}$ as 125 g.

Always grease cake tins very generously with butter and never margarine, as this causes cakes to stick.

If you are using a cooking non-stick spray, use it very generously. When working with yeast, *never use hot* liquids. They must always be lukewarm or blood heat. Yeast doughs must be kept out of a draught. If you observe these two rules, you need never be afraid to work with yeast as it is not at all finicky.

8 egg whites = 1 cup

Egg whites must always be at room temperature as they produce more volume. Egg whites freeze very successfully but thaw to room temperature before using.

To bake blind: Roll out your dough and place in greased pyrex dish, then place a piece of greaseproof paper over your dough and fill the shell with dried butter beans. This keeps the sides from collapsing.

APPLE CAKE

1 carton margarine 250 g (8 oz)
1 cup milk
1$\frac{1}{2}$ cups sugar
3 cups flour
4 eggs
3 teaspoons baking powder
  pinch salt
1 teaspoon vanilla
2 x 285 g (1 lb) tins pie apples
  cinnamon and sugar
1 tablespoon butter

Method: Cream margarine and sugar. Add eggs, sifted dry ingredients, milk and vanilla and beat till smooth. Pour the mixture into a large rectangular greased pyrex dish. Spoon apples on top. Sprinkle with cinnamon and sugar. About two tablespoons. Dot with butter and bake 180°C (350°F) oven 45 minutes. Serve warm with whipped cream.

Special hint: This is a large cake so be sure that the dish is adequate otherwise use 2 x 22 cm (9-inch) diameter pyrex dishes. This cake freezes very well.

AMBROSIA CAKE

Method: Sift together and set aside, 2$\frac{1}{2}$ cups flour, $\frac{1}{2}$ teaspoon salt, 3$\frac{1}{2}$ teaspoons baking powder.

Cream 175 g (6 oz) butter with 1$\frac{1}{2}$ teaspoons grated orange rind and 1$\frac{1}{4}$ cups castor sugar. Add 2 egg yolks, one at a time. Combine $\frac{3}{4}$ cup water with $\frac{1}{2}$ cup orange juice and 2 tablespoons lemon juice. Add the dry ingredients alternately with the liquid. Beat only until smooth. Then blend in $\frac{1}{2}$ cup coconut. Carefully fold in 4 stiffly beaten egg whites. Pour batter into 2 greased and floured 22 cm (9-inch) layer cake pans. Bake at 190°C (375°F) for 30 minutes or until tester comes out dry. Alternatively, cake may be baked in 1 tin at 190°C (375°F) for 45 minutes.

Decorate with orange butter icing and sprinkle thickly with shredded coconut.

ANGEL CAKE

1$\frac{1}{2}$ cups egg whites (12)
1$\frac{1}{2}$ cups flour
$\frac{1}{2}$ cup oil
2$\frac{1}{2}$ teaspoons baking powder
$\frac{1}{2}$ teaspoon cream of tartar

1 cup castor sugar
⅔ cup boiling water
1 teaspoon almond essence
 pinch salt

Method: Sift together flour, half the sugar, baking powder and salt. Make a well in the centre and add ½ cup unbeaten egg whites, water, oil and almond essence. Stir till blended, then allow to beat in mixmaster 8–10 minutes. Meanwhile beat the remaining egg whites in a large bowl till frothy. Add cream of tartar and beat till stiff, then gradually beat in remaining sugar. Fold the first mixture into the meringue mixture very lightly. Pour into ungreased chiffon cake tin and bake in 180°C (350°F) oven, middle shelf for 50 minutes. Invert over bottle and allow to cool completely before removing from tin. Slice through the middle and fill with whipped cream and strawberries and drizzle chocolate sauce over.

Special hint: Use a 410g (1 lb) tin of pitted cherries or youngberries when strawberries are out of season. When using the tinned fruit, strain juice and thicken with 2 tablespoons maizena mixed with a little cold water, then fold in fruit.

BEE STING CAKE

2 cups flour (not too full)
½ cup sugar
2 eggs
125 g (4 oz) butter
½ cup milk
1 teaspoon vanilla
3 teaspoons baking powder
 pinch salt

Topping:
60 g (2 oz) butter
¼ cup sugar
1 packet flaked almonds (100 g)
1 tablespoon milk

Method: Cream butter and sugar. Add vanilla, add eggs one at a time, beating well after each addition. Sift dry ingredients including baking powder, and add to mixture alternately with milk. Spread batter into a greased and floured 22 cm (9-inch) or 25 cm (10-inch) springform tin.

Prepare the topping by combining all the ingredients in a saucepan and heat till sugar has dissolved. Pour over cake, spread evenly with a knife and bake in 180°C (350°F) oven for 35 minutes. When cake is cool, split in half and fill with the following custard.

Custard:
2 egg yolks
¼ cup sugar
1 cup cream (½ pint)
3 tablespoons maizena
1 cup milk
1 teaspoon vanilla
25 g butter (1 oz)

Method: Scald milk and cream. Beat egg yolks with sugar till light and creamy. Add vanilla and maizena, then slowly add scalded milk and cream. Pour into double boiler and stir with a wooden spoon till thick. Stir in butter.

BLACK FOREST CAKE

For meringue:
6 egg whites (¾ cup)
1¼ cups ground almonds (125 g)
⅞ cup sugar
1½ tablespoons flour
1½ tablespoons maizena
 Pinch cream of tartar

Method: Beat the egg whites very stiffly, with cream of tartar, then gradually add the sugar and continue beating till very stiff. Sift the flour and maizena and fold into the meringue with the ground almonds. Divide into 3 portions and spread in greased, lined and greased again 22 cm (9-inch) diameter tins. Bake in a slow oven, 150°C (300°F), for about 45 minutes. The layers will harden on cooling.

For chocolate cake:
¾ cup flour
2 teaspoons baking powder
50 g (2 oz) butter or 2 tablespoons oil
¾ cup castor sugar
½ cup cocoa
½ cup milk
3 eggs
½ teaspoon vanilla

Method: Sift together the flour, cocoa and baking powder. Beat the eggs and sugar till thick and creamy. Place the butter and milk in a saucepan and bring gently to the boil, then slowly add to the egg mixture. Add the flour mixture and lastly fold in the vanilla. Pour into a greased and floured 22 cm (9-inch) diameter tin and bake 190°C (375°F) for 15–20 minutes. Cool and split in half.

To assemble: Whip 750 mℓ (1½ pints) cream with ½ cup icing sugar. Add 1 teaspoon vanilla. 2–3 tablespoons Kirsch and ¾ of a cup ground almonds. Melt a large slab of bitter chocolate in the top of a double boiler and spread a thin layer on one of the meringues. Pour the balance onto a foil lined 22 cm (9-inch) diameter tin, spread evenly and place in fridge to set.

Using the chocolate coated meringue as a base, alternate the layers of meringue with the chocolate cake using the cream and a bottle of cherry pie filling in between. Break the chocolate slab into pieces and place on top of the cake. Sprinkle with a little cocoa if desired.

Special hint: If you wish to make the black forest with the almond meringue layers only, then omit the chocolate cake altogether but use:
8 egg whites
1¼ cups sugar
1¾ cups ground almonds
2 tablespoons flour
2 tablespoons maizena

Proceed in exactly the same way, making 4 rounds instead of 3.

AUNTIE ROSIE'S BUTTER CAKE

175 g butter (6 oz) (can use half butter and half margarine)
1 cup sugar
1¾ cups flour
¼ cup maizena
2 full teaspoons baking powder
¾ cup milk mixed with ½ teaspoon vanilla
3 eggs

Method: Cream butter and sugar. Add eggs, one at a time. Add a little from the measured flour to prevent the mixture from curdling. Add sifted flour and maizena alternately with milk. Lastly fold in baking powder. Bake in greased and floured springform tin in 200°C (400°F) oven for 30 minutes. Dust with icing sugar when cool.

BUTTER CHOCOLATE CAKE

175 g (6 oz) butter
4 eggs
1½ cups milk
1¼ cups sugar
1 teaspoon vanilla
4 teaspoons baking powder
2 cups and 2 tablespoons flour
2 tablespoons cocoa

Method: Cream butter and sugar. Sift dry ingredients, except baking powder. Add eggs, milk, vanilla and sifted dry ingredients to creamed butter and beat in mixmaster for 7–10 minutes. Lastly fold in baking powder. Divide evenly into two greased and floured tins – 22 cm (9-inch) in diameter round or square – and bake in 180°C (350°F) for 30 minutes. Turn out immediately, cool and ice.

Icing: Cream 125 g (4 oz) butter with 1 packet (500 g/1 lb) icing sugar, 2 tablespoons cocoa, few drops vanilla and enough boiling water to make a nice spreading consistency. An orange icing is also nice with this cake. In which case, you would use orange rind and orange juice instead of the water.

CARNIVAL CAKE WITH PENUCHE ICING

2¼ cups sifted flour
1¼ cups castor sugar
2½ teaspoons baking powder
1 teaspoon orange extract
3 eggs
1 teaspoon salt
175 g (6 oz) butter
½ cup milk
½ teaspoon almond extract
¼ cup milk

Method: Sift together flour, sugar, baking powder and salt. Drop butter in. (Butter must be soft but not melted.) Pour in ½ cup milk, orange and almond extract and 1 egg and beat with mixer for a few minutes. Now add the ¼ cup milk and the remaining 2 eggs and beat 2 minutes longer. Pour into 2 × 22 cm (9-inch) greased and floured sandwich tins and bake 180°C (350°F) oven 25 minutes.

Penuche icing:
1½ cups brown sugar
125 g (¼ lb) butter
1½ cups castor sugar
2 tablespoons syrup
¾ cup milk
 pinch salt
1 teaspoon orange extract
1 cup chopped walnuts

Method: Combine sugar, syrup, milk, butter and salt in a saucepan. Bring slowly to full rolling boil, stirring constantly. Boil briskly for 2 minutes. Cool till lukewarm. Add orange extract and beat in mixmaster till thick enough to spread. Fold in nuts. Filling will be sufficient for the whole cake.

CARROT ALMOND TORTE

2 cups thinly sliced carrots
1 cup water
½ teaspoon salt
½ teaspoon sugar
175 g ground almonds (1¾ packet)
¾ cup flour
1 teaspoon baking powder
2 tablespoons orange liqueur, divided
6 eggs separated
1 teaspoon finely grated orange rind
500 mℓ cream (1 pint)
1 slab bitter chocolate 100 g (4 oz) sliced toasted almonds for garnish

Method: Boil carrots, water, sugar and salt till carrots are very tender about 30 minutes.

Mix ground almonds with flour, baking powder and a pinch salt, set aside. Drain carrots well and sieve or mash finely and stir in 1 tablespoon orange liqueur, set aside.

Beat yolks till very light, gradually adding 1¼ cups sugar, till pale and fluffy. Blend in carrots, orange rind and dry ingredients.

Beat whites stiffly and fold in lightly. Pour into two greased and floured 22 cm (9-inch) diameter sandwich tins or a springform tin. Bake in a 180°C (350°F) oven for 25–30 minutes.

Remove from oven and allow to cool then split each layer in half.

Melt the chocolate and when cool, fold into whipped cream with the orange liqueur. Sandwich the cake together with the chocolate cream and decorate with piped rosettes topped with a few toasted almonds.

CARROT CAKE

2½ cups flour
1¼ cups oil
1¼ cups sugar
3 cups finely grated carrots
2 teaspoons cinnamon
4 eggs
1 teaspoon bicarb
2 teaspoons baking powder
½ cup chopped pecan nuts
¾ teaspoon salt

Method: Beat eggs and sugar very well. Add oil and beat again, just till blended. Add sifted dry ingredients. Fold in carrots and nuts. Bake in two greased and floured 22 cm (9-inch) square or round tins for 40 minutes in a 180°C (350°F) oven. When cool, sandwich together and ice with the following:

Icing:
125 g (4 oz) butter
125 g cream cheese
500 g icing sugar (1 packet)
1 teaspoon vanilla

Method: Cream the butter and icing sugar. It must be a very stiff mixture. *Stir in by hand,* the cream cheese and vanilla. Do not stir too vigorously or the mixture will become very runny.

Decorate cake with pecan nuts and red and green cherries.

AUNT SYLVIE'S CHEESE CAKE

Pastry as given below for Cheese Cake

Filling:
750 g (1½ lb) cream cheese
250 mℓ (½ pint) cream
3 eggs and 1 white
¾ cup sugar
1 full dessertspoon flour
1 level dessertspoon custard powder
1 tablespoon brandy
1 tablespoon lemon juice

Method: Separate eggs. Mix all ingredients together by hand till smooth, excepting egg whites. Beat whites till stiff and lastly fold into the mixture. Pour into pastry shell and bake 180°C (350°F) oven for 20–25 minutes then switch oven off completely and leave for another 40–45 minutes.

CHEESE CAKE

2 cups flour
1 egg
125 g (¼ lb) butter
1 teaspoon baking powder
  pinch salt
50 g (2 oz) margarine
2 tablespoons sugar

Method: Sift dry ingredients, rub in butter and margarine and make into a dough with the slightly beaten egg. If necessary add a little cold water to the dough. Roll out and line greased rectangular pyrex dish. Mix together 1 dessertspoon flour and 1 dessertspoon sugar and sprinkle this over the unbaked pastry.

Filling:
1 kilo (2 lb) cream cheese
1½ cups sugar
4 eggs
4 tablepoons maizena, level
250 mℓ (½ pint) cream

Method: Place all ingredients for the filling in a bowl and blend by hand just until the mixture is smooth and there are no lumps. If you do use the mixmaster, blend only until the ingredients are well blended but do not allow your mixture to become watery. Your mixture must remain thick. You may add a little more cream or a bit of milk if you think it necessary.

Pour cheese into pastry shell and bake in 190°C (375°F) oven for 20 minutes, then *switch your oven off completely* and leave cake to set for 45–60 minutes. Remove from oven and cool.

Fruit topping for cheese cake:
Boil the juice of 1 x 410 g tin pineapple chunks. Thicken with 1 dessertspoon maizena mixed to a paste with cold water and 1 dessertspoon red jelly and add a few drops of red colouring.

Place pineapple and fresh strawberries in rows on top of cake, then spoon over the above sauce. You can, of course use any tinned fruit of your choice.

CHEESE CAKE PUFF

3 tablespoons sultanas
375 g cream cheese (¾ lb)
1 tablespoon flour
3 tablespoons thick cream
½ teaspoon vanilla
1 tablespoon sugar mixed with 1 teaspoon cinnamon
¼ cup flaked almonds
1½ tablespoons brandy
½ cup sugar or more to taste
1 egg beaten
1 teaspoon grated lemon rind
1 apple peeled cored and thinly sliced
1 egg yolk mixed with 1 teaspoon cream

Choux pastry:
125 g butter (4 oz)
1 heaped cup flour
1 cup water
4 eggs

Method: Combine butter and water in a saucepan over medium heat. Heat until butter is melted and mixture is boiling. Add flour all at once and stir vigorously until dough comes away from sides of pan and forms a ball. Remove from heat. Transfer to mixmaster and add eggs one at a time, beating well after each addition. Preheat oven to 190°C (375°F). Lightly grease and flour a baking sheet. Trace a 18 cm (7-inch) circle in the flour, using a plate or saucepan lid. Within the circle, spread a thin layer of choux pastry. Put the remaining pastry in a pastry bag and pipe a border of small mounds of paste around the edge of the circle.

Soak sultanas in brandy. Mix together cheese, sugar and flour. Stir in beaten egg, cream, lemon rind and vanilla. Add sultanas and brandy. Spoon this filling into the centre of the shell. Arrange apple slices on top. Sprinkle with sugar cinnamon mixture. Brush border with egg yolk mixture and sprinkle with almonds. Bake 180°C (350°F) oven for 50–60 minutes or till golden brown.

CHOCOLATE BLITZ TORTE

4 eggs
½ cup sugar
6 tablespoons milk
2 tablespoons cocoa

125 g (4 oz) butter
1 cup flour
2 teaspoons baking powder

Method: Cream butter and sugar well. Add yolks gradually. Beat constantly. Add sifted flour with salt and baking powder and cocoa. Add milk. Divide and spread in two 22 cm (9-inch) greased and floured tins. Put following meringue on top. Beat the four egg whites stiffly. Add $1\frac{1}{4}$ cups sugar gradually and then fold in 1 teaspoon baking powder. Spread over the chocolate mixture in both tins. Sprinkle with chopped nuts. Bake 180°C (350°F) oven for about 25–30 minutes. Cool slightly before removing from tins.

Sandwich together with the following:
Beat 1 cup cream with 1 tablespoon sugar. Add by hand, 1 tablespoon cocoa, 1 tablespoon drinking chocolate and $\frac{1}{4}$ teaspoon coffee. Alternatively use plain whipped cream and mix in chopped cherries, bits of bitter chocolate, marshmallows and nuts. You may also use whipped cream and cherry pie filling.

Special hint: A nice variation is to use the Grasshopper filling for this as well. (See Grasshopper cake)

CHOCOLATE CHEESE CAKE WITH SOUR CREAM TOPPING

1 packet tennis biscuits or chocolate marie biscuits
750 g ($1\frac{1}{2}$ lb) cream cheese
125 g melted butter (4 oz)
2 tablespoons maizena
3 eggs
$\frac{3}{4}$ cup sugar
1 tablespoon milk
1 slab milk chocolate (100 g)
1 level teaspoon instant coffee powder
1 heaped teaspoon cinnamon
250 ml whipped cream ($\frac{1}{2}$ pint)

Method: Crush biscuits and add melted butter. Press onto sides and bottom of 22 cm (9-inch) springform tin. Place chocolate, coffee and milk in top of double boiler and stir until smooth. Mix together by hand the cheese, sugar, eggs, maizena and cinnamon. Add cooled chocolate mixture and lastly fold in the cream. Pour into biscuit base and bake at 190°C (375°F) for 20–25 minutes.

Remove from oven and cool for 15 minutes. Increase oven temperature to 225°C (450°F).

Mix together – 1 cup sour cream, 1 tablespoon sugar, 1 teaspoon vanilla essence. Stir until sugar has dissolved. Spoon over cheese cake and bake at 225°C (450°F) for 3–5 minutes. Cool at room temperature and sprinkle with cinnamon.

CHOCOLATE CHESTNUT PYRAMID CAKE

6 eggs separated
$\frac{3}{4}$ cup sugar
2 tablespoons cocoa
2 tablespoons maizena

Method: Beat yolks with sugar till light and creamy. Add sifted cocoa and maizena. Lastly fold in stiffly beaten egg whites. Bake in two greased and floured small swiss roll tins, 35 cm x 25 cm (14 x 10 inches), 220°C (425°F) oven for 10 minutes. Turn out onto cloth and cut lengthwise into three even strips.

Filling: Cream 1 tin sweetened chestnut purée in mixmaster with 2 tablespoons brandy, till light and fluffy. Beat 500 ml (1 pint) cream till thick and fold into the chestnut mixture.

Alternative filling: Beat 500 ml (1 pint) cream with $\frac{1}{2}$ cup icing sugar, then fold in 2 tablespoons cocoa, 2 tablespoons drinking chocolate, 1 teaspoon vanilla and also 1 teaspoon instant coffee powder.

To assemble: Place three strips of cake on foil, side by side, cover with some of the filling, place the remaining strips of cake on top. Spread with more filling, then place a row of marashino or glace cherries along the centre. Place your hands underneath the foil and lift the two sides then press together to form a pyramid. Allow to set in fridge. Pour over the following glaze.

Chocolate glaze: Melt 3 tablespoons butter with 2 dessertspoons cocoa in a saucepan and stir till well blended. Blend 2 cups icing sugar with 1 unbeaten egg white, then add to saucepan with butter cocoa mixture and stir over low heat just till blended. Pour over cake immediately.

CHOCOLATE CHIFFON CAKE

5 eggs
1 cup flour
1 cup sugar
½ cup oil
  cinnamon
2 tablespoons cocoa
½ cup boiling water
2½ teaspoons baking powder
1 teaspoon vanilla
  pinch salt

Method: Separate whites from yolks. Beat whites stiffly. Add ½ teaspoon baking powder. Sift flour, salt and cinnamon, cocoa, sugar and baking powder (2 teaspoons) into mixmaster bowl. Make a well and add egg yolks, oil, vanilla and boiling water. Beat 7–10 minutes. Fold this mixture into the stiffly beaten whites. Pour into ungreased chiffon cake tin and bake 180°C (350°F) oven for approximately 40 minutes. Invert over a bottle to cool. Ice with chocolate icing or with a tin of caramelised condensed milk, by boiling closed for 3 hours.

PRALINE

Praline is a very useful decoration for cakes and is made as follows:

Melt 1 cup sugar over gentle heat with a few tablespoons of chopped nuts. Pour into an oiled swiss roll tin. Allow to set, then crush with a rolling pin and store in an airtight container.

LARGE CHOCOLATE CHIFFON CAKE

1½ cups flour
¾ cup oil
3 tablespoons cocoa
  pinch salt
8 egg whites, (1 cup)
1½ cups castor sugar
1 cup boiling water
1 teaspoon vanilla
  dash cinnamon
7 egg yolks
3½ teaspoons baking powder

Method: Separate whites and yolks. Place whites in a large bowl as your whole mixture will end up in this bowl. Into your mixmaster bowl sift flour, sugar, cocoa, baking powder (2½ teaspoons), cinnamon and salt. Make a well in centre add egg yolks, oil and boiling water. Beat 7–10 minutes.

Meanwhile beat whites stiffly with 1 teaspoon baking powder. Fold egg yolk mixture into whites. Pour into ungreased chiffon cake tin and bake 180°C (350°F) oven – 60 minutes.

Special hint: Can also use this cake with the Grasshopper filling (see Grasshopper Cake) for a special occasion.

CHOCOLATE FILLED BRAZIL NUTLOG

3 eggs separated
½ cup sugar
1 cup chopped toasted Brazil nuts
¼ teaspoon salt
½ teaspoon cream of tartar
¼ cup flour, sifted

Method: Beat yolks till light and fluffy. Add sugar gradually and continue to beat till all has been added. Blend in Brazil nuts. Add salt to egg whites, beat till fluffy. Add cream of tartar and beat till stiff. Fold into egg-Brazil mixture. Lastly fold in flour. Grease and then line a *small* swiss roll tin 35 cm x 25 cm (14 x 10 inches) with wax-paper extending 2 cm (1 inch) beyond pan. Pour in mixture and bake 190°C (375°F) for 10 minutes. Turn out onto damp cloth. Sprinkle cloth with castor sugar. Spread with filling and roll up.

Filling for Brazil nutlog:
2 squares bitter chocolate (±25 g)
¾ cup milk
4 tablespoons maizena
½ cup sugar
1 tablespoon butter
¼ teaspoon vanilla
½ cup chopped Brazil nuts

Method: Place chocolate and milk in double boiler and heat till chocolate has melted. Beat till well blended. Add small amount of chocolate mixture to maizena which has been sifted with the sugar. Return all to double boiler, stir till smooth and thick. Add butter, vanilla and nuts.

Chocolate glaze: Make a chocolate glaze by melting 50 g (2 oz) butter with 2 tablespoons cocoa. Stir till smooth. In a separate bowl, blend 1 unbeaten egg white with 1½ cups icing sugar. Blend the chocolate and icing sugar. Mix together till smooth and pour over cake. Decorate with chopped Brazil nuts, cherries and angelica.

COCA COLA CAKE

2 cups flour, sifted
250 g butter (½ lb)
3 tablespoons cocoa
2 beaten eggs
1 teaspoon vanilla
1½ cups sugar
1 cup Coca Cola
½ cup buttermilk
1 teaspoon bicarb

Method: Grease and flour a tube tin. Heat oven to 180°C (350°F). Combine flour and sugar in mixmaster bowl. Heat butter, cocoa and Coca Cola to boiling. Pour over flour and sugar mixture and beat for 2 minutes.

In a small bowl mix eggs, buttermilk, bicarb, vanilla. Add to first mixture and beat again, just a little. Batter will be thin. Bake for 55–60 minutes and allow to cool in the tin for 10 minutes before inverting onto cooling tray.

When cool, ice with the following:
125 g butter (4 oz)
3 tablespoons Coca Cola
1½ tablespoons cocoa
½–¾ box icing sugar (250–375 g)
½ cup chopped pecans

Method: Combine butter, cocoa and Coca Cola then heat to boiling. Stir in icing sugar and nuts. Cool a little before pouring over cake. This mixture will thicken as it cools.

COCONUT CHIFFON CAKE

1 cup egg whites
1⅓ cups sugar

2½ teaspoons baking powder
½ cup oil
¾ cup coconut extract, see note
1 cup toasted coconut
2 cups sifted flour
1 teaspoon salt
6 egg yolks
1 teaspoon vanilla
½ teaspoon cream of tartar

Method: Preheat oven to 180°C (350°F). Sift flour with sugar, baking powder and salt into mixmaster. Make a well in centre.

Add, in order, oil, egg yolks, coconut extract and vanilla. Mix with spoon till smooth, then beat for 5–7 minutes.

Meanwhile beat egg whites with cream of tartar until very stiff. Using a spatula and under-and-over motion, gently fold egg yolk mixture and toasted coconut into egg whites, just to blend.

Pour into ungreased chiffon cake tin and bake 50 minutes.

Invert cake over neck of bottle and allow to cool completely – 1½ hours approximately. Carefully loosen cake from pan. You may serve plain or lightly sprinkled with icing sugar or ice with a butter icing.

For a special occasion: you may fill this cake with the following:
Boil together in double boiler 1 cup orange juice with 16–20 coconut marshmallows. Allow to cool and then fold in 250 mℓ (½ pint) whipped cream.
Note – Pour 1 cup boiling water over 1 cup dessicated coconut and allow to infuse for 30 minutes, then place in strainer and press out coconut milk with spoon. If not sufficient to make up amount needed, add additional water.

CUSTARD SLICE

125 g butter (4 oz)
2–2½ cups flour
pinch salt
2 eggs
½ cup sugar
1 level teaspoon baking powder
½ cup thick cream

Method: Cream butter and sugar. Add eggs and cream and lastly sifted dry ingredients.

Roll out on lightly floured board and cut into 4 even rectangles 30 x 10 cm (12 x 4 inches) approximately. Place on greased and floured baking sheet and bake in 180°C (350°F) oven till golden brown.

Custard filling:
2 eggs
3 dessertspoons maizena
½ cup sugar
1½ cups milk
125 g butter (4 oz)
1 teaspoon vanilla

Method: Beat eggs and sugar till thick and creamy. Add maizena and beat till well blended. Scald milk and add slowly to beaten egg yolks beating all the time as you do so. Place in double boiler and cook stirring constantly, till thickened. When cooled add creamed butter little by little. Add vanilla. Allow to set in refrigerator before using.

Put the layers together with custard and pour a water icing over the top. Decorate with nuts and cherries.

Water icing: Mix together 2 cups icing sugar approximately 250 g with a little boiling water until of a nice spreading consistency.

DANISH CAKE

1¼ cups milk
½ cup sugar
2 eggs

4½ cups flour
1 teaspoon salt
1½ cakes yeast (30 g)
125 g butter (4 oz)

Method: Place milk and butter, sugar and salt in a saucepan and heat till butter and sugar have dissolved. Allow to cool to lukewarm. Liquify the yeast by mixing together with 2 teaspoons sugar and then add 1 tablespoon lukewarm water and allow to stand 10 minutes. Beat eggs in a separate bowl and set aside. Sift flour, make a well in the centre. Add butter/milk mixture, eggs and yeast and use another tablespoon lukewarm water to rinse out the yeast bowl. Mix by hand till blended, then knead in mixmaster till smooth.

Place in a large bowl or airtight container and leave to rise till double in bulk or overnight.

Using only a ¼ of the dough, line a 22 cm (9-inch) diameter cake tin, which has been lightly oiled, with a thin layer of dough. Cover with almond paste. Take another ¼ of the dough. Roll out into a rectangular shape. Spread with melted butter, sprinkle with cinnamon and sugar and washed dried fruit. Roll up as for a swiss roll, cut into slices, about 2 cm (1 inch) thick and place, cut side up, all round the base, about 7-8 pieces, then three slices in the middle. Allow to rise again for ¾-1 hour. Bake for 1 hour in a 180°C (350°F) oven, middle shelf. Cool and brush with apricot glaze made by boiling 1 cup smooth apricot jam with 2-3 tablespoons water. Sprinkle round the edges of the cake with shredded or flaked almonds.

Almond paste:
⅓-½ cup sugar
1 egg
½ teaspoon almond essence
2-3 tablespoons milk
100 g ground almonds (1 packet)
3 tablespoons marie biscuit crumbs

Mix together till smooth.

DANISH JAM PUFF CAKE

¾ cake yeast (15 g)
2 tablespoons lukewarm water
⅔ cup milk
175 g butter (6 oz)
3½ cups flour
½ cup sugar
 pinch salt
½ teaspoon finely grated lemon rind
1 egg and 2 yolks, lightly beaten together
 strawberry jam

Method: In a small bowl, liquify the yeast with 1 teaspoon sugar, then add the warm water. Set the bowl aside in a warm draught free place for 20 minutes or till the mixture is frothy.

Place the milk in a saucepan with the butter and sugar and stir till melted. Cool to lukewarm.

Sift the flour and salt, make a well in the centre and add the yeast, lemon rind, milk and butter mixture and the eggs. Stir the ingredients until all the flour has been incorporated and then knead in mixmaster or by hand, adding a little more warm water if necessary. Place the dough in an oiled bowl, sprinkle lightly with flour, and leave covered in a warm draught free place to rise till doubled in bulk. Punch the dough down and knead again for a few minutes then roll out to a rectangle about 1 cm (¼ inch) thick. Trim the sides and cut into 16 squares. Place a dessertspoon of jam on each square, gather up the sides of each square over the jam and press together to form a bundle.

Melt 50 g (2 oz) butter in a saucepan, and

dip each bundle in the melted butter, then place seam side down in a 22 cm (9-inch) springform pan, arranging bundles in a circular pattern. Dribble any remaining butter over the bundles. Cover the tin with a cloth and stand in a warm place for ½ hour. Sprinkle with 2 tablespoons sugar. Bake in a 180°C (350°F) oven for 30 minutes or till golden brown.

DEEP SOUTH PRUNE CAKE

2 cups flour
1¼ cups sugar
1 teaspoon bicarb
½ teaspoon salt
1 teaspoon cinnamon
1 teaspoon mixed spice
1 teaspoon nutmeg
3 eggs
1 cup oil
1 cup buttermilk
1 teaspoon vanilla
1 cup chopped pecans
1 cup finely chopped pitted prunes (Use the canned breakfast prunes)

Method: Preheat oven to 180°C (350°F). Sift dry ingredients together. Beat eggs and sugar till light and creamy. Add oil and beat again. Add sifted dry ingredients and buttermilk. Beat till smooth. Lastly stir in nuts and prunes. Bake in a greased rectangular pyrex dish or use a white fluted 25 cm (10-inch) diameter ovenware dish, for 45 minutes.

Prepare the topping given below and spoon over the cake, allowing the syrup to run down the sides of the dish by pushing cake away with a knife whilst spooning the syrup over.

Topping:
¼ teaspoon bicarb
¼ cup buttermilk
½ cup sugar
1 teaspoon syrup
50 g butter (2 oz)
½ teaspoon vanilla

Method: Dissolve bicarb in buttermilk, place all ingredients in a large saucepan and boil on low for 3 minutes. Pour over cake as directed above.

DOBOSCH TORTE

125 g butter (4 oz)
2 cups flour
3 eggs, separated
3 teaspoons baking powder
1 cup castor sugar
1 teaspoon vanilla
1 cup milk and water mixed

Method: Cream butter and sugar till light and fluffy. Add egg yolks. Sift flour and add alternately with milk and water. Stir in vanilla, fold in baking powder and lastly stiffly beaten egg whites. Grease and flour 6 x 22 cm (9 inches) diameter tins and divide mixture evenly between these tins. Bake in 190°C (375°F) oven for 10 minutes. Cool and sandwich together with the chocolate filling below. Make a caramel topping by melting ½ cup castor sugar. When golden, pour over top layer of cake, spread with a knife dipped in hot water and mark into wedges then decorate each wedge with a piped rosette, using the mocha cream for the latter.

Chocolate filling:
2 egg yolks
1 tablespoon brandy
½ cup castor
125 g (4 oz) bitter chocolate
250 g butter (½ lb)
½ cup milk
1 dessertspoon rum

Method: Dissolve ¼ cup castor sugar in milk on the stove. Beat egg yolks very well. Add the balance of the castor sugar and beat again. Pour milk mixture onto egg yolks beating continuously till cooled. Beat in the creamed butter a little at a time. Melt chocolate with brandy and rum, stir till smooth, allow to cool add to mixture then set in fridge before using.

FESTIVE FRUIT CAKE

250 g butter (½ lb)
1 cup castor sugar
7½ cups fruit
½ teaspoon ginger
1 teaspoon cinnamon
¼ cup syrup
6 eggs
3 cups flour
2 teaspoons baking powder
1 teaspoon mixed spice
⅓ cup brandy

Method: Wash fruit off the day before and allow to dry thoroughly. Sift dry ingredients, except sugar and mix very well with the fruit. Cream butter and sugar well. Add the eggs, one at a time, beating well after each addition. Add syrup and lastly stir in fruit and flour mixture, alternately with brandy. Pour into double lined and greased 25 cm (10-inch) diameter tin 8 cm (3½ inches) deep, or a large square tin and bake 180°C (350°F) for ¾ hour, then turn oven down to 125°C (250°F) and allow to bake for a further 2 hours, or longer if necessary. Test with a skewer. Allow the cake to cool overnight before covering with almond paste.

For the almond paste:
250 g ground almonds (½ lb)
250 g castor sugar (½ lb)
250 g icing sugar (½ lb)
1 whole egg
2 egg yolks
1 teaspoon almond essence

Method: Mix the castor sugar, icing sugar and ground almonds together. Make a well in the centre and place the egg, egg yolks and almond essence in. Start beating the eggs with a spoon drawing in the mixture gradually. When it becomes stiffer, mould and knead with your hands, to a smooth putty like paste. To coat the cake, roll out half the paste into a long strip that will fit round the sides of the cake. Brush with egg white or diluted apricot jam then press onto the cake by hand. Turn the cake on its side and roll it on a board to press the icing firmly on. Roll out the remaining icing to a round shape, slightly smaller than the size of the cake. Brush the icing and the top of the cake with egg white or jam, press onto cake and roll out with a rolling pin to the edges, keeping then even. Allow to stand for 24 hours before coating with ornamental icing.

Ornamental icing:
2 egg whites
500 g sifted icing sugar (1 lb)
3 or 4 drops glacial acetic acid.

Method: Mix all the above ingredients together, beating very well. Cover cake with a thin layer and use the balance to decorate with either a trellis pattern or rosettes.

FRUIT CAKE

250 g butter (½ lb)
6 eggs
3 cups flour
1 cup sugar

1½ kilo (3 lb) mixed fruit
1 tablespoon cream
1 tablespoon milk
2 tablespoons oil
2 teaspoons baking powder
250 g cherries (½ lb)
1 tablespoon ground almonds (optional)

Method: Cream butter and sugar, add eggs one at a time. Add cream, oil, milk, ground almonds, then add sifted dry ingredients. Lastly stir in fruit by hand. Bake in greased and lined tin (double layer greaseproof paper), for 2 hours. Bake for the first ½ hour on 190°C (375°F), then turn oven down to 125°C (250°F) and bake for a further 1½ hours. After removing from oven, pour over 2 tablespoons brandy. Cool before removing from tin.

FRUIT CAKE WITH EGG WHITES ONLY

16 egg whites (2 cups)
250 g glace cherries (red & green)
1 whole orange minced, skin and all
⅓ cup milk
4 cups flour
1 teaspoon salt
1½ kilos (3 lb) mixed fruit (sultanas, currants, raisins)
1 cup dessicated coconut
1 cup chopped pecans
¾ teaspoon bicarb
375 g butter (¾ lb)
1½ cups sugar
1 teaspoon cream of tartar

Method: Wash fruit off thoroughly the day before and leave on absorbent paper to dry.
Preheat oven to 180°C (350°F).
Combine the fruit with coconut, cherries, orange and pecans. Add to this the bicarb dissolved in milk.

Cream butter and sugar till light and fluffy. Sift together flour, salt and cream of tartar. Beat egg whites very stiffly and add to creamed butter alternately with sifted dry ingredients. When thoroughly blended, add fruit mixture and combine well.

Bake in 2 loaf tins or one 30 cm square tin, 10 cm deep (12-inches wide x 4-inches deep) which has been buttered and lined with a double thickness of waxproof paper. Sprinkle flaked almonds and press cherry halves on top. Bake for ½ hour on 180°C (350°F) then turn oven down to 125°C (250°F) and bake for a further 1½ hours. Allow to cool thoroughly before removing from the tin.

Spoon over 2–3 tablespoons brandy and store wrapped in foil till required.

Do not use at least a week so that the cake has time to mature.

Special hint: You may add glace pineapple and chopped preserved ginger or apricots or use any additional fruits of your choice.

GERMAN CHOCOLATE CAKE

250 g butter (½ lb)
125 g cooking chocolate (½ slab) dissolved with ½ cup hot water
2½ cups flour
1 teaspoon vanilla
1½ cups sugar
4 eggs, separated
1 cup buttermilk
1 teaspoon bicarb
pinch salt

Method: Heat oven to 180°C (350°F). Cream butter and sugar and add egg yolks, one at a time, beating well after each addition. Dissolve bicarb in ½ cup buttermilk and add. Add sifted flour and salt, chocolate, vanilla and remaining ½ cup buttermilk. Fold in stiffly beaten egg whites. Bake in 2 greased and floured 22 cm (9-inch) sandwich tins for about 40 minutes.

Sandwich together and top with the following filling:
1 cup sugar
125 g butter (¼ lb)
1 cup evaporated milk
3 egg yolks
1 teaspoon vanilla
1 cup coconut
1 cup chopped pecans

Method: Mix together sugar, butter, milk and well beaten egg yolks. Cook, stirring constantly until thick. Fold in vanilla, coconut and pecans.

GINGER CAKE

250 g butter (½ lb)
3 eggs
4 teaspoons ground ginger
1 teaspoon mixed spice
1 teaspoon bicarb
1 cup sugar
2 tablespoons syrup
¼ cup cold water
2 cups flour
¾ cup milk
  pinch salt

Method: Cream butter and sugar. Add egg yolks, syrup, ginger and mixed spices. Sift flour and add alternately to mixture with milk. Dissolve bicarb in water, and add to mixture. Lastly fold in stiffly beaten egg whites. Pour into greased and floured fluted tin or loaf tin and bake 180°C (350°F) oven 45–50 minutes.

Icing: Make a plain vanilla frosting and add to this a few tablespoons of the syrup from the preserved ginger and a few pieces of chopped ginger. Do not make the icing too thick as this must be spooned onto the top of the cake and allowed to drip down the sides. Of course, this cake may be left plain and dusted with a little icing sugar before serving. I must admit, I prefer it plain.

GINGER CHIFFON CAKE

½ cup oil
6 egg yolks
¾ cup cold water
1½ teaspoons bicarb
4 teaspoon ginger
1 teaspoon cinnamon
1 teaspoon mixed spice
2 tablespoons syrup
2 cups flour
1¼ cups sugar
½ teaspoon cream of tartar
7 egg whites

Method: Beat egg yolks and sugar till light and creamy. Add oil, syrup, water with bicarb dissolved in it, and sifted dry ingredients, except cream of tartar, and beat again till smooth.

Beat egg whites till frothy, add cream of tartar and beat till stiff. Pour egg yolk mixture gently over whites and fold in. Pour into ungreased chiffon cake tin and bake 180°C (350°F) oven 50–60 minutes.

Invert over a bottle till completely cool before removing from tin. Pour over a butter icing to which you have added 1–2 teaspoons ground ginger and allow to drip down the sides of the cake.

Alternatively split through the middle and fill with whipped cream, caramelised condensed milk and slices of preserved ginger. Repeat on top of cake.

To caramelise condensed milk, boil tin in water for 3 hours, adding more water as it boils away.

GRASSHOPPER CAKE

5 eggs
1 cup flour
1 cup castor sugar
½ cup oil
   dash cinnamon
2 tablespoons cocoa
¾ cup boiling water
2½ teaspoons baking powder
1 teaspoon vanilla
   pinch salt

Method: Separate whites from yolks and place the whites in a large bowl as you will end up mixing the whole mixture in this bowl. In your mixmaster bowl sift the flour, sugar, salt, cinnamon, cocoa and baking powder. Make a well in the centre and add the oil, egg yolks, vanilla and boiling water. Stir by hand then beat in mixmaster for 7-10 minutes. Meanwhile beat the egg whites till frothy, add an additional ½ teaspoon baking powder to this and continue beating till *very stiff*. Fold chocolate mixture over egg whites very lightly and pour into ungreased chiffon cake tin and bake 190°C (375°F) oven for 40 minutes. Invert over bottle to cool. Remove from tin, cut through the middle and spread with half the grasshopper filling, using the balance on top of the cake. Allow to set in fridge.

Grasshopper filling:
12 quartered white marshmallows
2 tablespoons creme de cacao
2 tablespoons creme de menthe or peppermint liqueur
   few drops green food colouring

Method: Place all the above ingredients in a double boiler and cook till the marshmallows have completely dissolved. Allow to cool in fridge and then fold into 250 mℓ (½ pint) whipped cream.

Cover the sides of the cake with marshmallow frosting, made as follows:
Place 1½ cups sugar, ⅔ cup water and a pinch of cream of tartar in a saucepan. Stir till sugar has dissolved. Allow to boil gently till sugar spins a thread and then pour slowly onto two stiffly beaten egg whites. Beat till mixture is of a good spreading consistency.

Special hint: Use a double strand of cotton to cut through the cake, by using a sawing movement.

KIRSCH GATEAU

Meringue cake:
5 egg whites
100 g ground almonds (1 packet)
1 tablespoon flour
½ cup castor sugar
1 tablespoon maizena

Method: Beat egg whites very stiffly, gradually adding the sugar. Lightly fold in the ground almonds (reserve 1 tablespoon), flour and maizena.

Line 2 round 22 cm (9-inch) sandwich tins with oiled greaseproof paper. Divide mixture in half and spread in each tin. Bake in hot oven, 200–220°C (400–450°F) for 15 minutes or till golden brown. Remove paper whilst hot.

Sponge cake:
5 eggs
1 cup sugar
50 g butter (2 oz)
1 cup plus 2 tablespoons flour
2 tablespoons maizena
⅓ cup milk and water together
2 slightly rounded teaspoons baking powder
1 tablespoon maraschino or Kirsch liqueur

Method: Beat eggs and sugar till thick and creamy. Place milk and butter in a saucepan and bring to the boil. Sift flour and maizena and add with the butter mixture to the beaten eggs. Add liqueur and lastly fold in baking powder. Pour into 2 greased and floured 22 cm (9-inch) sandwich tins and bake in 200°C (400°F) oven 20–25 minutes.

Butter cream:
250 g butter (8 oz)
1 tablespoon Kirsch
250 g icing sugar ($\frac{1}{2}$ packet)
  few drops cochineal

Method: Beat together till light and fluffy.

To assemble the cake: Spread one almond cake with butter cream. Sprinkle the sponge cake with Kirsch and place on top of the almond cake. Spread with a thin layer of butter cream and again top with sponge cake which has been sprinkled with Kirsch. Spread with a thick layer of butter cream and top with remaining meringue layer.

Cover the top and sides with the remaining butter cream. Press flaked toasted almonds round the sides and dredge the top with the reserved tablespoon of ground almonds. Dredge again with icing sugar and then, using the back of a knife, mark the top in the traditional diamond pattern.

KRANSKUCHEN

2 cups flour
2 teaspoons baking powder
250 ml ($\frac{1}{2}$ pint) cream, whipped till thick
  with 1 teaspoon lemon juice
1 egg
1 heaped tablespoon sugar
50 g butter (2 oz)
  pinch salt
  cherries, nuts, mixed fruits

Method: Sift dry ingredients and rub or grate in butter. Add cream and egg. Place in refrigerator for $\frac{1}{2}$ hour or a little longer. Roll out into rectangular shape, spread with apricot jam. Sprinkle with cinnamon and sugar, fruit and nuts. Roll up and cut at 5 cm (2-inch) intervals, then place on baking tray and curve into horse shoe. Twist cut edges to show the inside. Brush top with beaten egg and bake 190°C (375°F) oven for 35–40 minutes. Whilst warm, make water icing and pour over. Decorate with nuts and cherries.

Special hint: Another lovely shape for this is to roll into rectangular shape, place on baking tray then spread jam, cinnamon, sugar, fruit and nuts down the centre only. Cut diagonally at 5 cm (2-inch) intervals down both sides and plait one piece over the other all the way down. Curve into horseshoe and bake as directed.

ORANGE CHIFFON CAKE

$2\frac{1}{4}$ cups flour
1 teaspoon salt
$\frac{1}{2}$ cup oil
$\frac{3}{4}$ cup cold water
  rind of 2 oranges
$1\frac{1}{2}$ cups sugar
$\frac{1}{2}$ teaspoon cream of tartar
6 egg yolks
8 egg whites (1 cup)
3 teaspoons baking powder

Method: Sift the flour, salt and sugar. Make a well in the centre and add the egg yolks, oil, water and orange rind. Beat for 5–7 minutes. Meanwhile beat the egg whites till frothy, add the cream of tartar and continue to beat until very stiff.

Fold the baking powder into the egg yolk mixture and then fold this mixture gently over the well beaten egg whites.

Pour into ungreased chiffon cake tin

and bake in 180°C (350°F) oven for 1 hour.

Invert over neck of bottle and allow to hang free until thoroughly cooled. Remove from tin with a metal spatula or long sharp knife.

Split cooled cake crosswise into two layers, using cotton to cut. Spread filling between layers.

Orange custard filling:
(Optional) otherwise use as plain cake and just ice.
2 egg yolks
2 tablespoons maizena
$\frac{1}{4}$ cup orange juice
   finely grated orange rind
$\frac{1}{3}$ cup sugar
$\frac{3}{4}$ cup milk, scalded
1 tablespoon lemon juice
1 tablespoon butter

Method: Beat egg yolks and sugar till light and creamy. Add maizena and beat in. Add scalded milk beating all the time as you do so.

Pour mixture into double boiler and cook stirring constantly with a wooden spoon till thickened.

Remove from heat and stir in butter, orange rind and juice and lemon juice. Stir well. Cool and use as desired.

Orange butter icing:
500 g icing sugar (1 packet)
125 g butter (4 oz)
3–6 tablespoons orange juice, to blend.

Method: Cream butter. Add icing and orange juice and beat till smooth.

PINEAPPLE CHEESE CAKE

Method: Drain a small tin (410 g) pineapple chunks. Thicken juice with 1 dessertspoon maizena mixed to a paste with water. Cool.

Pastry:
250 g butter ($\frac{1}{2}$ lb)
6 tablespoons sugar

Method: Cream in the mixmaster. Add 2 eggs, 1 teaspoon baking powder and 2 cups flour. Grease a rectangular pyrex dish and line with the dough. Pastry will be soft and sticky, so work with floured hands or spread with a knife.

Cheese:
500 g cream cheese (1 lb)
2 eggs, separated
$\frac{3}{4}$ cup cream (175 mℓ)

Method: Combine 2 egg yolks with the cheese, cream, 1 tablespoon flour, 3 tablespoons sugar, $\frac{1}{4}$ cup milk, and 1 teaspoon vanilla. Then fold in the beaten egg whites.

On top of the pastry place pineapple, then the thickened juice, then the cheese mixture and top with crushed corn flakes. Bake 190°C (375°F), 20 minutes. Turn oven off completely and leave in oven another 45–60 minutes.

PINEAPPLE CREAM CAKE

$1\frac{1}{2}$ cups flour
$2\frac{1}{2}$ teaspoons baking powder
$\frac{1}{2}$ teaspoon salt
40 g butter ($1\frac{1}{2}$ oz)
4 eggs separated
$\frac{7}{8}$ cup castor sugar
1 teaspoon vanilla
$\frac{1}{2}$ cup milk and water mixed (125 mℓ) or 6 tablespoons milk and 2 tablespoons water

Method: Sift together the flour, baking powder and salt. Set aside till needed. Separate eggs and beat whites till very stiff. Add egg yolks and beat in well. Add sugar very gradually and beat until mixture is pale lemon-coloured. Add vanilla essence and then sifted dry ingredients. Lastly stir in milk and butter mixture which has been brought to the boil. Bake in two greased and floured heart shaped tins in 190°C (375°F) oven for 20 minutes. When cool, sandwich together with whipped cream and pineapple chunks. Decorate the top of the cake with cream, pineapple, cherries and chocolate sprinkles.

QUICK & DELICIOUS MARBLE CAKE

1 carton margarine (250 g)
1 cup milk (250 mℓ)
3 cups flour
3 teaspoons baking powder
1 teaspoon vanilla
2 tablespoons cocoa, mixed to a paste with boiling water
1½ cups sugar
4 eggs
   pinch salt

Method: Cream margarine and sugar. Add eggs, sifted dry ingredients, milk and vanilla and beat till smooth. Divide the mixture in half. Add the cocoa mixture to the one half. Grease and flour a fluted or large loaf tin, grease with butter not margarine, otherwise the cake will stick, spoon mixture in, alternating vanilla and chocolate layers. Zigzag through mixture with a knife and then bake in 180°C (350°F) oven for 1 hour. Turn out and cool, then pour over chocolate glaze as given for "Chocolate Chestnut Pyramid Cake". This is also a very good recipe for cookies. These would be baked in a 180°C (350°F) oven for approximately 15 minutes. It is preferable to use cookie or muffin trays, as the paper cups tend to absorb the fat from the cake, making them dry.

RASPBERRY OR LOGANBERRY ROLL

2 cups flour sifted
2 tins berries thickened with maizena
4 teaspoons baking powder
1 egg
1 tablespoon sugar
   pinch salt
125 g butter (4oz)
1 cup milk
3 tablespoons melted butter or more

Method: Preheat oven to 200°C (400°F). Grease and flour a swiss roll tin. Sift flour, baking powder, sugar and salt together in a mixing bowl. Rub or grate in the butter. Add beaten egg and milk to make a soft dough. Roll out onto a floured board into a 30 x 40 cm (12 x 16-inch) rectangle about 1 cm ($\frac{1}{4}$ to $\frac{1}{2}$ inch) thick. Spread with thickened raspberries or loganberries, and roll up as compactly as possible. Seal ends of roll, press together with fork. Place on greased baking tray, brush top with melted butter. Bake for 10 minutes at 200°C (400°F) then reduce heat to 180°C (350°F) and continue baking about 45 minutes or till crust is brown. To serve, cut roll in thick slices, serve warm with cream.

RUSSIAN TORTE

1½ cups flour
3 teaspoons baking powder
   pinch salt
45 g butter (1½ oz)
4 eggs separated
$\frac{7}{8}$ cup castor sugar
1 teaspoon vanilla
6 tablespoons milk
2 tablespoons water
1 dessertspoon instant coffee powder

Method: Sift together flour, baking powder and salt. Separate eggs and beat whites stiffly. Add egg yolks and beat very well. Gradually add sugar and beat till mixture is pale lemon coloured. Add vanilla essence and then sifted dry ingredients. Bring milk, water, coffee and butter to the boil and lastly stir into cake batter. Bake in 2 greased and floured 20–22 cm (8 or 9-inch) diameter tins in 200°C (400°F) oven for 20 minutes. Cool and split each layer in half.

Filling:
3 egg yolks
1 cup strong hot coffee
1 cup stiffly beaten cream
$\frac{1}{4}$ cup chopped glacé cherries, red and green
$\frac{1}{2}$ cup sultanas soaked in rum
$\frac{1}{4}$ cup chopped pistachio nuts
1 tablespoon maizena
$\frac{1}{2}$ cup sugar
1 teaspoon vanilla
6 chopped walnuts

Method: Beat egg yolks and sugar till light and creamy. Add maizena. Add hot coffee, beating all the time as you do so. Place in double boiler and cook till thickened, stirring constantly with a wooden spoon. Cool thoroughly. Add vanilla and fold in cream. Add cherries, sultanas and nuts.

SEMOLINA CAKE

375 g ($\frac{3}{4}$ lb) butter, soft
1 cup of sugar
   grated rind of 1 orange
1 cup orange juice
6 eggs separated
3 full teaspoons baking powder
   whole cloves
1 cup Semolina or Cream of Wheat
$\frac{1}{2}$ cup chopped pecan nuts
2 cups flour, well rounded
   pinch salt

Syrup:
1$\frac{1}{2}$ cups sugar
1 cup water
$\frac{1}{4}$ cup brandy

Method: Sift flour, baking powder and salt. Stir in Semolina and nuts. Beat egg yolks with $\frac{1}{2}$ the sugar till light and creamy then add butter and continue beating till very light and fluffy. Add orange rind, and sifted dry ingredients alternately with orange juice. Beat egg whites until frothy then gradually beat in remaining $\frac{1}{2}$ cup sugar till very stiff. Fold into egg yolk mixture. Pour into a greased 22 x 33 cm (9 x 13-inch) baking tin and bake in 180°C (350°F) oven for 45–50 minutes. Cool and cut into squares. Place a clove in the centre of each square. Boil water and sugar together for 3 minutes. Add brandy and pour syrup over cake.

STRAWBERRY SPICE SHORTCAKE

175 g butter (6 oz)
2 eggs
2 level teaspoons cinnamon
$\frac{1}{4}$ teaspoon nutmeg
$\frac{3}{4}$ cup castor sugar
$\frac{1}{4}$ teaspoon mixed spice
1$\frac{3}{4}$ cups self raising flour

Method: Cream butter and sugar. Beat in eggs, one at a time. Fold in sifted flour and spices. Divide mixture into 3 x 22 cm (9-inch) greased and floured tins and bake in 190°C (375°F) oven for 20 minutes. Sandwich together with whipped cream and strawberries and garnish with whole strawberries. Use apricots when strawberries are not in season.

STRAWBERRY VACHERIN

125 g butter (4 oz)
1½ packets ground almonds (150 g)
1½ cups sugar
8 egg whites, (1 cup)
1¼ cups flour
500 mℓ cream (1 pint)
   strawberries

Method: Melt butter and leave until cool but not set. Very lightly fold the almonds, sugar and sifted flour into the stiffly beaten egg whites. Carefully fold in butter. Spread the mixture on four rounds in lined and oiled baking tins and bake until biscuit coloured in 180°C (350°F) oven for approximately 20–30 minutes. Sandwich together with whipped cream and strawberries. Top with the glaze given below and decorate with piped cream rosettes and whole strawberries.

Topping:
¼ cup sugar
1 tablespoon water
1 dessertspoon jelly (red)
1 dessertspoon maizena
12–15 strawberries, diced

Method: Simmer sugar and water together for a few minutes, add strawberries and continue to cook for a few minutes longer. 5–10 minutes. Add jelly and maizena mixed with a little cold water. Cool thoroughly before using.

SWEDISH CAKE

Sponge Cake
2 eggs
1 cup flour
75 g butter (3 oz)
1 heaped teaspoon baking powder
½ cup milk and water mixed
¾ cup sugar

Method: Beat eggs and sugar till light and creamy. Add sifted dry ingredients. Melt butter in milk and bring to the boil. Add to mixture. Bake in greased and floured 22 cm (9-inch) diameter tin. Allow to cool and cut through into two rounds. Temperature 190°C (375°F) for 20–25 minutes.

Marzipan
2½ cups ground almonds
1 cup castor sugar
2 unbeaten egg whites

Method: Mix ground almonds and sugar together. Add egg whites and a few drops of almond essence, optional, then knead well. Roll out and line a 22 cm (9-inch) springform tin, which has also been lined with greaseproof paper.

Vanilla Cream
1 cup milk
2 tablespoon sugar
1 teaspoon vanilla
125 mℓ whipped cream (½ cup)
1½ tablespoons maizena
3 egg yolks
2 teaspoons gelatine

Method: Beat egg yolks and sugar till light and creamy. Add maizena and blend in well. Add scalded milk, beating all the time as you do so. Place in double boiler and cook till thickened. Remove from heat and stir in gelatine which was softened in 2 tablespoons cold water and then 1 tablespoon boiling water. Allow to cool completely and then fold in whipped cream and vanilla.

To Assemble: Pour half the vanilla cream into marzipan lined tin. Place one layer of sponge cake on top, which you can spread with jam, then the balance of the vanilla cream and top with the remaining layer of cake. Place in fridge to set. Turn out onto a round cake platter and garnish with

whipped cream or icing squeezed into a diagonal pattern with a piping tube and the "windows" filled with lemon curd and/or jam.

SWISS ROLL

5 eggs
1 cup sugar
1 cup plus 2 tablespoons flour
½ cup maizena
50 g butter (2 oz)
⅓ cup milk and water mixed
2 teaspoons baking powder

Method: Beat eggs and sugar till light and creamy. Add sifted dry ingredients except baking powder. Add boiled milk and butter and lastly fold in baking powder. Pour into large greased and floured swiss roll tin and bake in 200°C (400°F) oven for 8–10 minutes. Turn out onto damp cloth which has been sprinkled with sugar. Spread quickly with warmed apricot jam, then roll up and leave in cloth till cool.

TROPICAL CARROT CAKE

3 cups flour
2 teaspoons baking powder
1 teaspoon bicarb
2 teaspoons cinnamon
1 teaspoon salt
1¼ cups sugar
1½ cups oil
4 eggs
3 cups grated carrots
1 cup crushed pineapple
½ cup dessicated coconut
¾ cup chopped pecan nuts

Method: Preheat oven to 180°C (350°F). Sift flour with baking powder, bicarb, cinnamon and salt. Butter well and flour 2 x 22 cm (9-inch) square tins. In mixmaster beat sugar, oil and eggs till well blended. Add carrots, pineapple, coconut and nuts. Mix well.

Gradually add flour mixture, beating just until well combined. Batter will be thin. Pour into prepared tins and bake for 45 minutes. Turn out. Cool and ice with cream cheese icing.

Cream Cheese Icing:
125 g butter (4oz)
500 g Icing sugar (1 lb)
1 teaspoon vanilla
50–100 g cream cheese (2–4 oz)

Method: Beat butter, icing sugar and vanilla together. The mixture will be crumbly. Stir in by hand the cream cheese. Do not beat too much as the mixture becomes watery when you do so after adding cheese. Decorate with additional chopped pecans, red and green cherries.

TWO TONE PYRAMID CAKE

1½ cups flour
3 teaspoons baking powder
½ teaspoon salt
40 g butter (1½ oz)
1 heaped tablespoon cocoa, mixed with hot water to a paste
4 eggs, separated
⅞ cup castor sugar
1 teaspoon vanilla
4 tablespoons milk
2 tablespoons water

Method: Sift together flour, baking powder and salt and set aside till needed. Separate eggs and beat whites in mixmaster till stiff. Add egg yolks and beat in well. Add sugar very gradually and beat until mixture is pale lemon coloured. Add vanilla and sifted dry ingredients. Bring milk and butter to boil and stir in. Pour half the mixture into one of two greased and floured small 35 x 25 cm (14 x 10-inch) swiss roll tins. Mix the cocoa paste into remaining batter and pour into 2nd swiss roll tin. Bake in 200°C (400°F) oven for 10 minutes. Cool and cut each cake into half lengthwise. Place three layers, (white, chocolate, white) on a large piece of foil, side by side, spread with mocha cream. Place remaining chocolate layer on top of first chocolate layer (i.e. in the centre). Spread with more mocha cream. Place a row of maraschino cherries along centre of top chocolate layer. Put your hand under the foil and press the two white layers together to form a pyramid. Allow to set in fridge. Pour over chocolate glaze and decorate as desired.

MOCHA BUTTER CREAM

4 egg yolks
250 g butter ($\frac{1}{2}$ lb)
$\frac{1}{2}$ cup sugar
3 teaspoons instant coffee powder
3 tablespoons water
1 tablespoon brandy

Method: Cream the butter and set aside. Beat the egg yolks till thick and lemon coloured. Place the sugar, water and coffee in a saucepan and stir till sugar dissolves. Allow to boil briskly until sugar spins a thread and then pour in a slow stream onto the egg yolks, beating all the time, until mixture thickens and cools to room temperature. Add butter, beating in 1–2 tablespoons at a time and lastly stir in brandy.
Chocolate Glaze: Melt 50 g (2 oz) butter in a saucepan with 2 heaped tablespoons cocoa Fold 2–3 cups icing sugar into 2 unbeaten egg whites. Stir till smooth. Pour into saucepan and blend well with cocoa butter mixture.

VANILLA SLICE

Biscuit Layers:
3 cups flour level
pinch salt
1 dessertspoon custard powder
2 teaspoons baking powder
2 eggs
1 cup sugar
250 g butter ($\frac{1}{2}$ lb)
1 teaspoon vanilla

Method: Sift dry ingredients. Grate in butter. Add slightly beaten egg and vanilla and form into dough. Roll out into 4 even oblongs and bake on biscuit pan, which has been greased and floured in 180°C (350°F) oven till golden brown, for about 10–15 minutes. Cool and sandwich together with the following:

Filling:
2 egg yolks
$\frac{1}{4}$ cup sugar
1 teaspoon vanilla
2 tablespoons soft butter (50 g)
3 tablespoons maizena
$1\frac{1}{2}$ cups milk
$\frac{1}{2}$ cup cream

Method: Scald milk and cream. Beat egg yolks with sugar, till light and creamy. Add vanilla and maizena, then slowly add scalded milk and cream. Pour into double boiler and stir with a *wooden spoon* till thick. Stir in the butter till custard is smooth and creamy.

Make a water icing for the top of the vanilla slice, using 1 cup icing sugar, a few drops of lemon juice and enough boiling water to form a smooth mixture. Pour over and decorate with chocolate sauce or nuts and cherries.

VENETIAN TORTE

125 g butter (4 oz)
4 egg yolks
3 tablespoons milk
½ cup sugar
1 heaped cup flour
1 teaspoon baking powder
1 teaspoon vanilla

Method: Cream butter and sugar. Add the egg yolks, one at a time, beating well after each addition. Sift flour and baking powder and add alternatively with milk and vanilla. Spread batter in two greased and floured heart shaped tins or round 20 cm (8-inch) diameter tins.

Topping:
¾ cup sugar
4 egg whites
chopped nuts, cinnamon

Method: Beat the egg whites, stiffly, gradually adding sugar. Spread on top of cake batter, sprinkle with cinnamon and nuts. Bake in 180°C (350°F) oven for 25 minutes. When cool, sandwich together with the following:
Filling: In a double boiler, place 1 beaten egg, 1 tablespoon sugar, 250 ml sour cream (½ pint) and 1 tablespoon maizena. Stir over heat till very thick. Allow to cool and stir in half a small tin (± 100 g) crushed pineapple and 1 teaspoon vanilla.

WALNUT LAYER CAKE

3 cups flour
250 g butter (8 oz)
⅔ cup sugar
2 eggs, slightly beaten
½ teaspoon cinnamon
 pinch salt
use a little cold water, if necessary

Method: Sift together flour, sugar and salt. Rub or grate in butter and form into a dough with the egg and water. Divide into 5 parts and roll each into rounds approximately 20–22 cm (8–9-inch) in diameter. Bake on greased and floured baking sheet in 180°C (350°F) oven till golden brown. Cool and sandwich together with the following:

Filling:
500 mℓ whipped cream (1 pint)
¾ cup icing sugar
1 teaspoon vanilla
1½ tablespoons brandy
2 x 100 g packets chopped walnuts (¼ lb)
50 g grated bitter chocolate (2 oz)

Method: Spread top layer with warmed apricot jam. Sift icing sugar over jam. Mark into eight wedges, and sprinkle each alternate wedge with additional grated chocolate.

10. TARTS

BASIC TART DOUGH

2 cups flour
1 egg slightly beaten
125 g butter (4 oz)
1 teaspoon baking powder
50 g margarine (2 oz)
2 tablespoons sugar

Method: Sift dry ingredients. Rub or grate in butter and margarine. Knead into dough with slightly beaten egg. If necessary add 1–2 tablespoons cold water to bind.

APPLE SLICE

First Dough:
2 cups flour
1 egg
50 g margarine (2 oz)
 pinch salt
1 teaspoon baking powder
125 g butter ($\frac{1}{4}$ lb)
2 tablespoons sugar

Method: Sift dry ingredients. Rub or grate in butter and margarine and blend into a dough with the slightly beaten egg, if necessary use 1–2 tablespoons cold water to bind.

Second Dough
2$\frac{1}{2}$ cups flour
250 ml cream ($\frac{1}{2}$ pint) thick or sour
250 g butter ($\frac{1}{2}$ lb)

Method: Place flour in a bowl, rub or grate in butter and form into a dough with the cream. Leave in refrigerator overnight.

Apple Filling:
10–12 apples, only granny smith or ohenimuri
juice of 1 lemon
sugar to taste, about $\frac{1}{2}$ cup

Method: Peel apples, cut into quarters. Place in a saucepan with the lemon juice, cover and simmer over gentle heat till tender, but not a complete pulp. Add sugar and allow to simmer without the lid until the juice has almost cooked away. Cool thoroughly before using.

To Assemble: Roll out 2 strips of the first dough, about 12–15 cm (5–6-inches) wide and 25–30 cm (10–12-inches) long and place on greased and floured baking tray. Place apple filling down centre. Cut slices across 2nd dough (rolled out as for first dough) leaving a 2 cm (1 inch) border all round. Then cover with the strips of the 2nd dough. Brush edges with slightly beaten egg white. Press the sides down well together. Brush top with egg white and sprinkle with sugar. Bake in 190°C (375°F) oven till golden brown for about 35 minutes.

APPLE TART

2 cups flour
1 egg + 1 tablespoon cold water, slightly beaten
125 g butter ($\frac{1}{4}$ lb)
2 tablespoons sugar
1 teaspoon baking powder
50 g margarine (2 oz)

Method: Sift dry ingredients. Rub in butter and margarine and knead into a dough with the slightly beaten egg. Roll out dough and place in greased pyrex dish. You may either sprinkle with 1 tablespoon flour mixed with 1 tablespoon sugar or spread with a thin layer of jam. This seals the pastry and prevents it from becoming soggy underneath. You may either place strips of dough in a lattice pattern on top of the filling or you may slice unpeeled apple very thinly and place on top of stewed apples overlapping each other in a circular pattern. If you do this, brush with melted butter and sprinkle with cinnamon and sugar before baking and after removing from oven, glaze with a mixture of apricot jam, lemon juice and water. Bake in a 190°C (375°F) oven for 35–45 minutes, or till nicely browned.

Filling:
10–12 apples, granny smith or ohenimuri
   sugar to taste, about ½ cup
   juice of 1 lemon

Method: Peel apples and cut into quarters. Place in a saucepan with the lemon juice, cover and simmer over gentle heat till tender, but not a complete pulp. Add sugar and allow to simmer without the lid till the juices have almost cooked away.

APPLE TART DE LUXE

Pastry:
50 g butter (2 oz)
¼ cup sugar
1 level teaspoon baking powder
1 egg
1 tablespoon cream
1 cup flour
   salt
   vanilla essence

Method: Sift dry ingredients, blend in butter and egg and cream and make into soft dough. Line an oblong pie dish with pastry. Pour in the following:

Apple Mixture:
½ cup sugar
1 tablespoon flour
¾ cup sour cream
1 teaspoon vanilla essence
1 beaten egg
1 tin pie apples (410 g) or home cooked
   apples.

Method: Bake in 220°C (450°F) oven for 10 minutes. Remove from stove and top with the following:

Topping:
¼ cup flour
¼ cup brown sugar
35 g diced butter (1½ oz)

Method: Crumble this put on top of apple mixture and bake at 180°C (350°F) for 20–25 minutes.

APPLE TART WITH MERINGUE TOPPING

Dough:
125 g butter (¼ lb)
¾ cup sugar
2 eggs
2 teaspoons baking powder
½ teaspoon vanilla
2½–3 cups flour
   pinch salt

Method: Cream butter and sugar, add eggs, vanilla and mix well. Beat in flour sifted with baking powder and salt. Roll out and line greased pyrex dish. Spoon in apple filling and bake in 180°C (350°F) oven for 20–25 minutes.

Apple Filling:
1 large tin pie apples, mixed with
½ cup brown sugar
1 teaspoon cinnamon
   a pat of butter
1 dessertspoon apricot jam and
   some dried fruit (optional)

   Meringue Topping: 2 egg whites, beat till stiff, then add 4 tablespoons sugar a little at a time and lastly ½ teaspoon vanilla. Remove apple tart from oven, spread with meringue and return to oven for 10 minutes.

APRICOT PECAN SLICE

1 cup flour
$\frac{1}{2}$ cup maizena
$\frac{1}{4}$ cup icing sugar
1 teaspoon lemon juice
1 egg white
1 large can apricot halves (825 g or 2 lb)
1 cup self-raising flour
$\frac{1}{4}$ cup custard powder
250 g butter ($\frac{1}{2}$ lb)
$\frac{1}{4}$ cup approximately, soda water or ice water
apricot jam
chopped pecans

Method: Sift together the flour, self raising flour, maizena, custard powder, and icing sugar. Rub in the butter until mixture resembles fine crumbs. Add lemon juice and enough water to mix to a firm dough, then wrap and chill for 20 minutes. Roll out two thirds of the dough and line a lamington tin or swiss roll tin, 18 x 27 cm (7 x 11-inches) approximately, prick well and bake in 180°C (350°F) oven for 15 minutes. Drain apricots thoroughly. Warm 3-4 tablespoons apricot jam and spread a thin film over pastry.

Arrange apricot halves over pastry, brush with more apricot jam. Roll remaining pastry into strips and arrange, lattice fashion, over top. Brush strips with beaten egg white, sprinkle with pecans. Bake in 180°C (350°F) oven for about 15-20 minutes. Serve in a slab or cut into slices.

BELGIAN TART

210 g butter (7 oz)
2 tablespoons sugar
2 tablespoons oil
$\frac{1}{2}$ teaspoon vanilla
1 beaten egg
2 cups flour
pinch of salt
2 teaspoons baking powder

Method: Cream butter and sugar well. Add oil and vanilla and beat again. Add beaten egg. Add sifted flour, baking powder and salt. Place in fridge for about 2 hours. Grate half the dough into a greased springform tin. Spread with jam ($\pm$ 1 cup). Grate remaining dough on top. Bake in 180°C (350°F) oven for $\frac{1}{2}$–$\frac{3}{4}$ hour.

When cool, sieve over a few tablespoons icing sugar.

BENEDICT TART

175 g butter (6 oz)
1 egg
1 tablespoon oil
2$\frac{1}{2}$ cups flour
$\frac{1}{2}$ cup sugar
1 teaspoon baking powder
$\frac{1}{2}$ teaspoon salt
apricot jam

Filling:
2 packets flaked almonds (200 g)
$\frac{3}{4}$ cup sugar
3 tablespoons milk
145 g butter (4$\frac{1}{2}$ oz)
few drops almond essence

Method: Cream butter and sugar. Add egg and oil and beat a little longer. Add sifted dry ingredients. Press into a swiss roll tin which has been greased and floured, 30 x 20 cm (12 x 8-inches) approximately. Press the dough up the sides of the tin as well to form a ridge. Prick all over with a fork and bake 190°C (375°F) oven for 10-15 minutes. Remove from oven, spread with apricot jam, just to cover, not too thick, pour over filling, spread it evenly with knife, then return tart to the oven for a further 10 minutes. Allow to cool completely before removing from the tin. When you do remove from tin, first pry the edges loose with a sharp knife and shake the tin to make sure that the tart is loose.

Prepare the filling: Place the butter, sugar, milk and almonds into a saucepan and bring to the boil. Allow to simmer gently another 2–3 minutes then stir in the almond essence.

Special hint: It does seem improbable for the tart to be removed from the tin easily, but, in fact, this is the case.

CHERRY TART

Method: Make basic tart dough and bake blind in 190°C (375°F) oven for 15 minutes then remove the paper and bake another 10–15 minutes or till golden brown.

Filling:
1 vanilla instant pudding
¾ cup milk
¾ cup cream
1 dessertspoon brandy
1 bottle cherry pie filling
    whipped cream for decorating

Method: Pour milk and cream into a bowl, sprinkle over instant pudding and beat till thick. Lastly stir in brandy. Pour into cooled pastry shell, and place the cherry pie filling over this. Decorate with whipped cream.

COCONUT CUSTARD PIE

Pastry:
2 cups flour
2 tablespoons sugar
1 teaspoon baking powder
1 tablespoon cold water, only if necessary
125 g butter (4 oz)
50 g margarine (2 oz)
1 egg

Method: Sift flour, sugar, salt and baking powder. Grate in butter and margarine. Blend into dough with slightly beaten egg. Add water if dough is too crumbly to roll out.

Roll out on lightly floured board. Unroll into greased large round pyrex dish or ovenware dish. Cover with a sheet of waxproof paper and fill with butter beans. Bake in 180°C (350°F) oven for 15 minutes. Remove beans and paper and return to oven for another 10–15 minutes to brown.

Filling:
3 cups milk
4 tablespoons maizena
50 g butter (2 oz)
1 teaspoon vanilla
½ cup sugar
4 egg yolks
1½ cups dessicated coconut

Method: Scald milk. Blend sugar and maizena together in top of double boiler. Pour in hot milk a little at a time and stir till smooth. Beat egg yolks and slowly add milk mixture beating all the time. Pour back into double boiler and cook till thick. Remove from heat and stir in butter, coconut and vanilla. Cool.

Meringue topping:
4 egg whites
¼ cup sugar
½ cup coconut
    pinch salt
½ teaspoon vanilla

Method: Beat egg whites and salt together till they hold their shape. Add sugar gradually, beating all the time till smooth and stiff. Stir in vanilla.

Pour coconut filling into shell, cover with swirls of meringue and sprinkle the remaining ½ cup coconut on top. Bake in 210°C (425°F) oven for 5–6 minutes or till meringue is lightly browned.

GERMAN PLUM TART

1 cup flour
¼ cup sugar
½ cup ground almonds
1 heaped teaspoon cocoa
1 level teaspoon cinnamon
  pinch salt

Method: Rub or grate in 75 g (3 oz) butter. Knead into a dough with 1 slightly beaten egg. Grease a 22 cm (9-inch) diameter pie dish and line with the pastry.

Combine 2 tablespoons cinnamon sugar and 1 tablespoon ground almonds and sprinkle this mixture over the base of the pastry.

Use either:
1 kilo (2 lb) fresh pitted prune plums or
2 x 425 g tins drained Satsuma plums
Place over pastry in a circular pattern.

Dot with 1 tablespoon butter, sprinkle with 1 tablespoon cinnamon and sugar and bake in 200°C (400°F) oven for 15 minutes. Remove from oven and pour over custard given below:

Combine 150 mℓ (¾ cup) sour cream with 1 slightly beaten egg. Return to oven for another 10–15 minutes.

GRAPE TART

Prepare basic tart dough and bake blind in 190°C (375°F) oven for 15 minutes then remove the paper and bake another 10–15 minutes or till golden brown.

Filling:
1 vanilla instant pudding
¾ cup milk
¾ cup cream
1 dessertspoon brandy

Method: Pour milk and cream into a bowl, sprinkle over instant pudding and beat till thick. Lastly stir in brandy. Pour into cooled pastry shell and place the grapes in a circular pattern, alternating rows of black and green, over this. Brush over the grapes with the following glaze:
1 cup orange juice
2 dessertspoons red jelly powder
1 dessertspoon maizena
2 tablespoons sugar

Method: Boil orange juice and sugar, add jelly and thicken with maizena mixed to a paste with a little cold water. Allow to cool in refrigerator a while before using.

Decorate tart with whipped cream.

GROUND ALMOND TART

125 g butter (4 oz)
2 tablespoons oil
1 beaten egg
  pinch salt
2 tablespoons castor sugar
½ teaspoon vanilla
2 cups flour
2 teaspoons baking powder

Method: Cream the butter and sugar. Add the oil and vanilla and mix thoroughly. Add the beaten egg and then lastly, the sifted dry ingredients. Press into a 22 or 25 cm (9 or 10-inches) pyrex dish or spring-form pan.

Filling:
125 g butter (4 oz)
2 eggs
½ cup ground almonds
⅔ cup castor sugar
½ teaspoon almond essence
½ cup crushed marie biscuits

Method: Cream the butter and sugar well. Add the egg yolks and beat well. Stir in the almond essence, ground almonds and marie biscuits. Beat the egg whites stiffly then fold into the mixture.

Pour into pastry shell and bake in a 180°C (350°F) oven, middle shelf, 25–30 minutes. Whilst hot, pour over a glaze made of icing sugar and cold water, decorate round the edge with flaked almonds, and place a few cherries in the centre of the tart.

GUAVA TART À LA COCONUT CREAM

2 cups flour
1 egg
50 g margarine (2 oz)
1 teaspoon baking powder
125 g butter (4 oz)
2 tablespoons sugar
2 large tins guavas (2 x 450 g)

Method: Sift dry ingredients. Rub or grate in the butter and margarine, then knead into a dough with the slightly beaten egg. Roll out and line a 22 or 25 cm (9 or 10-inch) diameter pyrex dish. Bake blind for 15 minutes in a 180°C (350°F) oven. Remove paper and bake for a further 10–15 minutes or till nicely browned.

Drain the guavas very well, reserving the juice and scoop out the pips. Place the juice in a saucepan and thicken with 1 dessertspoon maizena mixed to a paste with a little cold water. Remove from heat and allow to cool. Brush a thin coating of the glaze evenly over the inside of the baked pastry case. Place the guavas in a circular pattern on the pastry, face down, slightly overlapping the halves so that the pastry is completely covered. Brush a little more of the glaze over the guavas and return to the oven for 10 minutes.

Coconut cream sauce:
¾ cup sugar
1½ cups cream
6 egg yolks
1½ tablespoons rum
⅞ cup water
1½ cups coarsely chopped or dessicated coconut
½ teaspoon vanilla

Method: Scald cream and place in liquidiser with coconut. Blend for a few minutes then pour into strainer lined with cheesecloth or muslin and squeeze the cloth to extract as much juice as possible. Place sugar and water in a saucepan, stir till dissolved. Allow to boil to soft ball stage. Remove from heat and pour in coconut cream in a thin slow stream, stirring constantly.

Beat egg yolks till light and creamy. Slowly add the coconut cream and then place in top of double boiler and cook until mixture has thickened or has the consistency of thick cream. Remove from heat and add vanilla and rum. Refrigerate sauce for at least 2 hours before serving. Can be stored in the fridge for a week.

LEMON MERINGUE TART

Use basic tart dough. Bake blind till golden brown.

Filling:
¼ cup maizena
1 cup sugar

⅓ cup lemon juice
1 tablespoon butter (25 g)
3 eggs separated
½ cup cold milk
1 cup hot milk
½ teaspoon finely grated lemon rind

Meringue:
3 egg whites
4 tablespoons sugar

Method: Mix maizena, sugar, pinch of salt and cold milk in the top of a double boiler. Add hot milk and cook till thick. Beat egg yolks till light and creamy. Add the hot mixture slowly to the egg yolks, beating all the time as you do so. Return the mixture to the double boiler and cook for a further 5 minutes. Stir in or add lemon juice, butter and rind. If too thin, cook a little longer. Pour into baked shell. Cool for 10 minutes and then cover with meringue made by beating the egg whites till stiff and gradually adding the sugar. Bake in 180°C (350°F) oven for 10–12 minutes or till lightly browned.

LINZERTORTE

1½ cups flour
¾ cup sugar
175 g butter (6 oz)
1¼ cups ground almonds
2 heaped teaspoons cocoa
  pinch salt
1 egg

Method: Sift all dry ingredients. Rub or grate in butter and then add slightly beaten egg. Roll out onto floured board and place in greased and floured small swiss roll tin 35 x 25 cm (14 x 10-inches). Do not use all the dough, leave some for the top. Spread thickly with Satsuma plum jam. Roll out balance of dough and cut into strips, then place diagonally both ways to form a criss-cross pattern. Sprinkle with chopped almonds and bake 180°C (350°F) oven for 45 minutes. When cool, sprinkle with icing sugar if desired.

PEACH KUCHEN

175 g butter (6 oz)
½ cup sugar
2 teaspoons baking powder
1½ cups flour
  pinch salt
1 large tin drained peach slices (897 g)
1 egg yolk
3 tablespoons thick cream
1 tablespoon sugar
4 tablespoons brown sugar
1 tablespoon butter (25 g)
1 teaspoon cinnamon

Method: Sift flour, baking powder, sugar and salt, then rub in butter to form a dough. Press into slightly greased pyrex dish and then place the very well drained peach slices in a circular pattern on the pastry. Sprinkle with the brown sugar, dot with the tablespoon of butter and dust with cinnamon. Bake at 190°C (375°F) in oven for 10 minutes, reduce heat to 180°C (350°F) and continue baking for another 15–20 minutes. Remove from oven. Blend egg yolk, cream and 1 tablespoon sugar, spoon over tart and return to oven for 5–8 minutes or till custard sets. Serve at room temperature.

QUICK DOUBLE CHOCOLATE TART

6 eggs separated
75 g butter (3 oz)
200 g dark chocolate (8 oz)
¾ cup sugar
100 g walnuts chopped (1 packet 4 oz)

Method: Melt chocolate in double boiler without stirring. Remove from stove and add butter. Beat egg yolks and sugar till light and creamy then beat in chocolate mixture. Lastly fold in stiffly beaten egg whites, and nuts. Pour half the mixture into a well greased round 22 cm (9-inch) diameter pyrex dish and bake in 180°C (350°F) oven for twenty minutes. Remove and allow to cool. The tart will sink, during cooling. When completely cool, top with the remaining chocolate mixture and chill for one day before using.

RHUBARB CREAM PIE

Pastry:
125 g butter (4 oz)
50 g margarine (2 oz)
2 teaspoons baking powder
   pinch salt
1 egg, slightly beaten
1½ cups flour
½ cup sugar
½ teaspoon cinnamon

Method: Sift dry ingredients. Rub or grate in butter and margarine, add egg. Form into dough, chill for approximately 20 minutes. Press into greased and floured dish.

Filling:
1 very large tin rhubarb (± 1 kilo)
1 tin pie apples (410 g)
1 tablespoon sugar
1 teaspoon lemon juice

Method: Combine these ingredients, spoon into pastry shell (no juice). Bake at 180°C (350°F) for 15 minutes. Remove from oven and pour over custard, made as follows:

Custard cream:
3 egg yolks
1 teaspoon vanilla
1 tablespoon maizena
¾ cup milk
1½ dessertspoons sugar
¾ cup cream

Method: Beat yolks and sugar till light and fluffy. Add vanilla and maizena. Scald milk and cream, add to egg mixture beating all the time. Pour into double boiler. Cook until thick. Pour over rhubarb and apple, return to the oven to bake a further 20–30 minutes.

TART À LA FLORENTINE

175 g butter (6 oz)
1 egg
1 tablespoon oil
2½ cups flour
½ cup sugar
1 teaspoon baking powder
¼ teaspoon salt

Method: Cream butter and sugar. Add egg and oil and beat a little longer. Add sifted dry ingredients. Press into a greased and floured swiss roll tin, 35 x 25 cm (14 x 10-inch) pressing the dough well up the sides of the pan to form a ridge. Prick all over and bake in 180°C (350°F) oven till golden brown 10–15 minutes. Cool thoroughly. Melt 100 g (4 oz) slab bitter chocolate in a double boiler, without stirring and spread in a thick layer over the biscuit crust. Allow to set hard, preferably in fridge.

Topping:
½ cup chopped glacé cherries, red and green
½ cup candied peel
¾ cup cake mix (i.e. sultanas, raisins, currants etc.)
1 packet shredded almonds (100 g)

½ cup flour
1 teaspoon lemon juice
1 tablespoon syrup
125 g butter (4 oz)
¼ cup sugar

Method: Combine the cherries, candied peel, cake mix and almonds, with the flour. Melt the butter, sugar, syrup and lemon juice in a saucepan. Stir in the fruit and flour mixture. Spread over the hardened chocolate and place in a 160°C (325°F) oven for a further 25 minutes. Cool thoroughly before removing from tin. Invert onto large tray and then back again onto serving platter.

11. SMALL CAKES & BISCUITS

AMBROSIA JIFFY CAKES

2⅔ cups flour
4 teaspoons baking powder
1 teaspoon cinnamon
125 g margarine (4 oz)
25 g butter (1 oz)
½ cup milk
   finely grated rind of 1 orange
   pinch salt
1 teaspoon mixed spice
1¼ cups sugar
2 eggs
½ cup orange juice

Topping:
75 g butter (3 oz)
2 cups dessicated coconut
¾ cup finely chopped orange pulp
1 cup brown sugar
   finely grated rind of one orange

Method: Sift flour with baking powder, salt and spices. Cream the margarine and butter with the sugar and orange rind, until fluffy. Add eggs and beat till well blended. Combine milk and orange juice and add flour mixture alternately with liquid, beginning and ending with flour. Grease and flour muffin tins and fill each with mixture until ½ full. Bake in moderate oven at 180°C (350°F) for 15–20 minutes or until golden brown. To make *ambrosia topping*, melt butter and brown sugar. Add orange rind, orange pulp and coconut and mix till well blended. Spread the mixture generously over baked cakes, turn the oven onto *grill* and place under broiler on the middle shelf of the oven. Grill in this manner until topping bubbles and coconut starts to brown.

BAKLAVA

750 g Phyllo pastry (1½ lb)
375 g melted butter (¾ lb)
250 g finely chopped walnuts or almonds (½ lb)
½ cup dry breadcrumbs
¼ cup sugar
1 teaspoon cinnamon
½ teaspoon ground cloves

Syrup:
2 cups sugar
1 cup water
   juice of ½ lemon

Method: Place 8 layers of phyllo pastry in a buttered rectangular pyrex dish or baking pan, brushing with melted butter between each layer. Mix together walnuts or almonds, breadcrumbs, sugar, cinnamon and cloves. Sprinkle top pastry sheet thickly with nut mixture, place two buttered sheets over this and repeat in this manner until the ingredients have been used up, ending with 8–10 pastry sheets. Brush top with remaining butter and trim edges. Cut diagonal lines to make diamond shaped pieces. Bake in 180°C (350°F) oven for 1 hour or until deep golden brown. Boil sugar, water and lemon juice for 10 minutes. Pour hot syrup over cooled baklava.

MERCIA'S RICH FEATHERLIGHT BUNS

10 cups flour
1½ cups sugar
4 eggs + 2 yolks
1 small tin evaporated milk (115 g)
250 mℓ thick cream (½ pint), if not thick, whip up
1½ cups lukewarm water
250 g butter (½ lb)
125 g margarine (4 oz)
4 tablespoons oil
2½ cakes yeast (50 g)
2 level teaspoons salt

Method: Liquify the yeast by placing in a small bowl and rubbing with 2 teaspoons sugar. Add 1 tablespoon lukewarm water and allow to stand in a warm place for 5–10 minutes. Meanwhile mix together the dry ingredients and make a well in the centre. Add the eggs and yolks, evaporated milk, cream, oil, melted butter and margarine, lukewarm water and the yeast liquid. Mix all together by hand and then knead in the mixmaster till smooth. If the quantity is too large for your mixmaster, divide into two and knead half at a time.

Place the mixture in a large bowl or pot, cover with a clean cloth, then wrap in a blanket and leave in warm draught free place to rise overnight. The following day, roll out 3 cm (1-inch) thick onto a lightly floured board, spread with melted butter, sprinkle with cinnamon and sugar and washed dried fruit, cut and form into shapes and then leave to rise in a warm place for another hour or two, till double in bulk and light and spongy to the touch. Paint with beaten egg, sprinkle with streusel and bake in a moderately hot oven, 180°–190°C (350°–375°F) for 15–20 minutes or till nicely browned.

Special hint: When working with yeast, it is most important that all liquids be only just lukewarm and also that the yeast dough is kept out of a draught; in the winter the buns may be placed in front of a heater and left there to rise. In summer, it is not necessary to cover mixture with a blanket, in fact it could be left in a large airtight container in the fridge till about midnight and then taken out and baked early in the morning. Mon and cheese filled buns can be baked in oiled patty tins. Sprinkle mon with streusel and cheese with cinnamon and sugar. The buns freeze beautifully, but must be warmed before serving.

Fillings for buns:
Mon (Poppy seed)
$1\frac{1}{2}$ cups poppy seeds ($\frac{1}{2}$ lb)
1 cup sugar
$\frac{1}{2}$ cup currants or sultanas
50 g butter (2 oz)
2 tablespoons honey
$\frac{1}{2}$ teaspoon cinnamon
$\frac{1}{2}$ cup milk

Method: Soak poppy seed in water overnight. Boil and throw all water off. Do this 2 or 3 times, until clean. Strain, place in a saucepan with the sugar, milk, honey, butter and cinnamon and cook on medium heat until thick. Add currants and allow to cool. You may mince the mixture if you want to but it is not absolutely necessary.

Almond paste filling:
$\frac{1}{3}$–$\frac{1}{2}$ cup sugar
1 egg
$\frac{1}{2}$ teaspoon almond essence
1 tablespoon milk
125 g ground almonds (4 oz)
3 tablespoons crushed marie biscuits

Method: Mix all ingredients together till smooth.

Cheese filling:
250 g cream cheese (8 oz)
1 egg
2–3 tablespoons sugar
1 level tablespoon flour
2 tablespoons cream

Method: Mix all ingredients together till smooth.

Streusel:
$\frac{3}{4}$ cup flour
2 tablespoons sugar
50 g butter (2 oz)

Method: Rub all ingredients together with fingertips, to form crumbs.

QUICK & EASY CINNAMON BUNS

2 cups flour
125 g butter (4 oz)
  pinch salt
3 teaspoons baking powder
1 tablespoon sugar
1 egg beaten in cup and filled with milk and cream, or just milk

Method: Sift dry ingredients, rub or grate in butter with fingers, and add egg mixture. Knead lightly. Roll out rectangular shape, spread with melted butter, cinnamon and sugar, roll up like swiss roll, slice, 3 cm (1 inch) thick and place in greased and floured patty tins. Brush top with more melted butter, sprinkle with cinnamon and sugar. Bake for 15 minutes in moderate oven 200°C (400°F).

CREAM HORNS

2½ cups flour
250 g butter (½ lb)
1 cup sour cream (250 ml)

Method: Rub butter into flour and make into a dough with the cream. Refrigerate overnight. Roll the dough into a rectangle and then cut into strips about 2cm (¾-inch) wide. Brush the one side of the strip with egg white and then roll around a well-greased baking cone. Place on a greased and floured tin and bake in 180°C (350°F) oven till light brown then remove cone and allow to dry out in the oven for a further 5–10 minutes. Fill with custard, jam and cream or fruit and cream. Dust with icing sugar.

MERCIA'S DANISH PASTRIES
(Even the Danish don't make them so good)

5 cups flour
2 cakes yeast (40 g)
1 cup milk
2 eggs, beaten
½ teaspoon finely grated lemon rind
¾ cup sugar
¾ cup lukewarm water
25 g butter (1 oz)
1 teaspoon salt
1 teaspoon vanilla
500 g (1 lb) chilled unsalted butter

Method: Liquify the yeast with 1 teaspoon sugar and then stir in a little of the measured lukewarm water. Cover and set aside.

Place remaining water, milk and butter in a saucepan and heat till butter has melted then allow to cool to lukewarm.

Sift flour, salt and sugar, make a well in the centre and add yeast mixture, milk/water/butter mixture, eggs, vanilla and lemon rind. Mix together to form a soft dough and then knead on a lightly floured board or in mixmaster for 10 minutes. Place in a bowl, cover with a damp cloth and allow to stand for 30 minutes. Remove butter from fridge, place in between plastic wrap and with a heavy rolling pin beat until pliable and 1 cm (¼ of an inch) thick. Roll dough into a rectangle, place butter on lower ⅔ of dough, leave a border of pastry around the butter, so that you can seal the butter inside the dough.

Fold the unbuttered third of the dough to the middle, bring the bottom third of the dough to the middle, complete with butter and seal edges by pressing firmly with rolling pin, three times one way and two the other, this distributes air evenly.

Turn the dough so that the fold is on your right, roll out to even thickness. Fold in three, seal, turn and roll out again as before. Repeat three or four times allowing dough to rest for 20 minutes in between rolling and folding. Place in plastic bag and leave in fridge overnight. Make into shapes and leave to rise for 30 minutes before baking. Bake in 180°C (350°F) oven for 15–20 minutes.

Almond filling:
½ packet ground almonds (55 g)
1 dessertspoon icing sugar
2 crushed marie biscuits
2 dessertspoons castor sugar
1 beaten egg
½ teaspoon almond essence

Method: Mix all the ingredients together.

Thick custard:
2 cups milk
2½ tablespoons custard powder
2 tablespoons sugar

Method: Mix custard powder with a little of the measured milk. Boil the rest with the sugar, pour over custard mixture, stirring vigorously. Return to low heat, stirring continuously until it thickens.

Pineapple custard filling: Grate 1 large pineapple. Boil together for 5 minutes with ½ cup sugar and ½ cup water. Remove from stove and stir in 2 tablespoons, custard powder, mixed to a paste with water. Return to stove till it thickens.

Use jam with custard and almond filling. Can also use pie apples and after baking glaze with melted apricot jam and water.

DOUGHNUTS

1¼ cups milk
½ cup sugar
1 teaspoon salt
1 cake yeast (20 g)
125 g butter (4 oz)
2 eggs
4½ cups flour

Method: Place milk and butter, sugar and salt in a saucepan and heat till butter and sugar have dissolved. Allow to cool to lukewarm. Liquify the yeast by mixing together with 2 teaspoons sugar and then add 1 tablespoon lukewarm water and allow to stand 10 minutes. Beat eggs in a separate bowl and set aside.

Sift flour, make a well in the centre. Add butter, milk mixture, eggs and yeast and use another tablespoon lukewarm water to rinse out the yeast bowl. Mix by hand till blended, then knead in mixmaster till smooth. Place in a large bowl or airtight container, cover with cloth and leave to rise till double in bulk or overnight.

Roll out dough about 1 cm (½ inch) thick, on a lightly floured board. Cut out with doughnut cutter. Can cut out little rounds, 5 cm (2 inches) in diameter as well. Leave to rise till spongy. Fry in hot oil and roll in castor sugar or pour over creamy cocoa frosting. The round can be split partly and filled with strawberry jam and whipped cream.

CREAMY COCOA FROSTING FOR DOUGHNUTS

25 g butter (1 oz)
½ teaspoon vanilla
1½ tablespoons cocoa
1½ cups icing sugar
1 tablespoon strong coffee

Method: Blend all together by hand till smooth, adding more boiling water if necessary to acquire the right consistency.

ECLAIRS

125 g butter (4 oz)
1 heaped cup flour (125 g)
1 cup water (250 ml)
4 eggs

Method: Bring water and butter to boil. Quickly stir in flour till mixture leaves the sides of the saucepan. Beat in eggs, one at a time, beating well after each addition. Drop by teaspoonsful or pipe onto a greased or floured baking sheet and bake 15–20 minutes in 180°C (350°F) oven, then turn oven off and leave another 10–15 minutes to dry out.

If you wish to make swans, then using a plain icing nozzle, pipe a few S-shapes for the head. It is very effective to serve these swans on a large mirror with lilies placed in between. Pour over a chocolate glaze or dust with icing.

Chocolate glaze: Melt 2 tablespoons butter with 2 tablespoons cocoa. Blend $1\frac{1}{2}$ cups icing sugar with 1 unbeaten egg white then add to the butter cocoa mixture and stir over heat till smooth and shiny.

MELT-IN-THE-MOUTH ASSORTED TARTLETS

125 g butter (4 oz)
50 g margarine (2 oz)
1 tablespoon cream of Wheat or Semolina
$1\frac{3}{4}$ cups flour
1 tablespoon maizena
2 tablespoons sugar
1 egg
1 level teaspoon baking powder

Method: Sift dry ingredients. Rub or grate in butter. Beat egg slightly and add to form a dough. Roll out onto a floured board. Cut into rounds. Place in greased and floured patty tins. Fill with any of the following:

First Filling: Washed dried *fruit* mixed with a little smooth apricot jam and brandy. Sprinkle with nuts or grate a little dough on top.

Second Filling: Fill with *jam* and top with *coconut* filling made by beating 3 egg whites with $\frac{2}{3}$ cup sugar, then stir in 2 cups dessicated coconut and 1 teaspoon vanilla.

Third Filling: Fill with sweetened stewed *apples*. Sprinkle with cinnamon and sugar and decorate with strips of dough placed in a lattice pattern on top.

Fourth Filling: Bake blind. Fill with vanilla instant pudding prepared with $\frac{3}{4}$ cup cream and $\frac{3}{4}$ cup milk. Stir in 1 tablespoon brandy. Top with fresh strawberries, gooseberries or tinned fruit and pipe rosettes of cream on top. Can make a glaze by melting $\frac{1}{2}$ cup jam with juice of half a lemon. Cool and spoon or brush over fruit.

Pecan Pies: Mix together 1 beaten egg with $\frac{3}{4}$ cup brown sugar and $2\frac{1}{2}$ tablespoons melted butter. Stir in $\frac{3}{4}$ cup chopped pecans and $\frac{1}{2}$ a teaspoon vanilla. Enough filling for 24 tartlets.

N.B. To use all the fillings, make double the quantity of dough.

ORANGE CHOCOLATE SQUARES

125 g butter (4 oz)
$\frac{3}{4}$ cup sugar
$\frac{3}{4}$ cup milk
$\frac{1}{4}$ teaspoon salt
$1\frac{1}{2}$ cups flour
2 teaspoons baking powder
2 tablespoons cocoa
2 eggs
$\frac{1}{2}$ teaspoon vanilla

Method: Cream the butter. Add all the remaining ingredients and beat well for

3 minutes. Pour into greased and floured 20–22 cm (8 or 9-inch) square tin. Bake 180°C (350°F) for 25–30 minutes. When cool, ice with the following

1½ cups icing sugar
1½ tablespoons orange juice
2 tablespoons butter

Method: Cream the butter and sugar very well. Add the orange juice. Cover the top of the cake only. Mark into squares with a fork. Place a cherry or nut onto each square and cut up, or leave whole if you prefer.

PETIT FOURS

125 g butter (4 oz)
2 eggs
1½ cups flour
  pinch salt
1 teaspoon cream of tartar
¾ cup sugar
¼ cup milk
½ teaspoon bicarbonate of soda

Method: Grease and flour an 20 cm (8-inch) square baking tin. Cream butter and sugar very well. Add the eggs, one at a time, beating well after each addition. Dissolve bicarb in milk and add to mixture. Sift in the flour, salt and cream of tartar and beat very well. Spread the mixture evenly in tin and bake 180°C (375°F) oven for about 20–25 minutes. When cold, cut into shapes, rounds, ovals, squares, triangles, etc. and coat with fondant frosting. Decorate with fancy piping of butter cream icing, bits of cherry, nuts, chocolate or coloured jubes.

Fondant frosting:
2 cups sugar
⅔ cup water
⅛ teaspoon cream of tartar
1 teaspoon glycerine

Method: Heat ingredients (except glycerine), slowly and stir until sugar has dissolved. When mixture begins to boil, add glycerine and then cover the pan and cook without stirring, until a small amount forms a soft ball, when dropped in cold water. Pour onto a lightly oiled swiss roll pan and cool until firm enough to retain a dent when pressed lightly. Fold mixture over and over with a spatula until cool enough to handle, then knead until smooth and creamy. Form into a ball and place in a glass jar, sealed and leave for 24 hours before using. When ready to use, melt fondants in small amounts over hot, not boiling, water, flavour and colour very delicately.

Chocolate: Add 50 g chocolate (2 oz), melted, to fondant, when kneading.

Coffee: Use strong coffee instead of water.

Quick tip: For a smooth coating, glaze shapes with melted apricot jam, mixed with 1 dessertspoon lemon juice and 1 dessertspoon water. Pour over petit fours. Allow to set then pour over fondant icing.

PITIKAS

1 tea cup water
  pinch bicarb
1 coffee cup oil
  approximately 2½ cups flour

Method: Sift flour and bicarb. Make a well in the centre and add the oil and water. Stir until blended and then knead till smooth. Roll into balls the size of a marble. Roll out the balls *very thinly*, cut into diamond shapes and fry in hot oil till golden brown. Drain well on absorbent paper. To serve, drizzle syrup or honey over and sprinkle with ground almonds and a little cinnamon if desired.

Special hint: Pitikas freeze beautifully and take just a few minutes to thaw. Drizzle with honey just before serving.

PRALINE NUT SQUARES

5 eggs
¾ cup sugar
1 teaspoon brandy or rum
1 teaspoon cinnamon
1 heaped cup finely minced hazel nuts (125 g)
1 heaped cup flour
2 teaspoons baking powder

Method: Beat eggs very well. Add sugar and beat again till very light and creamy. Sift the flour and cinnamon and add this and the nuts to the mixture, folding in lightly with a spatula. Add the brandy or rum and lastly fold in the baking powder. Pour into well-greased and floured square baking tin 22–25 cms (9-inch or 10-inch). Bake in 180°C (350°F) oven for 30–35 minutes. Cool and cut into squares. Cut each square through the middle and sandwich and ice with the following.

Chocolate filling:
2 egg yolks
1 tablespoon brandy
½ cup castor sugar
100 g (4 oz) bitter chocolate
250 g (½ lb) butter, creamed
¼ cup milk
1 dessertspoon rum

Method: Dissolve ¼ cup castor sugar in milk on the stove. Beat egg yolks very well. Add the balance of the castor sugar and beat again. Pour milk mixture onto egg yolks beating continuously till cooled. Beat in the creamed butter a little at a time. Melt chocolate with brandy and rum, stir till smooth, allow to cool, add to mixture then set in fridge before using.

Make the praline: by melting 1 cup sugar in a saucepan. Add ½ cup flaked or shredded almonds. Stir well then pour onto a well oiled biscuit tray and allow to cool completely. Crush with a rolling pin and use to decorate the sides of the squares.

VIENNESE BROWNIES

250 g cream cheese (8 oz), if it gets too thin, add 1 dessertspoon maizena
⅓ cup sugar
1 egg
¼ teaspoon almond extract
8 squares bitter chocolate (55 g)
125 g butter (4 oz)
2 eggs
½ cup sugar
1 cup flour
1 teaspoon baking powder
½ teaspoon salt
Sliced almonds

Method: Combine softened cream cheese, sugar, egg and almond extract. Melt chocolate and butter. Cool. Beat eggs, add sugar and chocolate mixture. Sift together flour baking powder and salt. Add to chocolate mixture and mix well. Pour half of chocolate mixture into greased 20 cm (8-inch) square pan, spread with cream cheese mixture. Top with remaining batter. Sprinkle with almonds. Bake at 180° (350°F) for 45 minutes. Cut into squares when cool.

WHITE TEIGLACH

3 eggs + 3 yolks
¼ cup oil
3 rounded teaspoons baking powder
1 dessertspoon ginger

½ cup sugar
2½ cups flour
500 g (1 lb) mixed fruit, pour over 2 tablespoons brandy

For the syrup:
3 cups sugar
4 teaspoons ginger
1 cup water

Method: Beat the eggs and yolks with the sugar till light and creamy. Add the oil and beat again, just a little. Add the sifted flour, baking powder and ginger. Roll out onto a floured board and sprinkle with the mixed fruit and brandy (you may add some red and green cherries as well). Roll up like a swiss roll, cut off little pieces and roll into a ball. Place on a greased and floured biscuit tray and bake in a slow oven about 160°C (325°F) approximately 15 minutes. They must not be too brown. Prepare the syrup by placing the sugar, water and ginger in a large shallow roasting pan, over two plates, if necessary. Boil till bubbly. Place teiglach in the syrup and boil for 3–4 minutes, making sure that they are all glazed. Remove from syrup and place on a big baking tray and pour the remaining syrup over.

Special hint: If you do not want them too sugary remove from syrup after 3 minutes. The glaze will only become apparent as they cool.

BISCUITS

CORNFLAKE KISSES

4 egg whites
1 cup sugar
1 cup coconut
pinch salt
½ teaspoon vanilla
3 cups cornflakes
1 cup chopped nuts

Method: Heat oven to 120°C (250°F). Beat egg whites with salt till stiff. Gradually beat in sugar. Fold in vanilla, coconut, nuts and cornflakes. Drop by spoonfuls onto greased tray. Bake 15–20 minutes.

BRANDY SNAPS

2 tablespoons flour, heaped
½ teaspoon ginger
2 tablespoons butter
¼ teaspoon lemon rind or juice
2 tablespoons syrup
2 tablespoons sugar
2 teaspoons brandy

Method: Melt butter, sugar, syrup together in a saucepan. Stir in sifted flour and ginger, then add lemon rind or juice and brandy. Pour mixture in very small dabs on a greased tin. Bake 10 minutes in 180°C (350°F) oven. Roll around handle of wooden spoon. If they harden, replace in oven for a few seconds till they soften. Store in a tin or glass jar and fill with whipped cream a few minutes before serving. Dust with icing sugar.

AUNT CELIE'S FRUIT SLICES

3 cups flour
1 dessertspoon custard powder
2 teaspoons baking powder
   pinch salt
1 cup sugar
250 g butter (½ lb)
1 teaspoon vanilla
2 eggs

Method: Sift dry ingredients. Rub or grate in butter. Add slightly beaten egg with vanilla. If desired add a little cream. Roll out, spread with apricot jam, sprinkle with washed dried fruit and nuts (optional). Roll up like swiss roll. Brush top with beaten egg and sprinkle with coconut. Bake 180°C (350°F) oven 15–20 minutes or till lightly browned. Cut into diagonal slices whilst hot.

CINNAMON SHORTBREAD

500 g butter (1 lb)
12 tablespoons sugar
1 dessertspoon mixed spice
$3\frac{1}{2}$–4 cups flour
4 egg yolks
1 dessertspoon cinnamon

Method: Cream butter and sugar. Add egg yolks and then sifted dry ingredients. Press into greased and floured swiss roll tin. Brush with egg white. Mark into squares, press an almond or cherry into the centre of each square. Bake 160°C (325°F) oven for approximately 40 minutes. Cut into squares whilst hot. Cool and remove from tin.

CRUNCHY CHOCOLATE NUT BALLS

175 g butter (6 oz)
1 teaspoon vanilla
2 tablespoons cocoa
1 box nutties, hazelnuts (optional)
$\frac{3}{4}$ cup sugar
$1\frac{1}{4}$ cups flour
1 cup cornflakes, crushed
  chocolate vermicelli
  melted chocolate

Method: Cream butter and sugar. Add vanilla, then blend in sifted flour and cocoa. Lastly add crushed cornflakes. Form into small balls. Press a nutty into the centre. Place on greased biscuit tray and bake 180°C (350°F) oven 15–20 minutes. Allow to cool and harden. Dip the top into melted chocolate and then chocolate vermicelli.

CURLED PECAN WAFERS

50 g butter (2 oz)
1 egg
$\frac{1}{3}$ cup very finely chopped pecan nuts
  pinch salt
$\frac{1}{2}$ cup brown sugar
1 tablespoon flour
$\frac{1}{4}$ teaspoon cinnamon

Method: Melt butter and sugar until sugar has partly dissolved. Cool. Quickly stir in egg and then add the sifted dry ingredients. Drop by teaspoonful on a thickly greased biscuit tray. Bake in 160°C (325°F) oven, centre shelf, for 7–10 minutes. Roll around the handle of a wooden spoon. If biscuits become too crisp to handle, return to the oven for a while till they soften. Cool and store in a glass jar. Before serving fill with whipped cream or with a chocolate cream made by beating 250 mℓ (1 cup) cream, with 2 tablespoons sugar. Stir in by hand, 1 tablespoon cocoa, 1 tablespoon drinking chocolate, $\frac{3}{4}$ teaspoon coffee.

CUSTARD BISCUITS

175 g butter (6 oz)
$1\frac{1}{4}$ cups flour
$\frac{1}{2}$ cup icing sugar
$\frac{3}{4}$ cup custard powder

Method: Cream butter and icing sugar very well. Add sifted flour and custard powder.

Roll into little balls the size of a marble, and place on greased and floured biscuit tray. Press with a fork dipped in icing sugar. Bake 180°C (350°F) oven 10–12 minutes or till very slightly browned. Bake on centre shelf. When cool, sandwich together with bitter chocolate, which has been melted in the top of a double boiler. You may roll the sides in hundreds and thousands.

FLORENTINES

$\frac{1}{2}$ cup chopped glaze cherries, red, green and yellow
$\frac{1}{4}$ cup mixed peel
1 teaspoon lemon juice
$\frac{3}{4}$ cup chopped almonds
$\frac{1}{2}$ cup chopped sultanas
$\frac{1}{2}$ cup flour
1 slab bitter chocolate (100 g)
$\frac{1}{4}$ cup sugar
125 g (4 oz) butter
1 tablespoon syrup
rice paper

Method: Combine the cherries, mixed peel, almonds and sultanas. Sprinkle the flour over and mix together. Melt the butter, sugar, syrup and lemon juice in a saucepan. Stir in the fruit and flour mixture. Drop by teaspoonfuls onto a biscuit tray covered with rice paper. Bake in 160°C (325°F) oven until the edges start to brown. When cool, ice the undersides with the melted chocolate and make wavy patterns with a fork. Allow to set before storing in cake tin.

Special hint: If you do not have rice paper you may make florentine squares by melting the chocolate (150 g) for this, and spread into the bottom of a well oiled 22–25 cm (9 or 10-inch) square tin. Allow to set thoroughly. Spread florentine mixture on top and bake in 160°C (325°F) oven 35–40 minutes. Cool and set in fridge. Cut into squares when cold. The squares will easily come clean out of the tin.

GINGER BISCUITS

125 g butter ($\frac{1}{4}$ lb)
1 cup sugar
1 tablespoon syrup
1 teaspoon cinnamon
finely grated rind of 1 orange
2 teaspoons ginger
$3\frac{1}{2}$ cups flour
$\frac{3}{4}$ teaspoon bicarbonate of soda
1 teaspoon baking powder
2 eggs
1 teaspoon mixed spice
2 teaspoons ginger
$\frac{1}{2}$ cup sultanas

Method: Cream butter and sugar. Add eggs, syrup, orange rind and sifted dry ingredients with enough flour to make a soft dough. Fold in sultanas. Roll into long rolls and place on greased and floured biscuit tray. Flatten slightly with a fork and sprinkle with sugar. Bake 180°C (350°F) oven 15–20 minutes. Cut in diagonal slices whilst hot.

GINGER SNAPS

125 g butter ($\frac{1}{4}$ lb)
$\frac{3}{4}$ cup sugar
1 egg
1 dessertspoon syrup
1 teaspoon ginger
$1\frac{3}{4}$ cups flour
$\frac{1}{2}$ teaspoon mixed spice
$\frac{1}{2}$ teaspoon bicarb
$\frac{1}{2}$ teaspoon cream of tartar

Method: Cream butter and sugar. Beat egg slightly with fork and dissolve bicarb in it. Add to creamed mixture. Add syrup, sifted dry ingredients. Roll into little balls. Press an almond into the centre and bake at 180°C (350°F) for 15–20 minutes or till golden brown.

GROUND ALMOND BISCUITS

1½ cups flour
125 g butter (¼ lb)
½ cup castor sugar
 pinch salt
¼ cup ground almonds
1 egg yolk
1 teaspoon baking powder

Method: Cream butter and sugar. Add egg yolk and lastly sifted dry ingredients. Roll out and cut into rounds. Bake on greased and floured biscuit tray in 180°C (350°F) oven for 10–15 minutes. Sandwich together with jam and ice the top with butter icing or sprinkle with icing sugar.

CRISPY COOKIE MAKER BISCUITS

Method: Beat together 250 g (½ lb) butter and 1 cup of sugar. Add 6 tablespoons oil, 2 tablespoons at a time, and beat very well, then add 2 eggs. Add sifted dry ingredients: 4 cups flour, 2½ teaspoons baking powder and 1 cup dessicated coconut.

Press into shapes onto baking sheet and bake 180°C (350°F) oven 10–15 minutes.

JOSEPH'S MANDELBRODT

Joseph is an African who has been in my sister-in-law's employ for the last umpteen years and I have never tasted mandelbrodt like the ones he makes. This is his recipe.

250 g (yellow) margarine
1 packet castor sugar (500 g)
6 beaten eggs
3–4 tablespoons oil
4 teaspoons baking powder
6 cups flour, enough to be able to roll dough
100 g (4 oz) nibbed almonds

Method: Cream butter and sugar. Add oil and beaten eggs. Add sifted flour and baking powder. Then lastly add nibbed almonds. Roll dough out into a large rectangular shape. Cut into four strips lengthwise. Fold each strip in half, lengthwise. Bake on greased and floured tin for 10 minutes in 180°C (350°F) oven. Remove from oven and cut into slices then return to oven for a further 10 minutes till golden brown and crisp.

KOURIABIDES

500 g butter (1 lb)
2 egg yolks
1 tablespoon brandy
4½ cups flour
5 tablespoons castor sugar
2 teaspoons baking powder
125 g coarsely chopped toasted almonds

Method: Cream butter and sugar till very light and fluffy. Add yolks and brandy and beat again. Add sifted flour and baking powder and lastly add almonds. Roll out pieces on a lightly floured board into a long sausage, then cut in slices diagonally, about 4 cm (1½ inch) long, then place on greased and floured biscuit tray. Place a clove in the centre of each biscuit and bake in 180°C (350°F) oven till light golden brown. Remove from oven and sprinkle sieved icing sugar over the biscuits, whilst on the baking tray. When cool, place on a serving platter, building up layer upon layer in pyramid fashion and sprinkling with a thick layer of icing sugar between each layer.

MOCK TEIGLACH

250 g butter (½ lb)
1 egg, beaten
1 cup sugar
¼ cup or more chopped walnuts or pecans
250 g (8 oz) dates, cut up
1 packet marie biscuits
1½ teaspoon ginger

Method: Melt butter. Add sugar, nuts, dates and ginger and stir all the time for 3 minutes. Remove from stove. Add beaten egg very slowly and stir well. Return to stove for another 3 minutes stirring constantly. Lastly add broken marie biscuits. Remove from stove and cool. Roll into little balls and toss in dessicated coconut or coat with melted chocolate.

PEPPERMINT BROWNIES

125 g butter (4 oz)
1 cup brown sugar
50 g melted chocolate (2 oz)
½ cup chopped pecans
½ cup flour
  pinch salt
2 eggs
1 teaspoon vanilla

Method: Heat oven to 180°C (350°F). Cream butter and sugar. Add eggs and beat again. Sift flour with salt and add to mixture. Add chocolate, pecans and vanilla. Spread 1 cm (½ inch) thick in a 22 cm (9-inch) square tin. Bake 30 minutes. Whilst still warm, spread the following topping over.

1¾ cups icing sugar
50 g butter (2 oz)
  few drops peppermint essence
  few drops green colouring
  boiling water
100 g bitter chocolate (4 oz)

Method: Sift icing sugar. Make well in centre, add butter and little boiling water to make a nice spreading consistency. Add peppermint essence and colouring. Allow this topping to set and then melt the bitter chocolate, spread this over the peppermint icing. Sprinkle with crushed peppermint crisp and allow to set in fridge before cutting into small squares.

ROMANY CREAMS

125 g butter (4 oz)
¼ cup sugar
⅔ cup drinking chocolate or quick chocolate powder
2 egg yolks
1 tablespoon milk
1 teaspoon vanilla
1½ cups flour
1 teaspoon baking powder
  pinch salt
1 cup dessicated coconut
100 g melted chocolate

Method: Cream butter and sugar. Add egg yolks, milk and vanilla and beat well. Add sifted flour, baking powder, chocolate powder and salt. Mix well into mixture. Lastly add coconut.

Drop by teaspoonful onto greased and floured baking sheets. Bake 180°C (350°F) on centre shelf of oven for 12–15 minutes. Cool and sandwich together with a thick layer of melted chocolate.

THIMBLE BISCUITS

125 g butter (¼ lb)
1 heaped cup flour
½ teaspoon vanilla
¼ cup brown sugar
1 egg yolk
   pinch salt
   chopped nuts – preferably almonds
   apricot and Satsuma plum jam

Method: Cream together butter and sugar. Add egg yolk and vanilla. Sift flour and salt and add to mixture. Roll into little balls, the size of a marble. Dip into the remaining slightly beaten egg white. Roll in chopped nuts and then place on greased and floured tray about 2 cm (1 inch) apart. With the handle of a wooden spoon, make an indentation in each biscuit. Fill half the biscuits with apricot jam and the other half with the plum jam. Bake in 180°C (350°F) oven for 10–15 minutes. You may fill with more jam after baking if necessary.

SHORTBREAD

250 g butter (½ lb)
2½ cups flour
½ cup maizena
½ cup castor sugar
   pinch salt

Method: Cream butter and sugar very well. Add remaining sifted dry ingredients. Press into a greased and floured biscuit tray, prick with fork. Bake in 150°C (300°F) oven for 30 minutes and cut into fingers whilst hot. Dust with castor sugar.

Special Hint: Also nice baked in 25 cm (10 inch) round tray and cut into wedges when cool.

12. BREAD, WAFFLES & SCONES

RICH SCONES

2 cups flour
4 teaspoons baking powder
1 beaten egg
  pinch salt
75 g (3 oz) butter
1 tablespoon sugar
1 cup sour cream

Method: Sift dry ingredients. Cut in the butter with a knife or grate in. Add beaten egg and cream. Drop spoonfuls into patty tins and bake 200°C (400°F) for 10–15 minutes.

SCONES

$\frac{1}{3}$ cup oil
$\frac{2}{3}$ cup milk
3 teaspoons sugar
1 egg
2 cups flour
4 teaspoons baking powder

Method: Sift flour, salt and baking powder. Mix the egg with the oil and milk and add to the dry ingredients. Lastly stir in the sugar. Drop in greased and floured patty tins and bake in a hot oven 200°C (400°F) for 10–15 minutes.

POPPY SEED ONION SQUARES

2 cups flour
1 teaspoon dried yeast
1 teaspoon oil
1 cup warm water
1 teaspoon salt

Method: Place yeast in shallow bowl. Pour over warm water and allow to stand 10–15 minutes. *Do not stir.* Place unsifted flour in a large bowl and make a well in centre. Stir the oil and salt into the yeast mixture then pour into the well and mix till all the flour has been incorporated. Knead well until smooth, approximately 5 minutes, cover with a cloth and allow to stand in a warm place overnight or till doubled in bulk.

Topping:
2 medium onions sliced
2 tablespoons butter
1 egg yolk, slightly beaten
$\frac{1}{2}$ cup sour cream (125 ml)
$\frac{1}{2}$ teaspoon salt
2 tablespoons poppy seed

Method: Fry onion in butter till golden brown. Add remaining ingredients. Roll out dough and press into oiled swiss roll tin. Spoon over topping. Bake 200°C (400°F) oven 30–45 minutes. Cut into squares.

HERBED BREAD – WHOLEWHEAT OR WHITE

Bread:
20 g yeast (1 cake)
1 cup lukewarm water
1 teaspoon salt
1 tablespoon oil
1 dessertspoon sugar
1 cup cake flour
2 cups special brown bread mix or wholewheat flour (for white bread use 3 cups cake flour only)

Herb butter:
2–3 cloves crushed garlic
2–3 spring onions, diced
  handful chopped parsley
125 g creamed butter ($\frac{1}{4}$ lb)
1 teaspoon coarsely ground black pepper

Method: Add all ingredients to creamed butter.

Glaze: Mix together in a small bowl, 1 beaten egg and ½ teaspoon salt.

Method: Liquify yeast by mashing with sugar stir in warm water. Set aside.

Place cake flour, special brown bread mixture and salt in mixmaster bowl. Add yeast mixture and oil and knead with dough hook for a few minutes. Rinse out yeast bowl with an additional tablespoon warm water and add to dough; knead in. Dough should be sticky but not wet.

Pat dough into smooth ball, place in oiled bowl and revolve to coat entire surface. Cover with a clean cloth and let rise in warm place about 1½ – 2 hours.

Oil a loaf pan 22 x 12 cm (9 x 5-inches) and dust with flour.

Roll out dough onto lightly floured board, almost to the length of the bread pan.

Spread with butter/herb mixture, leaving a 2 cm (1-inch) border all round. Roll up short end of dough, then pinch end seams well together. Place loaf, seam side down, in pan. Slash top deeply diagonally to reveal herb layers. Cover with cloth and leave in warm place till double in bulk, about 45 minutes to 1 hour.

Preheat oven to 190°C (375°F).

Brush dough with egg glaze and bake 35–45 minutes or till hollow sounding when rapped on bottom.

For extra crispness, brush lightly with water immediately after bread is removed from the oven. Place on wire rack to cool.

WHOLE WHEAT BREAD

2 cakes yeast (40 g)
1 cup milk
¼ cup honey
4 cups sifted flour
1¼ cups lukewarm water
3 tablespoons oil or butter
1 tablespoon salt
4 cups whole-wheat flour

Method: Soften yeast in lukewarm water. Scald milk and add oil or butter, honey and salt. Cool to lukewarm. Add softened yeast and flours. Knead well, cover and let rise in a warm place till doubled in bulk. Punch down, shape into loaves. Place in greased loaf pans. Cover and let rise until doubled in bulk. Bake in moderate oven, 190°C (375°F), about 1 hour. Makes 2 loaves.

N.B.: You may use 8 cups wholewheat flour instead of ½ and ½. You may also add crushed wheat to your dough for a rougher texture.

GARLIC BREAD

Method: Slice a french loaf three quarter way down into 5 cm (2 inch) slices. Mix 125 g (4 oz) butter with 4–5 crushed cloves garlic and ½ teaspoon dried herbs or parsley (optional) and spread between each slice. Wrap in foil and heat through in 180°C (350°F) oven for 10–15 minutes.

CRUMPETS

2 cups flour
2 teaspoons cream of tartar
1 teaspoon bicarbonate of soda
2 tablespoons syrup
2 teaspoons butter
2 eggs
1 cup milk

Method: Sift all dry ingredients. Make a well in centre. Add melted butter, egg yolks and syrup. Start stirring and gradually add the milk. Stir well until smooth and then add stiffly beaten egg whites. Drop by spoonfuls onto hot greased griddle. When bubbles appear on surface, turn over.

WAFFLES

2 cups flour
½ teaspoon salt
3 teaspoons baking powder
4 tablespoons sugar
2 eggs
1¾ cups milk
50 g melted butter (2 oz)

Method: Sift dry ingredients. Add egg yolks and milk and cooled butter. Lastly fold in stiffly beaten egg whites. Heat waffle iron and grease. Let rise for a while before closing.

13. TRADITIONAL JEWISH DISHES

CHEESE BLINTZES

3 eggs
2½ cups cold water
1½ cups flour
½ teaspoon baking powder
  pinch of salt

Method: Beat eggs and water well. Add flour, sifted with salt and baking powder. Beat till smooth. Grease pan with oil and fry on one side only till done. Stack one on top of the other whilst preparing filling.

Cheese Filling: ¼ kilo (½ lb) cream cheese mixed with 1 tablespoon cream, 1 dessertspoon flour, 1 egg, sugar to taste and dash cinnamon. Place 1 dessertspoon on filling in each blini, roll up and fry in oil or butter. Serve with a dollop of thick cream on top, sprinkled with cinnamon and sugar.

CHOPPED HERRING

2 salt herrings (cleaned and soaked overnight/12 hours)
3 granny smith or cooking apples, peeled
¼ of one onion
4 marie biscuits + 2 level tablespoons matzo meal
3 tablespoons vinegar
2 teaspoons sugar
2 hard boiled eggs
  white pepper – a dash

Method: Skin herrings and remove bones. Mince with apples, onion, marie biscuits and grate in one egg. Add vinegar, sugar and pepper. Decorate with the remaining egg by grating over it. Serve with Kichel.
  N.B. If you are freezing the herring, do not add the egg. This can be added after defrosting.

HERRING SALAD AND HERRING IN CREAM
Refer to Herring Section under "Fish"

CHOPPED LIVER

500 g chicken livers (1 lb)
3 onions, sliced
2 tablespoons chicken fat
2 tablespoons oil
3 hard boiled eggs
  salt and pepper to taste

Method: Boil chicken livers, which have been thoroughly washed, in water with salt and pepper for about 5 minutes. Drain off water and rinse with cold water. Fry onions in chicken fat and oil and mince with liver and 2 hard boiled eggs. Season to taste. Add a dessertspoon sherry if desired. Decorate with remaining egg.

GEFILTE FISH

2 kilos (4 lb) filleted mixed fish (hake and kingklip or hake and line fish)
Ask fishmonger for the skin and bones.
3 large onions, sliced and fried in 2 tablespoons butter and 2 tablespoons oil
1 tablespoon flour
2 tablespoons matzo meal
3 eggs
2 teaspoons salt
2 teaspoons seafood spice
1 teaspoon sugar
¼ teaspoon pepper
1 cup cold water

Method: Mince fish with carrots and lightly fried onions, adding the oil and butter that the onions have been fried in as well. Add all other ingredients and mix together very well. Shape in balls. Prepare the stock by boiling together the skin and bones, 3 sliced onions, pepper, salt and fish spice and a pinch sugar with 8–10 cups water for 1 hour. Strain into a clean pot, and add 2 sliced carrots and the fish balls and cook over gentle heat for $1\frac{1}{2}$ to 2 hours. Allow to cool before removing to serving bowl, add a few drops of egg yellow to the liquid, place a slice of carrot on top of each piece of fish and finally pour over the liquid.

Fish cakes: Sprinkle with cornflake crumbs, or matzo meal and fry in oil until golden.

MY GRANNY'S HELZEL

250 grams ($\frac{1}{2}$ lb) chicken fat, chopped finely, or suet, but preferably chicken fat
3 tablespoons sugar
1 tablespoon mielie meal
$1\frac{1}{2}$ cups flour
  salt, pepper to taste
1 tablespoon cinnamon

Method: Mix all the dry ingredients together. Rub the chicken fat very well into the dry ingredients. Stuff the necks of poultry and stitch up well. Boil in water for a few hours, not too much water, just to cover. Can also be baked in tzimmes. If you do not have poultry necks, then use muslin cloth instead.

KICHEL

4 eggs + 2 yolks
$\frac{1}{2}$ cup sugar
$\frac{1}{2}$ cup oil
3 cups flour
2 teaspoons baking powder

Method: Beat eggs and yolks with the sugar very well. Add oil and beat again. Add baking powder and beat a little longer, then lastly add the flour. Roll out a small amount at a time, they must be very thin. Prick with a fork, then brush with oil and sprinkle with sugar. Cut into diamond shapes. Grease a grilling tray very well with oil, place the kichel on these and bake in a hot oven, about 210°C (425°F) till golden brown, approximately 10 minutes.

KNEIDLACH – Refer to Soup Section

KREPLACH – Refer to Soup Section

MEAT BLINTZES – Refer to Soup Section

MEAT PIES – Refer to Soup Section

PESACH SPONGE CAKE I

12 eggs
2 tablespoons water
$\frac{3}{4}$ cup potato flour
$1\frac{1}{4}$ cups cake meal
2 cups sugar
  juice of 1 lemon (strained)
  cinnamon

Method: Beat egg whites, add egg yolks, lemon and water. Add dry ingredients. Bake in wax paper lined baking tin. Sprinkle cinnamon in the middle. Bake in 170°C (325°F) for $1\frac{1}{4}$ hours.

PESACH SPONGE II

6 eggs
1 cup sugar
1 tablespoon cold water
  juice of $\frac{1}{2}$ lemon
$\frac{1}{2}$ cup potato flour
$\frac{1}{2}$ cup cake meal

Method: Separate yolks and whites. Beat yolks with sugar, cold water and lemon juice till light and fluffy. Fold in potato flour and cake meal. Lastly add stiffly beaten egg whites. Bake in greased and wax paper lined tin in 180°C (350°F) oven for about 1 hour.

PESACH SWISS ROLL

Method: Beat 4 eggs with 1 cup sugar till light and fluffy. Melt 25 g (1 oz) butter with less than $\frac{1}{2}$ a cup milk. Add $\frac{3}{4}$ cup self raising flour and 2 tablespoons potato flour (level) and 2 tablespoons cake meal. Pour into greased and lined swiss roll tin and bake in 200°C (400°F) oven for 10 minutes. Turn out onto damp cloth which has been sprinkled with sugar, spread with jam whilst hot and roll up immediately.

Special hint: For choc roll use $1\frac{1}{2}$ tablespoons potato flour, $1\frac{1}{2}$ tablespoons cake meal and 3 rounded tablespoons cocoa. Roll up whilst hot. When cool, unroll, fill with whipped cream and re-roll.

TEIGLACH I

18 eggs less 5 whites
   finely grated rind of 2 oranges
2 teaspoons sugar
6 tablespoons oil
1 dessertspoon ginger
± 3 cups cake meal (packet)
1 tablespoon brandy

Method: Measure 3 slightly rounded cups of cake meal, place in a bowl and set aside. Place the eggs and sugar in your mixmaster bowl and beat till very light and frothy (about 5 minutes). Add orange rind and ginger and continue beating for another 15–20 minutes. Add the oil in a slow stream, beating all the time as you do so. Sift about half the cake meal from your bowl over the egg mixture, fold in with a spatula and leave to stand for a while, till it thickens. Continue adding the cake meal, till about $\frac{1}{2}$ cup remains. Use this remaining meal to sprinkle on your board and knead in a little at a time till your dough is soft but firm enough to handle. You will probably use all the cake meal from your bowl ± 1 or 2 tablespoons. Roll into little balls, the size of walnuts, make a hole in the centre with the handle of a wooden spoon and place in the *boiling* syrup.

Cook covered on high for 25–30 minutes then open the pot for the first time, give a stir with wooden spoon. Turn heat down to medium, and stir again about every 10 minutes. Turn down to low when necessary. They should be ready in about $1\frac{1}{4}$ hours or so. Remove one from the pot when it is nicely browned and, if it does not fall back, then they are done, otherwise allow to cook longer. Just before removing from syrup, stir in 2 dessertspoons ginger. Roll in crushed post toasties, coconut or finely chopped nuts, and place on cooling rack.

Syrup:
$1\frac{1}{2}$ kilos (3 lbs) syrup
6 cups sugar
6 cups water

Method: Prepare the syrup by placing the syrup, water and sugar into a large pot, stir now and then till sugar dissolves and then allow to boil. It must be boiling vigorously when you place the teiglach into the syrup.

Special hint: Tie a dish cloth over the lid of the pot to prevent the moisture accumulating and dripping over the teiglach.

TEIGLACH II

8 eggs (extra large)
 finely grated rind of 1 orange
4 tablespoons oil
1 dessertspoon ground ginger
 cake meal

Method: Measure 2 cups cake meal. Place in a bowl and set aside. You will not use more than this amount of cake meal, so put the packet with the remaining cake meal away. Place the eggs, oil, orange rind and 1 dessertspoon ginger in your mixmaster bowl and beat for about 5 minutes. Sift about ¾ of the cake meal from your bowl onto the eggs etc. and fold in with a spatula. Using some of the meal again from your bowl, sift a tablespoon or two onto a large wooden board. Place your mixture on the board and knead for a short while, adding more meal, if your dough is too soft. It should be about right, when there are two or slightly less tablespoons of cake meal remaining in your bowl. Roll into balls (about the size of a walnut) make a hole in the centre with the handle of a wooden spoon, and place in the *boiling* syrup. Cook covered on high for about 12 minutes, then turn down to medium and do not open the pot for the first 25 minutes. Stir quickly, with wooden spoon cover and then stir again every 10–15 minutes. Turn down to low eventually. Remove one from the pot, when it is nicely browned and if it does not fall back, then they are done, otherwise allow to cook longer. It usually takes about 1¼ hours. Just before removing from syrup, stir in the additional 2 dessertspoons ginger. Roll in crushed post toasties, coconut or finely chopped nuts, and place on cooling rack.

Syrup:
1 kilo tin syrup (2 lb)
4 cups sugar
4 cups water
2 dessertspoons ginger

Method: Prepare the syrup by placing the syrup, water and sugar into a large pot, stir now and then till the sugar dissolves and then allow to boil. It must be boiling vigorously when you place the teiglach into the syrup.

WHITE TEIGLACH

3 eggs + 3 yolks
½ cup oil
3 rounded teaspoon baking powder
1 dessertspoon ginger
2 tablespoons brandy
½ cup sugar
2½ cups flour
(1 lb) 500 g mixed fruit

Method: Place the fruit in a bowl and sprinkle with the brandy. Beat the eggs and yolks with the sugar till light and creamy. Add the oil and beat again just a little. Add the sifted flour, baking powder and ginger. Roll out onto a floured board and sprinkle with the brandied fruit (you may use some red and green cherries as well). Leave to stand for a while. Roll up as for a swiss roll, cut off little pieces and roll into a ball. Place on a greased and floured biscuit tray and bake in a 150°C (300°F) oven for approximately 15 minutes. They must not be too brown.

Syrup:
3 cups sugar
1 cup water
4 teaspoons ginger

Method: Prepare the syrup by placing the sugar, water and ginger in a large shallow roasting pan, over two plates, if necessary. Boil till bubbly. Place teiglach in the syrup and boil for 3–4 minutes, making sure that they are all glazed. Remove from the syrup and place on a big baking tray and pour the remaining syrup over. If you do not want them too sugary, do not pour over the remaining syrup.

TZIMMES

Peel and slice 8–10 carrots and place in a pot with $\frac{1}{2}$ kg (1 lb) brisket, cover with water and boil for 1 hour. Add:

2 cubed potatoes
$1\frac{1}{2}$ teaspoon salt
$\frac{1}{4}$ teaspoon pepper
$\frac{1}{4}$ teaspoon ginger
1 large slice pumpkin cut into a few pieces
$\frac{1}{4}$ teaspoon cinnamon
$\frac{1}{2}$ chicken cube
1 cubed sweet potato

When all the vegetables are tender and the water has been reduced to a quarter, add 2 tablespoons brown sugar and thicken with 1 dessertspoon maizena mixed with a little water. Pour into a casserole dish and place in the oven to brown. This dish may be prepared the day before and browned just before serving.

SALTENOSSES

Pastry:
2 cups flour
2 eggs
  pinch salt
$\frac{1}{2}$ cup water

Cheese filling:
500 g (1 lb) cream cheese
1 egg
1 tablespoon sugar
  pinch salt, dash pepper, dash cinnamon

Method: Make a fairly stiff dough and roll out thinly. Cut into oblongs 6 cm x 10 cm ($2\frac{1}{2}$-inch x 4-inch). Place a spoonful of cheese filling on each oblong and press edges firmly together.

Place in boiling salted water for 5 minutes. Drain and place in buttered pyrex dish. Pour over $\frac{1}{2}$ cup milk, 50 g (2 oz) butter, 250 mℓ ($\frac{1}{2}$ pint) sour cream and bake in a 180°C (350°F) oven for 30 minutes. Remove from oven, sprinkle with 2 tablespoons sugar and 1–2 teaspoons cinnamon and bake a further 10 minutes.

TEIGLACH III
(Made with ordinary cake flour)

12 extra large eggs – less 4 whites
 2 teaspoons sugar
 2 teaspoons ginger
   finely grated rind of one orange
 1 dessertspoon brandy
 4 tablespoons oil
 1 teaspoon baking powder
   approximately $3\frac{1}{2}$ cups flour

Syrup:
$1\frac{1}{2}$ kilos (3 lb) syrup
6 cups sugar
6 cups water

Method: Beat eggs and sugar till very light and fluffy. Add ginger and orange rind and continue to beat a little longer. Add brandy, oil and baking powder. Beat till blended and make into a soft dough with 3 cups flour, using the additional $\frac{1}{2}$ cup or so to knead in and for rolling on board. You may even find that you will require slightly less flour, depending on the size of the eggs etc. Roll into shapes, e.g. baigels, knots etc. Place the syrup, sugar and water in a large saucepan and add the Teiglach *only when the syrup is boiling vigorously.* Cover with lid (over which you have tied a clean dish cloth) and do not open the pot for the first 20 minutes. Give a quick stir and continue to stir at 10–15 minute intervals. The Teiglach should be ready in $1-1\frac{1}{4}$ hours. Before removing from syrup, stir in 2 dessertspoons ground ginger.

Remove with slotted spoon, roll in coconut, chopped nuts or cornflakes and place on cooling racks.

Teiglach may be frozen very successfully in airtight containers.

Special hint: You may also roll dough around pieces of preserved ginger or pitted prunes.

ALPHABETICAL CROSS INDEX

A

Ambrosia Cake – 113
Ambrosia Jiffy Cakes – 155
American Ground Beef Turnovers – 63
Angel Cake – 113
Appetisers – see "Section Index"
Apple Cake – 113
Apple Meringue – 97
Apple Slice – 143
Apple Tart – 143
Apple Tart De Luxe – 12
Apple Tart with Meringue Topping – 144
Apricot Glazed Baby Chicken – 43
Apricot Pecan Slice – 145
Artichoke Salad – 83
Artichokes, stuffed – 12
Asparagus À La Roquefort – 3
Asparagus, crumbed – 77
Asparagus Soup, Cream of – 19
Assorted Tartlets, Melt-in-the-mouth – 159
Auntie Celie's Fruit Slices – 162
Auntie Rosie's Butter Cake – 115
Auntie Rosie's Glazed Xmas Pudding – 96
Auntie Sylvie's Cheese Cake – 117
Avocado, baked, stuffed with Lobster – 25
Avocado Cream Cheese Dressing – 85
Avocado Dip – 3
Avocado Mould – 3

B

Baked Alaska – 89
Baked Avocado stuffed with Lobster – 25
Baked Butternut – 80
Baked Fish Au Gratin – 25
Baked Potato with Caviar – 77
Baklava – 155
Banana Custard Pudding Dessert – 98
Banana Waldorf Salad – 83
Barbeque Chicken – 43
Barbeque Lamb – 68
Barbeque Ribs – 70
Basic Tart Dough – 143
Bavarian Cream, three-tiered – 107
Bee Sting Cake – 114
Beef – See "Section Index"
Beef Olives – 57
Beef Stroganoff, Caviar Topped – 57
Beef Turnovers, American Ground – 63
Belgian Tart – 145
Benedict Tart – 145
Biscuits – see "Section Index"
Black Forest Cake – 114
Bogatsa – 89
Borscht – 17
Bouillabaisse – 17
Brandied Sauce for Ice-cream – 98
Brandy Snaps – 162
Brazil Nutlog, chocolate filled – 121
Bread – see "Section Index"
Breast of Veal, potato-stuffed – 72
Brisket with Prunes – 57
Buns, Mercia's rich featherlight – 155
Butter Cake, Auntie Rosie's – 115
Butter Cake, chocolate – 115
Butter Crunch Ice-cream Ring – 98
Butternut, baked – 80

C

Cabbage Blintzes – 63
Cabbage Pineapple Salad – 83
Cabbage Salad with piquant sour Cream Dressing – 83
Café Brulot – 90

Cakes – see "Section Index"
Carnival Cake with Penuche Icing – 116
Carrot Almond Torte – 116
Carrot Cake – 117
Carrot Cake, tropical – 138
Cassata Ice-cream Bombe – 99
Caviar Topped Beef Stroganoff – 57
Cheese Blintzes – 177
Cheese Blintzes, orange flavoured – 96
Cheese Bourekas – 3
Cheese Cake – 117
Cheese Cake, Auntie Sylvie's – 117
Cheese Cake, chocolate – 119
Cheese Cake, pineapple – 132
Cheese Cake Puff – 118
Cheese and Sour Cream Dip – 4
Cheese Soufflé – 4
Cherry Tart – 146
Chicken À La King – 43
Chicken Almondine, stuffed – 51
Chicken, apricot glazed – 43
Chicken, barbequed – 43
Chicken, breasts in cream and cider – 43
Chicken Casserole – 46
Chicken, chutney with bananas – 47
Chicken, fried – 48
Chicken, glazed banana stuffed – 48
Chicken, grilled marinated – 49
Chicken, with Kumquants and Mandarins – 47
Chicken Liver Risotto – 77
Chicken Maryland – 46
Chicken Paprika – 43
Chicken Pies – 47
Chicken Pie, upside down – 52
Chicken Soup – 17
Chicken, spicy casserole – 50
Chocolate Blitz Torte – 118
Chocolate Bowl Surprise – 99
Chocolate Cake, butter – 115
Chocolate Cake, Cassata – 100
Chocolate Cake, German – 128
Chocolate Charlotte Suisse – 100
Chocolate Cheese Cake/Sour Cream Topping – 119
Chocolate Chestnut Pyramid Cake – 119
Chocolate Chiffon Cake – 120
Chocolate Chiffon Cake, large – 120
Chocolate filled Brazil Nutlog – 121
Chocolate Leaves – Refer recipe "Chocolate Charlotte Suisse" – 101
Chocolate Mosaic Dessert – 101
Chocolate Mousse – 99
Chocolate Swiss Roll – Refer recipe "Chocolate Charlotte Suisse" – 100
Chopped Herring – 177

Chopped Liver – 177
Chutney Chicken with Bananas – 47
Cinnamon Buns, quick and easy – 157
Cinnamon Shortbread – 163
Coca-Cola Cake – 121
Coconut Chiffon Cake – 121
Coconut Custard Pie – 146
Coffee Ice-cream, easy – 103
Coquilles St. Jacques – 25
Cornflake Kisses – 162
Couer À La Creme – 101
Cream of Asparagus Soup – 19
Cream Cheese Caviar Blinis – 5
Cream Horns – 157
Cream of Mushroom Soup – 19
Creamed Fish in Rice Ring – 26
Creamy Caviar Mould – 4
Creamy French Dressing – 85
Creme Brullé – 101
Creme Caramel – 102
Crêpes Calypso – 90
        Delight – 90
        Florentine, stacked – 12
        Montmorency, flaming – 91
        Salmon – 35
        Seafood – 35
        Strawberry, flaming – 94
        Wholewheat with Salmon & Cream Cheese – 13
Crispy Cookie Maker Biscuits – 165
Crispy Fried Onion Rings – 78
Crumbed Asparagus – 77
Crumpets – 172
Crunch Crust Ice-cream Bombe – 102
Crunchy Chocolate Nut Balls – 163
Crusted Seafood Bisque – 19
Cucumber Yoghurt Salad – 83
Curled Pecan Wafers – 163
Curried Fish Balls – 26
Curry Meat Balls – 62
Custard Biscuits – 163
Custard Slice – 124

D

Danish Cake – 124
Danish Herring – 32
Danish Jam Puff Cake – 125
Danish Pastries, Mercia's – 157
Deep South Prune Cake – 126
Delicious Noodle Pudding – 91
Desserts – see "Section Index"
Dobosch Torte – 126

Double Chocolate Tart – 149
Doughnuts – 158
Duck, Bigarade – 48
Duck, Oriental – 49
Duck, Tropical – 52
Dutch Curried Pea Soup – 20

E

Easy Coffee Ice-cream – 103
Eclairs – 159
English Trifle – 103
Escargot – 5

F

Family Baked Fish – 27
Festive Fruit Cake – 127
Fillet Bearnaise – 59
Fillet en Boite – 58
Fish – see "Section Index"
Fish, Baked au Gratin – 25
Fish Balls, curried – 26
Fish, creamed in Rice Ring – 26
Fish, family baked – 27
Fish, Florentine – 27
Fish, Gefilte – 177
Fish Mould, Velvyt À La Newburg – 39
Fish Strudel – 27
Fish Supreme en Papilote – 30
Fish, whole baked Portugaise – 39
Flaming Crêpes Montmorency – 91
Flaming Strawberry Crêpes – 94
Floating Island Dessert – 103
Florentines – 164
French Dressing – 85
French Onion Soup, soufflèd – 20
French Salad – 84
Fresh Salmon Andalouse – 30
Friandises – refer recipe "Gateau St. Honoré" – 104
Fried Fennel – 77
Fried Chicken – 48
Fried Mushrooms – 77
Fruit Cake – 127
Fruit Cake, festive – 127
Fruit Cake with egg whites only – 128
Fruit Cobbler – 94
Fruit Slices, Auntie Celie's – 162
Fruited Lamb in Curry Sauce – 69
Fudge – refer "Topping" for "Mud Pie" – 106

G

Garlic Bread – 172
Garlic Steak/Anchovy Sauce/Chasseur Sauce – 59
Gateau St. Honoré – 104
Gefilte Fish – 177
German Chocolate Cake – 128
German Plum Tart – 147
Ginger Biscuits – 164
Ginger Cake – 129
Ginger Chiffon Cake – 129
Ginger Mousse – 104
Ginger Snaps – 164
Glazed Banana Stuffed Chicken – 48
Gnocchi, potato – 78
Gnocchi, spinach – 11
Granita De Café – 105
Grape Tart – 147
Grasshopper Cake – 130
Green Goddess Salad Dressing – 86
Granadilla Pudding – 105
Grilled Prawns/Langoustines – 31
Ground Almond Biscuits – 165
Ground Almond Tart – 147
Guava Tart À La Coconut Cream – 148

H

Halva Pudding – 105
Hamburgers – 62
Hawaiian Fillet of Beef, marinated – 62
Helzel, my Granny's – 178
Herbed Bread – Wholewheat or White – 171
Herring – see Fish in "Section Index"
Herring Chopped – 32
Herring in Cream – 32
Herring, Danish – 32
Herring Salad – 33
Hors D'oeuvres – see "Section Index"

I

Italian Liver – 59

J

Jewish Dishes – see "Section Index"
Joseph's Mandelbrodt – 165

K

Kabeljou, whole Mayonnaise – 40
Kaiserschmarren – 95
Kalamari – 33
Kichel – 178
Kirsch Gateau – 130
Kneidlach – 18
Kouriabides – 165
Kranskuchen – 131
Kreplach – 18
Kulibiak, Russian – 31

L

Lamb – see also "Meat" in Section Index
Lamb Barbeque – 68
Lamb Chops, Parmigiana – 69
Lamb Curry with Yoghurt – 70
Lamb Fruited in Curry Sauce – 69
Lamb in Phyllo – 72
Lamb Ribs, barbeque – 70
Lamb, Roast with Potatoes & Mint Sauce – 71
Langoustines, grilled – 31
Large Chocolate Chiffon Cake – 120
Lasagne, Meat – 64
      Tuna – 13
      Vegetarian – 80
Lebanese Cucumber Soup – 20
Lemon Cream – 105
Lemon Meringue Tart – 148
Linzer Torte – 149
Liver, Italian – 59
Liver Pâté Roll – 5
Lobster Soufflé in Shells – 33
Lobster Thermidor – 34
Loganberry Roll – 133

M

Mandelbrodt, Joseph's – 165
Marble Cake, quick and delicious – 133
Marinated Grilled Chicken – 49
Marinated Hawaiian Fillet of Beef – 62
Mayonnaise – 86
Meat – see also "Section Index"
Meat Balls, curried – 62
Meat Blintzes – 19
Meat Pies – 18
Melt-in-the-mouth Assorted Tartlets – 159
Mercia's Danish Pastries – 157
Mercia's Rich Featherlight Buns – 155
Mincemeat Loaf – 63
Minestrone – 21
Minted Meringue Sandwich – 105
Mock Teiglach – 166
Monkey Gland Steak – 65
Moussaka – 71
Mud Pie – 106
Mushroom and Cheese Quiche – 6
Mushroom Coquilles Mornay – 6
Mushroom Soup, Cream of – 19
Mussels with Wine & Cream – 7
My Granny's Helzel – 178

N

Noodle Pudding, delicious – 91
Nut Meringue Torte – 106

O

Onion Rings, crispy fried – 78
Onion Soup, French souffléd – 20
Onions, stuffed – 80
Orange Baked Alaska – 95
Orange Chiffon Cake – 131
Orange Chocolate Squares – 159
Orange Flavoured Cheese Blintzes – 96
Oriental Duck – 49
Oxtail with Baked Beans – 65

P

Paella – 34
Palm Heart & Artichoke Salad – 84
Pavlova – 107
Pea Soup, Dutch curried – 20
Peach & Cherry Flambé – 97
Peach Kuchen – 149
Pepper Steak – 65
Peppermint Brownies – 166
Pesach Sponge Cake – 178
Pesach Swiss Roll – 179
Petit Fours – 160
Pineapple Cheese Cake – 132
Pineapple Cream Cake – 132
Pitikas – 160
Pizza Italiano – 7
Pizza, quick and easy – 8
Poppy Seed Dressing – 86
Poppy Seed Onion Squares – 171
Potato, baked with caviar – 77

Potato Gnocchi – 78
Potato Latkes – 78
Potato Nests – 79
Potato Pudding – 79
Potato Salad in Green Peppers & Tomatoes – 85
Potato Stuffed Breast of Veal – 72
Poultry – see also "Section Index"
Praline – 120
Praline Nut Squares – 161
Praline Soufflé – 107
Prawns – In Cream & Wine – 35
          Grilled – 31
          Tropical Jambalaya – 38
          Lisboa – 35
          Sweet & Sour – 38
Prune Cake, Deep South – 126
Puff Pastry – 68
Pumpkin Fritters – 79

Q

Quiche, Cheese & Mushroom – 6
Quick Delicious Marble Cake – 133
Quick Double Chocolate Tart – 149
Quick Easy Cinnamon Buns – 157
Quick Easy Pizza – 8
Quick Puff Pastry – 68

R

Raspberry Roll – 133
Ratatouille – 79
Red Cabbage – 79
Red Kidney Bean Salad – 84
Rhubarb Cream Pie – 150
Rice Pudding – 97
Rich Scones – 171
Risotto, Chicken Liver – 77
Roast Lamb with Potatoes & Mint Sauce – 71
Roast Scotch Fillet with Herb Sauce – 66
Roast Turkey – 50
Roquefort Dressing – 86
Roman Lamb – 71
Romany Creams – 166
Russian Kulibiak – 31
Russian Torte – 133

S

Salads & Dressings – see "Section Index"
Salmon Andalouse, fresh – 30

Salmon Brioche – 9
Salmon Crêpes – 35
Salmon Pie – 10
Salmon Soufflé Roll – 10
Salmon in Wine Sauce – 36
Saltenosses – 181
Sauerbraten Beef Ring – 64
Savoury Tartlets, Asparagus, Cheese, Tuna – 8
Scones – 171
Scones, rich – 171
Scotch Fillet, Roast with Herb Sauce – 66
Seafood Casserole en Croûte – 36
Seafood Crêpes – 35
Semolina Cake – 134
Shortbread – 167
Shortbread, Cinnamon – 163
Small Cakes – see "Section Index"
Snoek Pâté – 9
Souffléd Cream & Caviar Blinis – 10
Souffléd French Onion Soup – 20
Soups – see also "Section Index"
Spaghetti with Clam Sauce – 37
Spicy Chicken Casserole – 50
Spinach & Feta Cheese Flan – 11
Spinach Gnocchi – 11
Spinach Salad – 84
Spring Rolls – 50
Stacked Crêpes Florentine – 12
Steak – Garlic/Anchovy Sauce – 59
          Monkey Gland – 65
          Pepper – 65
Strawberry Spice Shortcake – 134
Strawberry Vacherin – 135
Stuffed Artichokes – 12
Stuffed Chicken Almondine – 51
Stuffed Onions – 80
Stuffed Trout Amandine – 37
Stuffed Trout, Herb & Lemon Sauce – 37
Sumptuous Salad – 85
Sweet and Sour Prawns – 38
Swedish Cake – 135
Swiss Roll – 138

T

Tacos – 66
Taramasalata – 13
Tart À La Florentine – 150
Tarts – see also "Section Index"
Teiglach, I/II – 179 & 180
Teiglach, Mock – 166
Teiglach, White – 161
Teiglach, III – 181

Thimble Biscuits – 167
Thousand Island Dressing – 86
Three Tiered Bavarian Cream – 107
Tomatoes & Green Peppers with Potato Salad – 85
Tongue in Apricot Sauce – 67
Tournedos Rossini – 67
Traditional Jewish Dishes – see "Section Index"
Trifle, English – 103
Tropical Carrot Cake – 138
Tropical Duck – 52
Tropical Prawn Jambalaya – 38
Trout, stuffed Amandine – 37
Trout, stuffed with Lemon/Herb Sauce – 37
Tuna Lasagne – 13
Turkey, roast – 50
Turkish Oranges – 110
Two-tone Pyramid Cake – 138
Tzimmes – 181

U

Upside Down Chicken Pie – 52

V

Vanilla Slice – 139
Vareniky – 97
Veal – see also "Meat" in "Section Index"
Veal Birds – 57
Veal Breast, Potato stuffed – 72
Veal Chops, Parmigiana – 69
Veal Goulash – 73
Vegetables – see "Section Index"
Vegetarian Lasagne – 80
Venetian Torte – 140
Velvyt Fish Mould À La Newburg – 39
Viennese Brownies – 161

W

Waffles – 173
Walnut Layer Cake – 136
Wellington Boot – 68
White Teiglach – 159
Whole Baked Fish Portugaise – 39
Whole Baked Kabeljou Mayonnaise – 40
Wholewheat Bread – 172
Wholewheat Crêpes filled with Salmon & Cream Cheese – 13
Winter Soup – 21

X

Xmas Pudding, Auntie Rosie's, glazed – 96

Z

Zabaglione – 110

SECTION INDEX

APPETISERS AND HORS-D'OEUVRES

Asparagus À La Roquefort – 3
Avocado Dip – 3
Avocado Mould – 3
Cheese Bourekas – 3
Cheese Soufflé – 4
Cheese & Sour Cream Dip – 4
Creamy Caviar Mould – 4
Cream Cheese Caviar Blinis – 5
Escargot – 5
Liver Pâté Roll – 5
Mushroom Cheese Quiche – 6
Mushroom Coquilles Mornay – 6
Mussels with Wine and Cream – 7
Pizza Italiano – 7
Quick & Easy Pizza Dough – 8
Salmon Brioche – 9
Salmon Pie – 10
Salmon Soufflé Roll – 10
Savoury Pancakes – 5
Savoury Tartlets – 8
Snoek Pâté – 9
Souffléd Cream & Caviar Blinis – 10
Spinach & Feta Cheese Flan – 11
Spinach Gnocchi – 11
Stacked Crêpes Florentine – 12
Stuffed Artichokes – 12
Taramasalata – 13
Tuna Lasagne – 13
Wholewheat Crêpes with Salmon & Cream Cheese – 13

SOUPS

Borscht – 17
Bouillabaisse – 17
Chicken Soup – 17
Accompaniments to Chicken Soup:
　1) Kneidlach – 18
　2) Kreplach – 18
　3) Meat Blintzes – 19
　4) Meat Pies – 18
Cream of Asparagus/Mushroom Soup – 19
Crusted Seafood Bisque – 19
Dutch Curried Pea Soup – 20
Lebanese Cucumber Soup – 20
Minestrone – 21
Souffléd French Onion Soup – 20
Winter Soup – 21

FISH

Baked Avocado Stuffed with Lobster – 25
Baked Fish Au Gratin – 25
Coquilles St. Jacques – 25
Creamed Fish in Rice Ring – 26
Curried Fish Balls – 26
Family Baked Fish – 27
Fish Florentine – 27
Fish Strudel – 27
Fish Supreme en Papilote – 30
Fresh Salmon Andalouse – 30
Gefilte Fish – 177
Grilled Prawns/Langoustines – 31
Herring:
　Chopped Herring – 32
　Danish Herring – 32
　Herring in Cream – 32
　Herring Salad – 33
Kalamari – 33
Lobster Soufflé in Shells – 33
Lobster Thermidor – 34
Paella – 34
Prawns in Cream and Wine – 35
Prawns Lisboa – 35
Russian Kulibiak – 31
Salmon or Seafood Crêpes – 35
Salmon in Wine Sauce – 36
Seafood Casserole en Croute – 36
Spaghetti with Clam Sauce – 37
Stuffed Trout Amandine – 37
Stuffed Trout with Lemon Herb Sauce – 37
Sweet & Sour Prawns – 38
Tropical Prawns Jambalaya – 38
Velvyt Fish Mould À La Newburg – 39

Whole Baked Fish Portugaise – 39
Whole Kabeljou Mayonnaise – 40

POULTRY

Apricot Glazed Baby Chickens – 43
Barbecued Chicken – 43
Chicken À La King – 43
Chicken Breasts in Cream & Cider – 43
Chicken Casserole – 46
Chicken Maryland – 46
Chicken Paprika – 43
Chicken Pies – 47
Chicken with Kumquats and Mandarins – 47
Chutney Chicken with Bananas – 47
Duck Bigarade – 48
Fried Chicken – 48
Glazed Banana Stuffed Chicken – 48
Marinated Grilled Chicken – 49
Oriental Duck – 49
Roast Turkey – 50
Spicy Chicken Casserole – 50
Spring Rolls – 50
Stuffed Chicken Almondine – 51
Tropical Duck – 52
Upside Down Chicken Pie – 52

MEAT

Beef:
American Ground Beef Turnovers – 63
Beef Olives or Veal Birds – 57
Brisket with Prunes – 57
Cabbage Blintzes – 63
Caviar Topped Beef Stroganoff – 57
Curry Meat Balls – 62
Fillet Bearnaise – 59
Fillet en Boite I & II – 58
Garlic Steak with Anchovy/Chasseur Sauce – 59
Hamburgers – 62
Italian Liver – 59
Lasagne – 64
Marinated Hawaiian Fillet of Beef – 62
Mincemeat Loaf – 63
Monkey Gland Steak – 65
Oxtail with Baked Beans – 65
Pepper Steak – 65
Roast Scotch Fillet with Herb Sauce – 66
Sauerbraten Beef Ring – 64
Tacos – 66
Tongue in Apricot Sauce – 67

Tournedos Rossini – 67
Wellington Boot – 68

Lamb:
Barbeque Lamb – 68
Barbeque Ribs – 70
Fruited Lamb in Curry Sauce – 69
Lamb Chops Parmigiana – 69
Lamb Curry with Yoghurt – 70
Lamb in Phyllo – 72
Moussaka – 71
Roast Lamb & Potatoes & Mint Sauce – 71
Roman Lamb – 71

Veal
Potato Stuffed Breast of Veal – 72
Veal Birds – 57
Veal Chops Parmigiana – 69
Veal Goulash – 73

VEGETABLES

Baked Butternut – 80
Baked Potato with Caviar – 77
Chicken Liver Risotto – 77
Crispy Fried Onion Rings – 78
Crumbed Asparagus – 77
Fried Fennel – 77
Fried Mushrooms – 77
Potato Gnocchi – 78
Potato Latkes – 78
Potato Nests – 79
Potato Pudding – 79
Pumpkin Fritters – 79
Ratatouille – 79
Red Cabbage – 79
Stuffed Onions – 80
Vegetarian Lasagne – 80

SALADS & DRESSINGS

Artichoke Salad – 83
Banana Waldorf Salad – 83
Cabbage/Pineapple Salad – 83
Cabbage Salad with piquant sour Cream Dressing – 83
Cucumber/Yoghurt Salad – 83
French Salad – 84
Palm Heart/Artichoke Salad – 84
Potato Salad in Tomatoes & Green Peppers – 85
Red Kidney Bean Salad – 84
Spinach Salad – 84
Sumptuous Salad – 85

DRESSINGS

Avocado Cream Cheese – 85
Creamy French Dressing – 85
French Dressing – 85
Green Goddess Salad Dressing – 86
Mayonnaise – 86
Poppy Seed Dressing – 86
Roquefort Dressing – 86
Thousand Island Dressing – 86

DESSERTS

Hot
Apple Meringue – 97
Auntie Rosie's Glazed Xmas Pudding – 96
Baked Alaska – 89
Bogatsa – 89
Café Brulot – 90
Cheese Blintzes – 177
Crêpes Calypso – 90
Crêpe Delight – 90
Delicious Noodle Pudding – 91
Flaming Crêpes Montmorency – 91
Flaming Strawberry Crêpes – 94
Fruit Cobbler – 94
Kaiserschmarren – 95
Orange Baked Alaska – 95
Orange Flavoured Cheese Blintzes – 96
Peach & Cherry Flambé – 97
Rice Pudding – 97
Vareniky – 97

Cold
Banana Custard Pudding Dessert – 98
Brandied Sauce for Ice-cream – 98
Butter Crunch Ice-cream Ring – 98
Cassata Ice-cream Bombe – 99
Chocolate Mousse – 99
Chocolate Bowl Surprise – 99
Chocolate Cake Cassata – 100
Chocolate Charlotte Suisse – 100
Chocolate Mosaic Dessert – 101
Couer À La Creme – 101
Creme Brulle – 101
Creme Caramel – 102
Crunch Crust Ice-cream Bombe – 102
Easy Coffee Ice-cream – 103
English Trifle – 103
Floating Island – 103
Gateau St. Honoré – 104
Ginger Mousse – 104
Granita De Café – 105
Granadilla Pudding – 105
Halva Pudding – 105
Lemon Cream – 105
Minted Meringue Sandwich – 105
Mud Pie – 106
Nut Meringue Torte – 106
Pavlova – 107
Praline Soufflé – 107
Three Tiered Bavarian Cream – 107
Turkish Oranges – 110
Zabaglione – 110

CAKES

Apple Cake – 113
Ambrosia Cake – 113
Angel Cake – 113
Auntie Rosie's Butter Cake – 115
Auntie Sylvie's Cheese Cake – 117
Bee Sting Cake – 114
Black Forest Cake – 114
Butter Chocolate Cake – 115
Carnival Cake with Penuche Icing – 116
Carrot Almond Torte – 116
Carrot Cake – 117
Cheese Cake – 117
Cheese Cake Puff – 118
Chocolate Blitz Torte – 118
Chocolate Cheese Cake/Sour Cream Topping – 119
Chocolate Chestnut Pyramid Cake – 119
Chocolate Chiffon Cake – 120
Chocolate Chiffon Cake, large – 120
Chocolate Filled Brazil Nutlog – 121
Coca-Cola Cake – 121
Coconut Chiffon Cake – 121
Custard Slice – 124
Danish Cake – 124
Danish Jam Puff Cake – 125
Deep South Prune Cake – 126
Dobosch Torte – 126
Festive Fruit Cake – 127
Fruit Cake – 127
Fruit Cake with egg whites only – 128
German Chocolate Cake – 128
Ginger Cake – 129
Ginger Chiffon Cake – 129
Grasshopper Cake – 130
Kirsch Gateau – 130
Kranskuchen – 131
Mocha Butter Cream – 139
Orange Chiffon Cake – 131
Pineapple Cheese Cake – 132
Pineapple Cream Cake – 132
Praline – 120
Quick & Delicious Marble Cake – 133

Raspberry or Loganberry Roll – 133
Russian Torte – 133
Semolina Cake – 134
Strawberry Spice Shortcake – 134
Strawberry Vacherin – 135
Swedish Cake – 135
Swiss Roll – 138
Tropical Carrot Cake – 138
Two-tone Pyramid Cake – 138
Vanilla Slice – 139
Venetian Torte – 140
Walnut Layer Cake – 140

TARTS

Basic Tart Dough – 143
Apple Slice – 143
Apple Tart – 143
Apple Tart De Luxe – 144
Apple Tart with Meringue Topping – 144
Apricot Pecan Slice – 145
Belgian Tart – 145
Benedict Tart – 145
Cherry Tart – 146
Coconut Custard Pie – 146
German Plum Tart – 147
Grape Tart – 147
Ground Almond Tart – 147
Guava Tart À La Coconut Cream – 148
Lemon Meringue Tart – 148
Linzertorte – 149
Peach Kuchen – 149
Quick Double Chocolate Tart – 149
Rhubarb Cream Pie – 150
Tart-À-La-Florentine – 150

SMALL CAKES

Ambrosia Jiffy Cakes – 155
Baklava – 155
Cream Horns – 157
Doughnuts – 158
Eclairs – 159
Melt-in-the-Mouth Assorted Tartlets – 159
Mercia's Danish Pastries – 157
Mercia's Rich Featherlight Buns – 155
Orange Chocolate Squares – 159
Petit Fours – 160
Pitikas – 160
Praline Nut Squares – 161
Quick and Easy Cinnamon Buns – 157
Viennese Brownies – 161
White Teiglach – 161

BISCUITS

Aunt Celie's Fruit Slices – 162
Brandy Snaps – 162
Cinnamon Shortbread – 163
Cornflake Kisses – 162
Crispy Cookie Maker Biscuits – 165
Crunchy Chocolate Nut Balls – 163
Curled Pecan Wafers – 163
Custard Biscuits – 163
Florentines – 164
Ginger Biscuits – 164
Ginger Snaps – 164
Ground Almond Biscuits – 165
Joseph's Mandelbrodt – 165
Kouriabides – 165
Mock Teiglach – 166
Peppermint Brownies – 166
Romany Creams – 166
Shortbread – 167
Thimble Biscuits – 167

BREAD, WAFFLES & SCONES

Crumpets – 172
Garlic Bread – 172
Herbed Bread, Wholewheat or White – 171
Poppy Seed Onion Squares – 171
Rich Scones – 171
Scones – 171
Waffles – 173
Wholewheat Bread – 172

TRADITIONAL JEWISH DISHES

Cheese Blintzes – 177
Chopped Herring – 177
Chopped Liver – 177
Gefilte Fish – 177
Kichel – 178
Kneidlach – 20
Kreplach – 18
Meat Blintzes – 19
Meat Pies – 18
My Granny's Helzel – 178
Pesach Sponge Cakes – 178
Saltenosses – 181
Pesach Swiss Roll – 179
Teiglach – I/II 179 & 180
Teiglach III – 181
Tzimmes – 181
White Teiglach – 180